Habitat creation handbook for the minerals industry

Editors: Graham White and Jo Gilbert
Authors: Graham White, Jo Gilbert, Phil Benstead, Matt Fasham and Paul José

Citation

For bibliographic purposes this book should be referred to as White, G J and Gilbert, J C (eds) (2003) *Habitat creation handbook for the minerals industry*. The RSPB, Sandy.

The techniques described or referred to in this book do not necessarily reflect the policies of the partner organisations or individuals involved in its production. A great deal of the information presented originated from the experience of individual grassland managers and must therefore be considered on a site-specific basis.

No responsibility can be accepted for any loss, damage or unsatisfactory results arising from the implementation of any of the recommendations within this book.

The use of proprietary and commercial trade names in this guidebook does not necessarily imply endorsement of the product by the partner organisations.

Published by
The Royal Society for the Protection of Birds,
The Lodge, Sandy, Beds SG19 2DL

Design by
Creative Services, the RSPB

Figures by
Dan Powell

Printed by
Eclipse

RSPB ref: 24-931-01-02

ISBN: 1 901930 37 8

Contents

Appendices

Acknowledgements

A steering group, without whom the project would not have been possible, assisted the authors throughout the project. The steering group helped scope the content of the book and reviewed several drafts. Our thanks go to you all.

This group consisted of:
Tom Moat and Natalie Bennett (English Nature), Tom Simpson and Roger Orpin (DETR), Steve Fidgett and Jane Topliss (representing the CBI Minerals Committee), John Box (Wardell Armstrong), Andy Butler (Tarmac), Eleanor Cohn and Ian Trueman (University of Wolverhampton), Nigel Holmes (Alconbury Environmental Consultants) and Phil Putwain (University of Liverpool).

The following are thanked for their contributions and comments:
Nigel Ajax-Lewis (Glamorgan Wildlife Trust), Pete Akers (The RSPB), Penny Anderson (Penny Anderson Associates), Graham Atkins (BBOWT), David Atkinson (Cambridgeshire CC), Alison Barnes, Rebecca Barrett (The RSPB), British Ceramic Confederation, Clare Brooke, Jane Brookhouse (The RSPB), Dave Burges (The RSPB), Phil Burston (The RSPB), Phil Clark (Warwickshire Wildlife Trust), David Collins (ADAS), Clive Conroy (Wardell Armstrong), Nick Coppin (Wardell Armstrong), Ian Cromie (QPA), Martin Crow (Hanson Aggregates), John Day (The RSPB), Andrew Denley (Hanson Aggregates), Ian Douglas (Northumberland Wildlife Trust), Mark Dowdall (HJ Banks), George Elliot (Tarmac Quarry Products Ltd), Matthew Ellis (CCW), Jerry Facey (IMERYS Minerals Ltd), Ron Foster (Lafarge Aggregates), Jim Glover (The RSPB), Colin Grigg (IMERYS Minerals Ltd), Kiff Hancock (Somerset Wildlife Trust), Mike Harding (ELP), Jill Hatcher, Carl Hawke (The RSPB), Andy Hay (The RSPB), Duncan Hayden (Bardon Aggregates), Barry Hedges (French Jones), Tim Hill (LVRPA), Trevor Hind (UK Coal), Tony Hutson (The Bat Conservation Trust), Martin Isles (QPA), Mike Jukes (UK Coal), Tony Kendle (Eden Project), Jeff Kew (The RSPB), Janice Kirby (UK Coal), Dave Lamacraft (The RSPB), Steve Lowe (Northumberland Wildlife Trust), Ruth MacArthur (The RSPB), Ray Matthews, Anne McCall (The RSPB), David McDougall (ADAS Environmental), Clive Mellon (The RSPB), Sally Mills (The RSPB), Sarah Niemann (The RSPB), George Okuniewski (HJ Banks), Duncan Orr-Ewing (The RSPB), David Parker (CCW), Phil Parker (Philip Parker Associates), Kevin Peberdy (WWT), the late Peter Prince, Andy Roberts (Hanson Aggregates), Jeremy Roberts (The RSPB), Peter Robertson (The RSPB), Matt Shardlow (Buglife), John Sharpe (The RSPB), Dianne Shenton (HJ Banks), Norman Sills (The RSPB), Ken Smith (The RSPB), Heather Sohl (HMWT), Simon Stennett (The RSPB), Nick Stewart (Plantlife), Giles Strother (BBOWT), David Southgate (Hanson Aggregates), Valerie Standen (Durham University), Andrew Traill-Stevenson (ARC Environmental Study Centre), Mike Street (Milton Keynes Park Trust), Nigel Symes (The RSPB), Mark Thomas (The RSPB), Siobhan Walker (Ure & Swale Washlands Project), Paul Walton (The RSPB), Simon Warwick (Lower Ure Conservation Trust), Olly Watts (The RSPB), Mike Webb (The RSPB) Richard Williams (HJ Banks), Iolo Williams (The RSPB), Richard Winspear (The RSPB), Robin Wynde (The RSPB) and Simon Zisman (The RSPB).

Foreword

In the past the mineral extraction industry has created large areas of benefit to wildlife. This is demonstrated by the fact that some 600 Sites of Special Scientific Interest (SSSIs) are former mineral workings. These past achievements show the potential behind what can be a creative force in the countryside. But more can be done for wildlife. This handbook will enable mineral companies and their site managers to make an even more effective contribution to biodiversity conservation in the future. An increasing awareness of the role the industry can play in biodiversity conservation is illustrated by initiatives such as the Statement of Intent signed in July 1998 between English Nature, the Quarry Products Association and the Silica and Moulding Sands Association and also the Memorandum of Understanding signed in 2000 between Hanson Quarry Products Europe and English Nature.

This handbook is a 'call to arms'. The mineral industry can make a difference by seizing the opportunity represented by habitat creation and make a real contribution to biodiversity. At the same time, it can demonstrate a very real benefit associated with working minerals. Such contributions also fit into wider landscape and sustainable development strategies. All these strategies are backed by the philosophy of communication, joint action and partnership – an important approach in all spheres of human endeavour, none more so than successful business and conservation.

Alongside the significant habitat creation potential of mineral workings, the industry is also increasingly taking environmental responsibility for its considerable landholdings. There is much to be gained if ecological assessments were to be undertaken and management plans written for these holdings. This is equally important for land that is never to be worked, yet to be worked and in the process of being worked, as well as restored land. Improved management should be implemented and subject to regular monitoring and review.

Congratulations to everyone involved in the production of this handbook.

Chairman CBI Minerals Committee

INTRODUCTION

Preface

Background

Both nature conservation organisations and the minerals industry now recognise the significant contribution mineral extraction operations can deliver for biodiversity (English Nature *et al*, 1999). This handbook has been produced to aid the creation of valuable habitat on land that has been worked for minerals.

This handbook draws together and summarises relevant information from a wealth of published material as well as presenting new information and case studies. It recognises the important role surface mineral extraction can play in biodiversity conservation through the creation of priority habitats. The aim is to provide habitat creation guidelines that acknowledge the latest 'state of the art' information and present these in the form of practical recommendations. It is hoped that this handbook will prove useful to a wide range of people involved in the restoration of mineral extraction sites, from chief executives to mineral planners, restoration managers and site managers.

The handbook focuses on habitat design and creation techniques for a range of Biodiversity Action Plan (BAP) priority habitats. It should be stated from the outset that the emphasis is very much on creation and that restoration of degraded habitats is largely not considered. Semi-natural habitats are now so scarce in the UK that it is hoped the mineral planning system can assist in safeguarding those areas that remain.

Structure of this handbook

The handbook comprises five sections:

Section 1 sets the scene. It provides a background to the role the mineral industry should play in furthering the UK Government's BAP process. It briefly summarises the nature of the industry and examines relevant planning and wildlife legislation.

Section 2 highlights the importance of planning when undertaking creation projects. It explains how to evaluate a site, make decisions and plan for a project. The range of physical, chemical, wildlife and legal factors affecting planning is outlined. This section also deals with the complicated issue of ensuring appropriate long-term management of nature conservation areas created by the mineral industry.

Section 3 suggests ways in which the wildlife interest of a site can be managed during the operational phase of mineral extraction in order to benefit the final restoration. The issues of minimising detrimental impacts as well as encouraging compatible wildlife are addressed. The section also describes the use of best practice in soil management and landforming. Aspects of soil storage, avoidance of soil compaction and the role of soil fertility in habitat creation are described.

Section 4 forms a major component of the handbook and examines the design and creation of priority habitats. The section divides these into grassland, woodland, heathland, wetland and field margin habitats. It also deals briefly with the creation of a range of other habitats and the creation of features beneficial to priority animals.

Section 5 contains a selection of case studies illustrating the possibilities for habitat creation, which have been planned or achieved around the UK.

Throughout the handbook, jargon has been avoided where possible, but a glossary is included for terms that may be unfamiliar (Appendix 1). Abbreviations used in the text are given in full in Appendix 2 and scientific names of species mentioned in the text are listed in Appendix 3.

A plea

Habitat loss and fragmentation will no doubt continue to have a negative impact on the UK's wildlife and as a result, habitat creation schemes will become increasingly important. While writing this handbook, it became apparent that although it was often acknowledged that techniques used to create habitats were experimental, there was a distinct lack of an appropriate scientific approach. It would be prudent in the future to approach rigorously each creation project as an opportunity to learn and share best practice.

In an ideal world the proper recording and publication of the results of habitat creation projects involving mineral extraction sites would be a fixed condition of all mineral planning consents.

Disclaimer
References are made to many habitat creation schemes throughout this handbook. The authors are not responsible for approving or disapproving of any of the schemes mentioned.

1 RESPONSIBILITIES AND OPPORTUNITIES

1.1 Habitat creation potential of the minerals industry

The mineral industry (surface extraction) can play an important role in the conservation of species and habitats in the UK (Bate *et al*, 1998). It has large landholdings, which include many important nature conservation sites and, equally important, the process of winning minerals allows new habitats to be created through site restoration.

A survey of six counties in England showed that mineral workings were associated with an average of 13% of the biological SSSIs in these counties (Box *et al*, 1996). Features that benefit wildlife can also be incorporated into end-uses that do not have specific nature conservation objectives, such as agriculture, amenity and recreation, eg watersports and angling. However, habitat creation is not a substitute for *in situ* conservation of semi-natural habitats. Irreplaceable wildlife sites in the ownership of mineral companies should be safeguarded from extraction and managed appropriately wherever possible.

For the purposes of this handbook, surface mineral extraction includes winning of the following materials:

- sand and gravel
- clay and brick-making material
- soft rock, such as chalk
- hard rock, such as limestone and igneous formations
- opencast coal
- peat.

R Wilmshurst (rspb-images.com)

Plate 1.2
A tenth of the peregrine population nests in quarries.

Past mineral extraction practices, whether by accident or design, have resulted in the creation of some very good habitats for wildlife, including:

- gravel pits, which have become important in the UK for breeding and wintering wildfowl populations (Plate 1.1)

G McCarthy (rspb-images.com)

Plate 1.1
A significant percentage of the wintering population of the gadwall is found on flooded gravel pits.

G J White

Plate 1.3
Diverse grasslands can develop in chalk and limestone quarries.

- hard rock quarries, used as nest sites by cliff-nesting birds such as the peregrine and chough (Plate 1.2)
- chalk and limestone quarries, which often develop spectacular grassland communities (Plate 1.3). Quarries can support diverse floras, a sample of 48 English quarries, between 15 and 100 years old, yielded 428 species of vascular plant (Davis, 1982b)
- chalk quarries with cave systems, which can support populations of rare bats such as the barbastelle
- flooded brickpits that have become important sites for rare amphibians such as the great crested newt (Plate 1.4).

Creation of new habitats will help mitigate the historical legacy of loss and fragmentation of natural habitats in the last century. Habitat creation has several important roles:

- contributing to increasing biodiversity and the achievement of Biodiversity Action Plan targets
- linking fragmented areas of semi-natural vegetation in an otherwise intensively used landscape
- buffering existing semi-natural areas
- expanding existing sites, so making their management more practicable or economically viable
- providing new areas which can serve as local amenity and educational resources and which can draw people away from fragile habitats.

R Wilmshurst (rspb-images.com)

Plate 1.4
Flooded brick pits can be important for amphibians, such as the great crested newt.

During the post-war period, most restoration has been to agricultural land, not wildlife habitat. The exception is sand and gravel extraction, which often resulted in the creation of open water habitats unsuitable for farming. These open water habitats have since become nationally important, particularly for wintering wildfowl, and support considerable biodiversity. Design specifications and techniques for maximising the benefits for wildlife after sand and gravel extraction were formulated in the 1980s and resulted in a number of habitat management and creation guidelines (eg Street, 1989; Andrews and Kinsman, 1990; Giles, 1992).

An increasing proportion of mineral workings are being restored to the broad category 'amenity use', which includes nature conservation. With the introduction of a new, target-led approach to biodiversity conservation, the industry's role and commitment in achieving the habitat creation targets set out in the UK Habitat Action Plans are being recognised – not least by the production of this handbook. This is backed by a ground swell of public opinion in favour of nature conservation after-uses.

Box 1.1 Some definitions

Throughout this handbook the following definitions have been adopted.

- Restoration is used in its broadest sense, ie the return of land to some beneficial after-use. (In MPG7 the term 'reclamation' is used.)

- Creation is defined as the construction of interesting and attractive ecological communities on sites which currently support little or no nature conservation interest (Parker, 1995). The bulk of this book deals with the creation of habitats under this definition. The current state of knowledge of habitat creation does not allow it to be used as compensation for the loss of scarce habitats. Ecologists question whether habitat creation can play a significant role in conserving species and biodiversity generally or whether authentic communities with full species complements can ever be a feasible goal. It is clear however that the creation of semi-natural habitat, when carried out well, will usually have a positive impact on biodiversity. Semi-natural habitats are now so scarce and fragmented that habitat creation is required to buffer and re-connect them. However, it is important that the process of habitat creation is not used to justify the destruction of existing semi-natural habitat (Hopkins, 1989).

- Translocation is defined as the removal of habitat from a donor to a receptor site – this subject is dealt with briefly in section 3.3.4. Translocation is an option of last resort, where the adverse impacts of a minerals development cannot be avoided, nor mitigated. Moreover, the success of translocation schemes is highly variable (Gault, 1997). Translocation cannot be advocated as a method for preserving habitats. Changes will usually occur in communities that have been moved – as the physical and chemical conditions of the donor and recipient site are rarely the same. At best, it is the optimal use of available biological material where an adverse impact cannot be avoided. Translocation should never be used to justify the development of an important nature conservation site.

1.2 Opportunities for the minerals industry to contribute to achieving BAP targets

Mineral extraction can provide the opportunity to replace increasingly sterile agricultural habitats with habitats of real value to nature conservation. The minerals industry should also take appropriate action to maintain irreplaceable habitats such as ancient semi-natural woodlands, peatlands and limestone pavement that exist on sites in their ownership.

By working with nature, planning long-term and employing flexible designs, habitat creation can achieve realistic ecological objectives and be affordable. If creation and maintenance costs are reduced by adopting this approach, then habitat creation becomes an increasingly attractive proposition (Gilbert and Anderson, 1998).

1.2.1 What is biodiversity?

Biodiversity encompasses the whole variety of life on Earth. It is not restricted to rare or threatened species, but includes the whole of the natural world from the commonplace to the critically endangered. It includes the plants and animals familiar to us all in the places where we live or work, wherever that may be (HMSO, 1995).

1.2.2 The UK Biodiversity Action Plan

The Convention on Biological Diversity was one of several major initiatives stemming from the Earth Summit in Rio de Janeiro in 1992. Together, these initiatives form an International Agreement on Sustainable Development, Agenda 21. The United Kingdom was one of 150 signatories to the Convention, which reflects a worldwide concern that human activities are changing and destroying habitats and natural ecosystems on an increasing scale and rate, resulting in an unprecedented loss of species. Signatories agreed to develop national strategies, plans and programmes for the conservation and sustainable use of biological diversity, and to share resources to help implement such programmes.

The UK is now well advanced in developing and implementing a national action plan. The Government's response to the Biodiversity Convention, *Biodiversity: The UK Action Plan* (HMSO, 1994), sets out the broad strategy for conserving and enhancing wild species and wildlife habitats in the UK. The overall goal of the UK Biodiversity Action Plan (BAP) being: to conserve and enhance biological diversity within the UK; and to contribute to the conservation of global biodiversity through all appropriate mechanisms. The UK Biodiversity Action Plan has now been re-enforced (in England and Wales) by the Countryside and Rights of Way (CRoW) Act (2000), in particular by section 74 of this Act.

One of the main outcomes of the UK Biodiversity Action Plan was the identification of those species and habitats that were most in need of conservation action in the UK and the setting of quantifiable biological targets for these priority species and habitats. Costed UK Biodiversity Action Plans (BAPs) have now been produced for 391 species and 45 habitat types. In addition, various measures have been put in place to encourage and assist the implementation, monitoring and reporting of progress of these UK BAPs.

The selection of priority species and habitats was based on an appraisal of their status, including an assessment of former losses or rates of decline, and threats to their survival. In many cases, the BAPs for habitats include targets for the restoration of existing habitat and the creation of 'new' habitat. It is recognised that this creation of habitat, on land that is currently under different land-use, does not directly compensate for past habitat loss but it may help to improve the conservation status of the habitat overall. Creation targets for priority habitats relevant to this handbook include, for example:

- creation of 1,200 ha of reedbed, in blocks of at least 20 ha by 2010, predominantly in south-east Britain on land of low conservation interest (HMSO, 1995) (Plate 1.5).
- creation of 6,000 ha of lowland heathland by 2005 (HMSO, 1995) (Plate 1.6).
- creation of 2,500 ha of coastal and floodplain grazing marsh (HMSO, 1995).

For a list of broad habitat groups considered under the BAP and in this handbook, together with creation targets for these habitats see Table 1.1. The text of all the published UK BAPs, including the targets, can be found on the UK Biodiversity website (www.ukbap.org.uk). BAP species that could potentially benefit from restoration following surface mineral extraction are listed in Appendix 4.

Although an organisation (known as Lead Partner or Lead Agency) has been identified to co-ordinate the implementation of each BAP, the Government is keen to encourage species and habitat 'champions' from the private sector. Champions can assist by providing sponsorship, services, land or other contributions depending on circumstances, and in return can benefit from positive publicity, profile, staff motivation etc. Implementation of the UK BAP is now a devolved responsibility and there are separate country biodiversity groups in England, Wales, Scotland and Northern Ireland. Concepts such as English Nature's Natural Areas approach and Scottish Natural Heritage's Natural Heritage Zones may help to influence the direction of habitat creation. The creation and restoration of habitats is an important method for linking the remaining islands of semi-natural habitat, reversing effects of past fragmentation.

The priorities and targets contained within the UK BAPs are translated into Regional and Local BAPs (Figure 1.1), and it is often at these levels that habitat creation can best be targeted. Local BAPs also identify habitats and species of local importance and resonance in addition to the UK priorities. It is important that in developing habitat creation projects consideration is given not only to what benefits can be achieved for UK priority species and habitats but also for those of local importance.

G J White

Plate 1.5 (left) Gravel pits have the potential to help meet creation targets for reedbed and for Plate 1.6 (below) lowland heathland.

D Kjaer (rspb-images.com)

Figure 1.1 Biodiversity action planning from national to county level.

This ensures that national targets are translated into action on the ground at a local level.

UK Biodiversity Plan ➔ (HMSO, 1995) | South-west Regional ➔ Biodiversity Plan (Cordrey, 1997) | Cornwall's Biodiversity ➔ vols 1,2 and 3 (Cornwall Wildlife Trust, 1998) | The Cornwall Heathland Habitat Action Plan (Gault, 1998)

Table 1.1 The classification, distribution and creation targets of the BAP priority habitats considered in this handbook.

BAP category and National Vegetation Classification (NVC) communities (after Rodwell, 1991 et seq)	Distribution	BAP creation target
Broadleaved, mixed and yew woodland NVC: W1-W17 and W19	Widespread.	Initiate colonisation and/or planting of 3,000 ha of lowland beech and yew woodland on unwooded sites. Complete half by 2010 and all by 2015*. Initiate colonisation and/or planting of 6,750 ha of wet woodland on unwooded sites. Complete half by 2010 and all by 2015*. By 2002, initiate the expansion of 500 ha of wood pasture and parkland in appropriate areas to reverse fragmentation and reduce generation gap between veteran trees*. Initiate colonisation and/or planting of 6,000 ha of upland mixed ash woods on unwooded sites. Complete half by 2010 and all by 2015*.
Coastal and floodplain grazing marsh NVC: MG8, MG9, MG10, MG11, MG12, and MG13. Drainage channels include aquatic communities A1-A6, A8-A13, A15, A16 and A19-A21 and swamp communities S4-S8, S12-S14, S16-S18, S20-S23, S25, S26 and S28.	Widespread along suitable river floodplains. Coastal areas are largely along south and east coast of England.	Reversion of 2,500 ha of arable land to wet grassland (outwith of agri-environment schemes which have separate targets).
Neutral grassland NVC: MG1-MG5, MG8.	Widespread.	Re-establish 500 ha of lowland meadow of wildlife value by 2010. Attempt to re-establish 50 ha of upland hay meadow of wildlife value by 2010*.
Calcareous grassland NVC: CG1-CG11.	Lowland calcareous grassland is widespread but scattered on lime-rich soils overlying limestone rocks, including chalk. Upland calcareous grasslands are found on lime-rich soils, mostly above 250–300 m.	Attempt to re-establish 1,000 ha of lowland calcareous grassland of wildlife value at carefully targeted sites by 2010*. Initiate pilot attempts to re-create at least 200 ha of upland calcareous grassland by 2005 with particular emphasis on reducing fragmentation through linking small, vulnerable and discontinuous sites.
Acid grassland NVC: U1-U6.	On nutrient-poor, free-draining soils, such as sands and gravels, usually below 300 m.	Attempt to re-establish 500 ha of lowland acid grassland of wildlife value at carefully targeted sites by 2010*.
Lowland heathland NVC: M15, M16, H1-H6, H8-H10, H12, H16.	Found below 300 m, the majority being in south and south-west England. Usually on sand.	Re-establishment of 6,000 ha of heathland by 2005, preferably linking existing habitat, with emphasis on the following counties: Cornwall, Devon, Dorset, Glamorgan, Gwynedd, Hampshire, Norfolk, Pembrokeshire, Staffordshire, Suffolk and Surrey (HMSO, 1995).
Upland heath NVC: M15, M16, H4, H8-H10, H12, H16, H18, H21.	Found above 300 m, usually on peat.	Initiate management to re-create 5,000 ha of upland heath by 2005 where heathland has been lost due to agricultural improvement or afforestation with particular emphasis on reducing fragmentation.

Continued overleaf ▸▸▸

▸▸▸

Fen, marsh and swamp NVC: S4, M22, M24, S24-S28, S1-S28, M4-M14, M21, M26-M38.	Vegetation that is groundwater fed, and permanently, seasonally or periodically inundated peat, peaty or mineral soils where grasses do not predominate. Does not therefore include wet grassland (with the exception of purple moor-grass, reed or *Glyceria* dominated habitats.	Create 1,200 ha of new reedbed by 2010. The creation of new reedbed should be in blocks of at least 20 ha with priority given to creation in areas near to existing habitat and linking to this wherever possible (HMSO, 1995). Maintain existing area of fen, carr, marsh swamp and reedbed habitats and identify those suitable for restoration. Create new reedbeds on land of low conservation importance. Identify priority fen sites in critical need of, and initiate, rehabilitation by the year 2005. All rich fen and other sites with rare communities should be considered. Ensure appropriate water quality and quantity for the continued existence of all SSSI/Area of Special Scientific Interest (ASSI) fens by 2005.
Bogs NVC: M1-M3, M15-M20 and M25.		Creation not technically possible.
Standing open water and canals NVC: A1-A24.	Widespread	Maintain and improve the conservation interest of standing open waters, through use of integrated management plans, and the sensitive management of adjacent lands. Create new standing open waters, of maximum wildlife benefit where possible. Maintain existing environmental quality of all canals (remaindered, derelict and navigable) in the UK and enhance the wildlife interest of the habitats associated with key canals through upgrading and improving water quality and quantity and restoration of bankside features
Rivers and streams NVC: A2, A8, A9, A11-A20.	Widespread	Maintain and improve the quality, state and structure of all UK rivers and streams and their associated floodplains. Restore degraded river and streams taking account of water quality and quantity, structure and hydraulic connection with the floodplain.
Saline lagoon NVC: SM1 and marine biotopes.	Natural or artificial bodies of saline water partially separated from the adjacent sea. They retain a percentage of their sea water at low tide and may develop as brackish, fully or hyper saline waterbodies.	Create, by the year 2010, sufficient lagoon habitat to offset losses over last 50 years – perhaps 120 ha in total (HMSO, 1995).

*UK Biodiversity Group, 1998

1.2.3 The minerals industry and the BAP process

The minerals industry has a huge potential to contribute to the BAP process and the habitat and species targets. A key aspect of BAPs is that although they are based on a scientific understanding of the status and threats to the relevant species and habitat, their implementation is based on a partnership approach. The involvement of a wide range of organisations, groups and individuals, including the minerals industry and locals communities, is therefore important. Individual minerals operators could play a valuable role by becoming a 'champion' for an appropriate species or habitat.

G J White

Plate 1.7 Mineral extraction in the Lee Valley Park, Herts/Essex, an older quarry that was left with spits and islands of reject gravels – now rich in wildlife.

Where there are a number of options for the restoration of a particular mineral site, the local BAP is likely to provide good guidance. However, strategic planning for meeting the targets within a BAP is also required in many cases, and again the industry can contribute. A ground-breaking development in the 1990s was the full involvement of representatives from the minerals industry in the formulation and implementation of the Cotswold Water Park BAP. This approach is becoming more common. There are increasing examples of strategic and targeted restoration over wider areas, such as river valleys (see Box 1.2), and an extension of this approach would be highly beneficial.

Feedback within the BAP process is also important. The minerals industry is urged to consider organising a system of reporting that could be used to share information about the outcome of habitat creation schemes.

Box 1.2 Examples of strategic planning

1) The Lee Valley Regional Park

The Lee Valley Regional Park stretches along 25 miles of the River Lee in London, Essex and Hertfordshire (Plate 1.7). The Park has a remit to provide opportunities for leisure, sports and recreation and to be the guardian of the valley's environment and wildlife. The valley includes over 100 individual waterbodies, mostly formed from mineral extraction. A Water Management Strategy was developed to inform the process of reviewing the Park Plan. This provided a framework to:

- allocate nature conservation and recreational uses to different sites
- establish broad principles for future development and management
- establish the further potential of the Park as a nature conservation and water recreation resource for the region.

The Water Management Strategy was itself informed by a thorough review of the existing and potential value of the Park for wildlife (and recreation) and the parallel development of a local BAP. Both documents helped guide the restoration and management of new sites as the Park was seen to have great potential for helping to meet national and regional BAP targets for a number of key wetland habitats and species, such as open waters, reedbeds, the bittern, otter and water vole. In 2000, the Lee Valley was classified as a Special Protection Area (SPA) and Ramsar Site, primarily as a result of the wintering waterbird populations which the valley supports.

2) The Swale and Ure Washlands

The Swale and Ure Washlands Project was set up following consultation on North Yorkshire County Council's Minerals Local Plan, when a number of consultees suggested the need for a broader, more strategic view of mineral site restoration. Gravel workings in particular were seen as having great potential for wildlife. However, all too often that crucial potential was not fully realised.

The aims of the Project are to:

- develop a strategic view of the after-use of mineral extraction sites down the Swale and Ure washlands
- identify priorities for increasing biodiversity (in line with the local BAP, see section 5.4)
- encourage the restoration of degraded land to productive use
- involve communities in the development of projects.

It is managed by the Lower Ure Conservation Trust (a registered charity) and guided by a steering group with representatives from the local authorities, operators and environmental organisations.

1.3 Surface mineral extraction in the UK

Various mining activities cover large areas of land in the UK, for example in 2000, the total area of land in England with planning permission for surface mineral workings was 113,644 ha (ODPM 2002). The six most extensive mineral types in 2000 were sand and gravel, vein minerals, ironstone, limestone/dolomite, clay/shale and peat. These accounted for 81% of the total permitted area. Most sites are restored to a beneficial after-use once extraction has ceased. In England during the period 1994-2000, 50% of land reclaimed went to agriculture, amenity uses including nature conservation accounted for 36%, forestry for 6% and other uses 8%. This continues a trend of increasing proportions of land returned to amenity uses and a reduction in that reclaimed for agriculture.

There are obvious environmental considerations and concerns relating to surface mineral and aggregate extraction, not least is the potential for destruction of irreplaceable semi-natural habitats and plant/animal communities. It is essential that new mineral workings should not affect key areas of nature conservation importance. Documents such as the RSPB *Good Practice Guide to Mineral Restoration* provide advice to operators. This handbook concentrates on the potential for habitat creation after mineral extraction.

1.3.1 Types of mineral extraction

Most extraction processes involve three phases.
Phase 1: stripping off the soil and overburden above the desired material and removing it to a storage area.
Phase 2: removal of the mineral, aggregate or fuel.
Phase 3: replacement of overburden and soil and restoration of land to a beneficial after-use.

Surface mineral extraction sites can be divided into four types. The way these types of extraction are linked to the different minerals is shown in Table 1.2.

1.3.2 Sand and gravel extraction

Many sand and gravel extraction sites are located in river floodplains throughout the lowlands of the UK (Plate 1.8) but some, in glacial and other deposits, are situated elsewhere. The materials were derived from the deposition and sorting of fluvial (and glacial) sediments over many millennia. Extraction usually takes place over a short timescale compared with most other surface mineral operations. Extractions are most numerous where there has been most need for their products especially in south-east England. Permitted sand and gravel extraction workings in England in 2000

Table 1.2 Types of excavation associated with various mineral extraction industries.
(after Coppin and Bradshaw, 1982)

	Excavation type			
Mineral	Shallow pits with little overburden	Shallow pits with lots of overburden	Deep quarries or pits with little overburden	Deep quarries or pits with lots of overburden
Stone quarries			•	
Chalk quarries	•		•	
China clay				•
Ball clay		•		•
Clay and shale	•	•		
Sand and gravel	•	•	•	
Slate				•
Coal		•		•

G J White

A K Nelson

Plate 1.8
Sand and gravel extraction sites are mainly located in river floodplains throughout the lowlands of the UK.

Plate 1.9
The black-tailed skimmer dragonfly quickly colonises new gravel workings.

R Revels (rspb-images.com)

G J White

Plate 1.10
The breeding population of great crested grebes has benefited greatly from flooded gravel workings.

Plate 1.11
Nationally important populations of wintering waterbirds, such as tufted ducks and pochards, can use flooded gravel workings.

totalled 27,007 ha (ODPM, 2002) – 24% of all land affected by surface mineral working. An estimated 400-500 ha of flooded pits were created each year during the 1980s (Andrews and Kinsman, 1990). The creation of these flooded workings has greatly benefited wetland wildlife, for example:

- some species of dragonfly, such as the black-tailed skimmer, have extended their range through use of these sites (Plate 1.9)
- about 60% of breeding little ringed plovers and over a third of great crested grebes (Plate 1.10) depend on flooded sand and gravel workings
- internationally important numbers of wintering waterfowl, including gadwalls, tufted ducks and pochards use flooded sand and gravel workings. In some cases single pits, such as Bowmoor Lake in the Cotswold Water Park, can support nationally important numbers of wintering waterfowl (Plate 1.11).

Some deposits are found along ridges and high ground, due to glacial or other geological processes, and these can be worked without de-watering. Such extraction may involve significant changes to landform, but offers the chance to create

G J White

Plate 1.12
Sand quarries have the potential for the creation of grassland habitats on diverse landforms – Sandy Heath Quarry.

heathland and acid grassland habitat, eg Sandy Heath, Bedfordshire (Plate 1.12).

Restoration following sand and gravel extraction has great potential to deliver biodiversity targets for lowland wet grassland and reedbed creation, as well as continuing to provide open water habitats. Many quarries currently in operation, eg the Hanson-RSPB wetland project at Needingworth in Cambridgeshire (section 5.1) and Langford Lowfields in the Trent Valley (section 5.7), are being designed in partnership with conservation bodies to ensure serious contributions to meeting UK BAP targets are set for reedbed.

The winning of silica and moulding sand is a low-volume (an average of 4.4×10^{12} tonnes per annum), but high value,

P Benstead

Plate 1.13
Ball clay extraction is geographically suited for restoration to heathland habitats.

production process involving small quarries at just a few locations and is not considered further. Habitat creation options and techniques for such quarries are likely to be the same as for other sand and gravel extraction processes. Extraction of silica sand is covered by MPG15 *Provision of silica sand in England.*

1.3.3 Clay extraction

The brick-making industry quarries clay, usually in large volumes over long timescales from very deep pits, which often become deep lakes. These are usually unsuitable for nature conservation after-use, although carefully planned infilling and re-profiling of steep sides can create potential. Some shallower excavations have developed their own wildlife interest after being worked. For example, great crested newts, bearded stonewort and greater bladderwort are found in brickpits in the Peterborough area, Cambridgeshire.

The pottery industry in the UK is historically centred on Stoke-on-Trent, around which there are many old and a few active clay extraction sites. Today, clay extraction occurs more widely across the UK, but especially in England. Clay extraction was also formerly associated with cement-making. The cement industry now uses shales, but many old workings exist, eg Cliffe Pools (Box 4.7), and have the potential to be managed for nature conservation.

Ball clay occurs in nationally important, localised deposits in the Bovey Basin in South Devon, the Petrockstowe Basin in North Devon and the Wareham area in Dorset (Plate 1.13). Ball clay has mainly ceramic applications and 70% of production is exported, mostly to Europe. Because of their soil characteristics and geographical location, former ball clay sites have particular potential for restoration to heathland, eg Gadle Knapp, Dorset (Hill and Box, 1999). Many supported heathland before extraction.

1.3.4 China clay extraction

Extraction of China clay or kaolin occurs on the edges of moors, mainly in Devon and Cornwall on the heather moorland of Dartmoor, Bodmin Moor and the Hensbarrow Downs. In southern England, heather moorland is a threatened habitat restricted to just three counties: Devon, Cornwall and Somerset. Kaolin deposits are produced by hydrothermal degradation of granite from below during its formation. Deposits extend therefore to considerable depths and individual quarries can be worked for long periods. Only a small proportion of the granite (the feldspars) breaks down into kaolinite, leaving large amounts of waste: undecomposed rock, mica and predominantly quartz sand. The waste to product ratio is in the order of 7:1. The deposits are removed by high pressure water jets in open pits. The mica settles out in lagoons and the sand and rock is deposited in large heaps. This has resulted in a complex of pits, lagoons and tip heaps covering 90 km^2 in Cornwall and Devon (Plate 1.14). The industry moves some 20 million tonnes of material annually, much of which is waste. Some waste material is re-used as bulk fill for road and other construction purposes or as a building product in its own right, for use in block-making and for the manufacture of concrete or concrete products.

China clay deposits are rare and the industry is seen as vital to the economy of the south-west. Restoration in the past has been mainly to agricultural land, but increasingly the potential to restore heathland and moorland is being realised in restoration plans. A unique example of restoration of a China clay workings is the Eden Project (Box 3.1), which has completely revived the local economy.

1.3.5 Limestone quarrying

Limestone, including chalk, is quarried for aggregate in construction and to provide material for making cement. Cement consists of limestone or chalk (80–90%) and shale or clay (10–20%), which is blended and heated to partial fusion. The resultant clinker is then ground with gypsum. Energy-saving considerations have given rise to the increased use of the drier materials, limestone and shale. UK production has consequently contracted to just 20 factories mainly in the Midlands and northern England.

Limestone and chalk quarries often have deep workings and little overburden is produced. Natural succession can take over 50 years to achieve complete vegetation cover. In the process, bare chalk and limestone substrates often support interesting pioneer communities, which include rare and scarce plants such as gentians, pasque flowers, man orchids, bee orchids and fly orchids (Plate 1.15). Several chalk quarries with old cave systems in southern England support very important populations of rare bat species, such as the barbastelle. Scrub and woodland develops in the absence of any management and these undisturbed areas are important for wildlife.

Some chalk quarries are excavated below the water-table resulting in clear marl lakes that often support interesting floras and

Imerys Minerals Ltd

J Gilbert

Plate 1.14 (above top) Complex of pits, lagoons and tip heaps covering 90 km² in Cornwall and Devon resulting from China clay extraction.

Plate 1.15 (above bottom) Natural regeneration may be slow but can provide excellent results – Hopton Quarry, Derbyshire.

invertebrate faunas, eg College Lake in Buckinghamshire which has good bird and invertebrate interest (Box 2.2). Unvegetated areas around such chalk quarries, where seepages of water occur from the rock, attract pioneer invertebrates, eg the scarce blue-tailed damselfly.

1.3.6 Acid rock quarrying

Part of the UK demand for aggregates is met by 'acid rock' quarrying. 'Acid rocks' provide about 42% of crushed rock aggregates (the rest being limestone and dolomite) or about 25% of all aggregates won (including sand and gravel). Production is centred on dispersed sites mainly in the west and north of the UK.

Acid rock quarrying has fewer benefits to wildlife but does, along with limestone, create breeding sites in the form of inaccessible cliffs, for scarce birds such as the peregrine and chough in some areas. Acid rock quarries are even harsher environments for plants than chalk quarries and can take many decades to achieve higher plant succession (Hodgson, 1982).

1.3.7 Opencast coal mining

Opencast coal mining started during the Second World War. Since then a range of restoration techniques have been developed. Currently opencast coal accounts for one quarter of all coal produced in the UK, although coal production is generally declining (Plate 1.16). The high ratio of overburden to coal, which can be as much as 30:1, means that land can usually be restored to its original form.

Plate 1.16 Opencast mining.

J Gilbert

Privatisation of the coal industry in 1994 left most of the opencast coal industry in the hands of a few operators. There were 42 opencast sites producing more than 15 million tonnes in 1999, 24 were owned by just three companies: RJB Mining (now UK Coal), Celtic Energy and the Scottish Coal Company Ltd.

Since the introduction of the more restrictive Mineral Planning Guidance (MPG3 *Coal mining and colliery disposal*, DoE, 1999), many opencast coal site (OCCS) planning applications have been refused in England. Current policies in England favour mining applications on sites already affected by previous mining activities, such as old colliery tips from former deep mines. Opencast coal mining is already playing a role in the reclamation of such former mines. The current situation in Scotland is very different. Despite the revision of National Planning Policy Guideline NPPG16 *Opencast coal and related minerals* (Scottish Office Development Department, 1999), applications are being given permission and the area being mined is increasing. Currently some of the largest opencast coal sites in Europe are in Scotland.

In the past opencast coal sites have been largely restored to agriculture, amenity and commercial woodland, but more recently sites have been restored to wetland, heathland and upland habitats. Clay deposits are often associated with coalfields making surface water wetland creation possible after extraction. Coal extraction has also led to the creation of large overburden tips in some areas, which can be restored to habitats such as acid grassland or heathland (see Fairburn Ings case study, section 5.8).

British opencast coal mining restoration has a worldwide reputation for its quality, although there is still plenty of room for improvement of restoration to nature conservation and the integration of biodiversity conservation into other fields of restoration, eg agriculture and amenity. Environmental problems can develop because of opencast coal mining, especially associated with the re-establishment of the hydrological regime following restoration eg at Hauxley, East Chevington. Two principal effects can occur:

- the collapse and settlement of backfilled material, as a consequence of physical weathering due to groundwater contact. Subsidence is usually only a problem where backfill has been inadequately compacted and may be beneficial from a nature conservation perspective (Plate 1.17).
- groundwater pollution from contact with physically and chemically weathered rockfill materials, particularly through the weathering of pyrites in the backfill. This can create very acid conditions and is particularly prevalent in Scotland (Reed and Singh, 1986).

G J White

T Melling (rspb-images.com)

Plate 1.17 (above top) Mining subsidence may be beneficial to nature conservation where shallow wetlands result.

Plate 1.18 (above bottom) Peat extraction is severely damaging to wildlife habitats.

1.3.8 Peat extraction

Mechanical peat extraction severely damages wildlife habitats, both on the extraction site and potentially in the surrounding area (Plate 1.18). This is due to the extensive drainage required to allow machinery onto the site and the widespread removal of vegetation to clear the surface for extraction. The authors of this handbook do not support peat extraction, but recognise there is a need to restore areas where the peat has already been taken.

Most commercial peat extraction occurs on the lowland raised peat bog type. MPG13 *Peat guidance* (paragraphs 42–43) gives priority to wetland restoration and the report's Annex D provides guidelines for the rehabilitation of raised bogs. This should be the priority target for the conservation after-use of any raised bog: only 6% of the original raised bog habitat remains in the UK and the EU Habitats Directive requires the restoration of degraded sites to their former habitat. Raised bog restoration does however require a suitable depth of ombrotrophic peat upon which to commence conservation management. If this peat is not available, other nature conservation objectives may be considered.

Until the 1960s peat was largely extracted by hand digging. The subsequent mechanisation of commercial peat extraction has greatly increased the damage to extracted peatlands. Several techniques may be used. Block cutting, the 'traditional' method of commercial extraction, is a large scale, mechanised version of hand cutting. Peats are cut from long trenches and laid on the higher, uncut face to dry. Sausage extraction is a variation on this method that turns out the cut peat in long 'sausages' for drying. Small peat operators may simply use an excavator to dig the wet peat, which is then spread and left to dry on higher ground or taken away and stock-piled. This method leaves a series of wet pits that are usually suitable only for non-peatland habitat creation. The most common peat extraction method used today is milling. This requires the entire bog surface to be stripped of vegetation and a regular grid pattern of drains installed. These define the milling fields from which the surface peat is then scraped, dried and removed. These extensive, bare, flat surfaces require a large scale approach to restoration, such as that being undertaken at Thorne and Hatfield Moors in South Yorkshire by English Nature.

Ham Wall in Somerset, where sedge peat has been extracted from under agricultural land, is an example of restoration to wetland habitats, particularly reedbed (section 5.5).

1.4 Legislation relating to surface mineral extraction and restoration options

Mineral planning legislation and the bodies responsible for its implementation throughout the UK are outlined in Table 1.3. In this handbook, the term Mineral Planning Authority (MPA) is used to cover all UK authorities responsible for mineral development control and policy.

1.4.1 Planning procedure

The legislative framework of mineral planning is provided by:
- the Town and Country Planning Act 1990 (as amended by the Planning and Compensation Act 1991 and the Environment Act 1995) in England and Wales
- the Town and Country Planning (Scotland) Act 1997 in Scotland
- the Planning (NI) Order (Article 112) in Northern Ireland.

The legislative framework is supported by a series of Government Guidance Notes on planning policy.

- In England, Planning Policy Guidance notes (PPGs) and especially Mineral Planning Guidance notes (MPGs) are produced by the Office of the Deputy Prime Minister (ODPM). There is also a series of Regional Planning Guidance notes (RPGs) that cover minerals issues.
- In Scotland, there is a series of National Planning Policy Guidelines (NPPGs), which are supported by Planning Advice Notes (PANs) and Circulars.
- In Wales, Minerals Planning Policy Wales (MPPW) (National Assembly for Wales, December 2000) provides guidance on mineral planning issues.
- In Northern Ireland, guidance is provided by Planning Policy Statements (PPSs) and Development Control Advice Notes (DCANs), although there are none relating to minerals. Minerals are treated like any other proposed development and are decided upon by the planning authority.

Planning permission is required to carry out mineral extraction. This is granted by the MPA or, on appeal, by the relevant national administration. In granting permission, conditions will always be imposed in respect of restoration and aftercare.

Decisions on mineral extraction applications are made in accordance with the development plan, unless material considerations indicate otherwise ('the plan-led system', Sec 54a Town and Country Planning Act 1990, and Sec 25 of the Town and Country Planning (Scotland) Act 1997). MPAs should prepare a Minerals Local Plan (MLP) in respect of the winning and

Table 1.3 Responsible bodies and legislation relating to mineral extraction and restoration planning.

	Body responsible for mineral planning	Relevant mineral planning legislation
England	Mineral Planning Authority (County Council or Unitary Authority)	Town and Country Planning Act 1990
Wales	Mineral Planning Authority (Unitary Authority)	Town and Country Planning Act 1990
Scotland	Development Control Authority, the District Authority or (in one-tier areas) the Regional or Island Council	Town and Country Planning (Scotland) Act 1997
Northern Ireland	Department of Environment Northern Ireland (DoENI)	Planning (Northern Ireland) Order 1991*

* Legislation lacks provision for statutory aftercare.

working of minerals or the deposit of mineral waste. In Scotland these policies are usually contained within the development plan, however, some local planning authorities choose to produce specialised subject mineral plans. These plans should identify relevant international, national and local nature conservation interests, and should ensure that these interests are properly protected and enhanced in development and land-use policies.

In England, detailed advice on restoration and aftercare schemes together with guidance in the use of planning obligations and the financial provisions is contained in MPG7 *The reclamation of mineral workings*. Advice on nature conservation is also contained within PPG9 (1994) *Nature conservation*. Paragraph 42 states that: 'Extraction of minerals can create new types of habitat in areas where they were formerly rare or absent, while quarry faces may provide a valuable supplement to natural rock outcrops since features of geological importance may be revealed during quarrying operations. MPAs and mineral companies should bear in mind opportunities for habitat creation and enhancement even where nature conservation is not the primary end-use of a site. Planning conditions, particularly on longer-life sites, may need to allow for some flexibility to accommodate changes to schemes should these become necessary. Consideration should also be given to arrangements for continuing management of restored nature conservation sites, beyond the end of the aftercare period'.

1.4.2 Mineral Permission Review Procedure

The appreciation that many old mineral workings had little or no restoration or aftercare provisions led to a number of legislative mechanisms to ensure that old permissions were reviewed and the problem addressed. The problem was initially tackled by the Town and Country Planning (Minerals) Act 1981 (later part of the Town and Country Planning Act 1990). A review of its effectiveness was undertaken in 1991, and the subsequent Planning and Compensation Act 1991 introduced new measures to deal with the 1943–1948 permissions (Interim Development Orders – see below). Later, under the Environment Act 1995, new measures to review and update mineral permissions granted between 1948–1982 and periodic reviews of all sites were introduced.

1.4.3 Interim Development Orders

Interim Development Orders (IDOs) were permissions granted between 1943 and 1948 and were not required to be registered with MPAs. Under the 1991 legislation all IDO permission holders were required to register sites with the MPA and submit modern restoration and aftercare conditions for approval. No compensation was liable to be paid in respect of restoration and aftercare conditions. However where conditions are imposed that affected asset value, these could only be put in place by agreement with the operator or by the use of orders which could involve compensation.

1.4.4 Environment Act 1995

Extensive reviews of the 1981 legislation in relation to post-IDO permissions led to the 1995 Act, which requires submission of updated planning conditions for approval; failure to submit results in the loss of permission. Again, modern restoration and aftercare conditions can be applied on the updating of planning permission. The Act also provides for review of all mineral permissions every 15 years to keep pace with modern best practice. If conditions are imposed which would affect the economic viability or asset value of the site, compensation would be payable. Many old permissions granted between 1943 and 1982 have now been updated through the IDO or Environment Act procedures.

Both these mechanisms offer potential to deliver nature conservation benefits. Many sites have been re-surveyed or audited for the first time – a process that is highlighting the importance of the mineral sites for conservation at regional and national levels. There are many cases of co-operation between BAP groups and operators at a local biodiversity planning level during the re-evaluation process. Other issues may already be resolved or underway (noise, traffic etc) so attention focuses on restoration and long-term management planning. MPG14 (in Scotland Circular 34/1996) provides guidance on the inclusion of modern day standards of environmental control into updated work programmes of sites with old permissions.

1.4.5 Aftercare

Schedule 5 of the 1990 Town and Country Planning Act (Schedule 3 of the 1997 Act in Scotland) provides powers to enable MPAs to 'impose' aftercare conditions on the grant of planning permission in relation to land which is to be used for agriculture, forestry or amenity following mineral workings. The need for aftercare conditions stems from the recognition that land which is to be fully reclaimed needs not only the replacement of soils or soil-making materials, but also needs cultivation and the initial establishment and maintenance of vegetation (Plate 1.19). The ultimate aim behind the concept of aftercare is that, over time, the land will be brought to a standard whereby it does not have to be treated differently from undisturbed land. The aftercare period should be for a maximum of five years but can be extended beyond this period by mutual consent between the operator, the mineral planning authority and the landowner. MPG7 *The reclamation of mineral workings* provides further details. Comments on aftercare of amenity sites are also included in *Effectiveness of provisions for the aftercare of mineral workings* (DETR, 2000).

Plate 1.19 Aftercare – management of vegetation is often crucial to achieving restoration objectives.

G J White

For short-term workings, such as most sand and gravel and opencast coal sites, the after-use will be specified in the planning application. A working and restoration scheme will be part of the application for consideration by the MPA. Longer-term workings, such as hard rock quarries, may have outline proposals for reclamation. However, it is important to have some scheme at an early stage of long-term workings as certain aspects of habitat creation can be built in from commencement.

1.4.6 Legal agreements

Planning obligations (legal agreements) may be entered into under the terms of the section 106 of the 1990 Town and Country Planning Act (Section 75 of 1997 Act in Scotland), as amended by the Planning and Compensation Act 1991. These may be a unilateral undertaking by a developer as well as by an agreement between a developer and a local planning authority. Use is made of planning obligations in mineral planning to deal with issues which cannot adequately be controlled by planning conditions. Examples include:

- retention of the after-use – to guarantee that the proposed after-use will be implemented or maintained into the longer term
- long-term maintenance and management – for land to be returned successfully to beneficial use it is important that it is managed beyond the statutory five year aftercare period. For some after-uses, such as nature conservation, which may not generate sufficient funds to be self-sufficient, it may be appropriate to seek a planning obligation to secure such funding.
- maintenance of water levels – some nature conservation sites may require regular flooding to maintain habitat.
- provision of facilities for nature conservation and other amenity uses.

In the case of long-term use and management of land, Section 39 of the Wildlife and Countryside Act 1981 may be appropriate. These Acts allow an authority to enter into a legally binding agreement with an operator and/or owner to cover matters that are unrelated to the planning permission itself. The agreements offer greater security for the long-term management of land for a specified timescale.

1.4.7 Wildlife legislation

In some cases available options for creation may be constrained by the protected status, under national or international legislation, of existing wildlife, eg where a protected species occurs which may be affected by a creation project. Such species are primarily protected under the Wildlife and Countryside Act 1981. Since 1994, the wildlife conservation provisions of the Act have to be read alongside the Habitats Regulations 1994, which ensures that the UK complies with the requirements of the EU Habitats Directive. Species listed in Annex IV of the Habitats Directive are termed 'European protected species of animal'. In November 2000, the CRoW Act came into force in England and Wales. The wildlife measures of the CRoW Act strengthen both the protection of SSSIs and the enforcement provisions for protected species, as well as providing some backing to the current Biodiversity Action Plan process.

Protected species should be identified during preliminary desk and site investigations and the relevant agencies, such as the statutory nature conservation bodies, should be contacted (Plate 1.20). In the case of new mineral extraction sites, it is likely that the presence of such species will result in permission being refused, but many long-term operational sites, eg hard rock quarries, may contain interesting flora and fauna. Operations should be designed to prevent damage to designated sites eg SSSIs, SPAs, Special Areas of Conservation (SACs) or Ramsar sites, Scheduled Ancient Monuments or National Parks.

1.4.8 Water resource legislation

The Environment Agency has the statutory responsibility in England and Wales for water resource management, pollution control, flood defence, fisheries, navigation, recreation and conservation. This includes regulation of all abstraction and discharges and the monitoring of water quality. In certain areas of England and Wales, Internal Drainage Boards (IDBs) are responsible for agricultural land drainage and flood defence. In Scotland, the Scottish Environmental Protection Agency (SEPA) does not have the same statutory responsibilities as the Environment Agency. SEPA is responsible for pollution control, including monitoring and regulation of discharges, but abstraction is not licensed in Scotland. SEPA does have duties to conserve water resources as far as possible and to undertake gauging of river flows. When asked, SEPA must advise planning authorities on flood risks, but responsibility for flood defence lies with local authorities and private landowners. In Northern Ireland, water resource responsibilities are split between various departments: Department of Environment Northern Ireland, DoENI, (water quality), the Department of Regional Development (drinking water and sewerage) and the Department of Agriculture and Rural Development (flood defence and fisheries).

The Environment Agency and the IDBs also have a statutory responsibility for conservation under section 16 of the Water Resources Act 1991 and section 12 of the Land Drainage Act 1991. They are both obliged to:

- conserve and enhance the natural beauty, wildlife, geology and physiographical features of special interest
- protect and conserve buildings, sites and objects of archaeological, architectural and historic interest
- preserve public rights of way.

S Knell (rspb-images.com)

Plate 1.20
The presence of protected species, such as bats, will require specialist advice.

Although SEPA does not have the same statutory responsibilities, it does have a duty to promote conservation and enhancement of the natural beauty and amenity of controlled waters and associated land as well as the conservation of related flora and fauna.

Wetland creation schemes often involve the manipulation of water to create conditions beneficial to wildlife. These must be designed to prevent any adverse affect on hydrological conditions off-site. Consultation with the appropriate water resource authority is essential at an early stage in the planning process. In England and Wales any abstraction over 20 m^3 per day requires a licence. Abstraction licensing will be introduced in Northern Ireland and Scotland as the EU Water Framework Directive is implemented.

For a summary of water legislation and conditions relevant to wetland creation projects see Table 1.4.

Table 1.4 Water legislation and conditions relevant to wetland creation projects.

Legislation	Extent of coverage	Provisions
Water Framework Directive	European Union	WFD establishes an obligation on Member States to prevent deterioration in the status of water (surface water and ground water) and to restore water to 'good status' by 2015. Status is measured by a combination of chemical and ecological factors, ensuring that the biological condition of surface waterbodies will become a much more important driver in all water management policies in the future. The Directive has provisions to support the water needs of Protected Areas (such as Natura 2000 sites), including wetlands, and to ensure that the water needs of wetlands dependent on groundwater are met. It also provides a major opportunity to promote floodplain restoration and wetland creation as a tool to achieve better ecological conditions in inland and coastal waters.
Reservoirs Safety Provisions Act 1975	England, Scotland and Wales (and its provisions are followed in Northern Ireland)	It imposes safety provisions on reservoirs and artificial lakes capable of holding more than 25,000 m^3 above the natural surface of the land or where dam height exceeds 4.5 m. All such waterbodies must be constructed in accordance with the design and under the supervision of a qualified civil engineer (appointed to a Panel under the Act). These waterbodies must also be inspected annually by a Supervising Engineer and at least every 10 years by a Panel Engineer (MAFF, 1996). Clearly engineering advice should be sought if restoration schemes are likely to involve the impoundment of large volumes of water.
Land Drainage Act 1991	England and Wales	Requires any works that interfere with an existing drainage system, eg dams across drainage channels, to have land drainage consent. Water resource authorities must be supplied with the details of proposed work. Before the authority can issue consents they have to be satisfied that there will be no knock-on effects to third parties or that third parties accept the consequences of the proposal.
Water Resources Act 1991	England and Wales	Licence is required to abstract water from any source of supply (even small scale and one-off abstractions). Section 25 of the Act requires an impoundment licence if for example on-stream water is impounded or an existing watercourse is diverted. Licences are required to discharge water. Water quality details must be provided.
Water (Scotland) Act 1980	Scotland	Similar provisions as above regarding water abstraction and impoundment licences, although abstraction licences not generally required at the current time.
Water and Sewerage Services Act 1973	Northern Ireland	Similar provisions as above regarding water abstraction and impoundment licences, although abstraction licences not generally required at the current time.
Control of Pollution Act 1974	Scotland	Licences required to discharge water. Water quality details must be provided.
Northern Ireland Water Act 1972	Northern Ireland	Licences required to discharge water. Water quality details must be provided.

2 ASSESSING THE POSSIBILITIES

Mineral planning authorities will require detailed restoration plans at some stage during the working. For most short-term workings the after-use will be specified in the application. Although after-use is only one factor to be considered in a planning application, it is important that restoration schemes are well thought through, practical and achievable. They can generate positive public relations for the mineral company. BAP strategies (section 1.2) aid mineral developers by identifying possible avenues of opportunity for habitat creation on sites where there is no existing nature conservation interest. If in doubt, mineral extractors should contact the relevant statutory nature conservation agency to find out which habitat is most appropriate in a given area and should consult their local BAP co-ordinator, county ecologists or the local Wildlife Trust. This is one of many points at which interested parties can influence the mineral extraction planning process in favour of producing benefits to biodiversity (Figure 2.1 and sections 2.2.1 and 2.2.3)

This section deals largely with the planning of habitat creation schemes. Currently in the UK there are many schemes designed to reclaim derelict land; the restoration planning approach described below, and summarised in Box 2.1, could be used in these circumstances.

Figure 2.1 Mineral extraction and restoration process.

Stages marked ✪ are where the restoration outcome can be influenced

Potential for extraction identified
↓
Consideration of freehold/mineral rights acquisition
↓
✪Obtain site information
↓
✪Consultation
↓
✪Formulate restoration strategy
↓
Planning application
↓
Assessment of application
↓
Consultation on application
↓ ↑
Consultees
↓ ↓
REFUSAL OR
↓
Approval of application based on conditions of restoration
↓
Phasing of extraction including overburden management
↓
Development of macro-features during extraction
↓
Creation of micro-features using on-site machinery
↓
Vegetation establishment
↓
Ongoing long-term management

Box 2.1 The process of formulating objectives and project planning

The following is shown as a simple linear process, however, there are often occasions where activities are repeated or run in parallel. For example, consultation is generally an ongoing activity.

Collation of site information (2.1.1)

Scoping of habitat creation possibilities (2.1.2)

Feasibility study (2.1.3)

Consultation (2.2.1)

Choosing an appropriate habitat to create (2.2.2 and 4)

Setting the objectives (2.2.3)

Project planning (2.2.4)

Planning for long-term management (2.3)

2.1 Information gathering

The first step in any planning exercise is the collation of site information that will identify and evaluate the existing wildlife interest. This in turn will allow the identification of constraints, provide the baseline information for monitoring purposes and enable the formulation of realistic objectives. Finally, it will enable the selection of habitat creation options and inform decisions on the most appropriate techniques to use. Information can be gathered as part of a desk study coupled with site investigation by experienced practitioners.

2.1.1 Collation of site information

Initial desk study appraisal

Information should be gathered from the following sources.

- Examination of maps provides information on a site's topography, soil, underlying geology, and land-use history, and gives information on hydrology, hydrogeology and infrastructure features. Production of accurate base maps is essential as these are used from the feasibility study to the final monitoring. Putting the maps onto a Geographical Information System (GIS) to overlay different features should be considered.
- Aerial photographs are excellent for identifying features not obvious on the ground. They allow accurate location of vegetation features and boundaries. Site survey staff should have access to recent photographs.
- The aspect and general landscape of the area should be considered as part of the desk study for the area.
- Neighbours and tenants can often provide local information.
- Site occupants or previous owners can provide information on previous site management regimes.
- The relevant water resource agency can provide information on site variables such as climate, water resource availability and water quality.
- Wildlife records are a valuable source of information and are available from the bodies listed in Table 2.1.
- Relevant legislation and associated legal requirements can be ascertained by contacting the relevant statutory nature conservation and water management bodies (section 1.5).

Site investigations

Data gathered during field investigations should build on information collected during the desk study. Possible areas for investigation are outlined below and may require specialist involvement. All survey workers should work from standard base maps. A careful assessment of all risks involved should be undertaken and appropriate health and safety measures implemented to protect fieldworkers. The following subjects are often investigated during site studies:

- existing flora and fauna
- landform design
- adjacent land-use
- hydrology
- water quality
- palaeoecological interest
- archaeological and geological interest
- potential for control of fire
- engineering requirements
- safety
- access for livestock and machinery
- landscape
- existing site use by local people.

Existing flora and fauna

Assessing existing biological interest is a vital part of any restoration strategy. Existing features of special interest, eg tunnel systems with protected bat species, may have to be safeguarded during the extraction and restoration phases. Biological surveys allow:

- identification of important or protected species and communities present
- identification of potential conflicts between existing interest and extraction and restoration strategy
- assessment of potential for natural regeneration (ie presence nearby of potential colonists or pioneer communities already present) and biological resources valuable during subsequent restoration (Table 2.2)

Table 2.1 Key consultees and other relevant bodies for the formulation of restoration plans.
(adapted from Wheeler and Shaw, 1995)

Agency or body	Subject area
Key consultees Land and mineral owners (and neighbouring landowners), local community	Involvement and co-operation in restoration schemes. Legal aspects of site leases. Future plans for land following extraction.
Mineral Planning Authority	Guidance on planning and conservation issues e.g. from development plans. Site planning constraints, eg rights of way. Existing statutory (eg common land, National Nature Reserves – NNRs, Scheduled Ancient Monuments – SAMs) and non-statutory designations eg local nature reserves. Possible financial support for restoration work.
Statutory nature conservation agencies, ie English Nature (EN), Countryside Council for Wales (CCW), Scottish Natural Heritage (SNH), DoENI and the Countryside Agency	Statutory designations eg NNRs, SSSIs, ASSIs, Areas of Outstanding Natural Beauty (AONBs) etc. Will advise on the occurrence of protected species eg great crested newt or adder and also general wildlife value of site. Provide advice on restoration techniques, especially species translocations/introductions. Possible practical or financial help (especially with species identified as priorities in BAPs).
Environment Agency, IDB, SEPA and Rivers Agency and Environment and Heritage Service (NI)	Management of water at the catchment level. Consent requirements for water abstraction, impoundment and discharge, as well as management affecting drainage or flood defence. Pollution potential of discharges. Possible practical, advisory and financial help with restoration. Water resource information.
Agriculture and forestry agencies eg Dept for Environment, Food and Rural Affairs (DEFRA), Scottish Executive Environment and Rural Affairs Department (SEERAD), Department of Agriculture Northern Ireland (DARD), and the Forestry Commission (FC)	Current usage and possible effects on adjacent land. Advice on agri-environment schemes. Agricultural land quality information.
English Heritage, Historic Scotland, Environment and Heritage Service, County Archaeological Officers	Advice on archaeological interest and survey. Location and details of SAMs. Possible practical and financial support for restoration.
Other useful bodies Local Authority Record Office	County series Ordnance Survey (OS) maps. Estate plans and early documents relating to site history.
Local authority archaeologists or Archaeological Trust, Council for British Archaeology, wetland archaeological specialists	Site history, information and advice, possible practical support for survey and restoration work.
English Heritage, Royal Commission on Historical Monuments of Wales, Royal Commission on Historical Monuments of Scotland, Environment and Heritage Service	Repositories of the National Archaeological Record, which holds information on archaeological sites and the National Building Record, which includes the National Record of Industrial Monuments.
Joint Nature Conservation Committee (JNCC) The Wildlife Trusts, Scottish Wildlife Trust, Ulster Wildlife Trust	Existing records for specific sites (including the Invertebrate Site Register). Advice on the conservation of specific species. Existing records for specific sites, amenity and wildlife value of specific sites. Advice on wildlife and habitat management.
Council for the Protection of Rural England (CPRE), Council for the Protection of Rural Wales (CPRW)	Landscape, wildlife, and historical details relating to specific sites.

Continued overleaf ▸▸▸

▸▸▸

The RSPB	Ornithological records for specific sites. Advice on conservation and management for particular birds. Habitat management advice, especially wetland and heathland creation and management.
National invertebrate specialist groups (eg Royal Entomological Society, British Entomology and Natural History Society, Balfour-Brown Club, British Arachnological Society, British Dragonfly Society, British Butterfly Society)	Invertebrate records for specific sites. Advice on species conservation and management.
Biological Records Centres	Biological records for specific sites. Species evaluation.
Health and Safety Executive (HSE)	Health and safety issues on site.
Meteorological Office	Climatic records and information.
Centre of Ecology and Hydrology	Hydrological information and advice.
Scientific literature, local journals	Related information on general and specific restoration issues, as well as information on conservation and local issues.

Table 2.2. Biological resources that can be stored and used during restoration.
(Andrews *et al*, 1992)

Resources include:
- soil from semi-natural habitats
- seed from heaths and grasslands
- turf
- sediments from waterbodies
- boles of mature trees, especially damaged and decaying individuals – these will have to be stored in a suitable microclimate, ie in a woodland
- individual plants.

These resources should only be used when it is agreed that the area from where they will be removed is due to be damaged.

- identification of areas with potentially undesirable colonists
- retention of existing important features on non-operational land, eg habitats that cannot be re-created
- collection of data for comparison with subsequent monitoring efforts.

Botanical surveys should identify vegetation communities (as well as rare and scarce plants) occurring on, and adjacent to, the site and should at least conform to Phase 1 Habitat Survey (NCC, 1990) (Plate 2.1). Many limestone quarries, for example, harbour important grassland communities in areas peripheral to operation. It is important to identify possible refugia for vegetation and invertebrate communities that could be safeguarded during extraction and subsequently used to provide material for re-colonisation. Consultation may be required with statutory nature conservation agencies and specialists after field surveys in order to assess wildlife value.

Plate 2.1
Habitat surveys allow the identification of important species or communities.

G J White

Landform design

This includes:

- size and shape and extent in relation to surrounding habitat
- topography
- soils.

Soils are particularly important to the restoration scheme. A detailed soil survey is required with soil analysis. A clear understanding of the physical and chemical characteristics of the soil needs to be determined. If sites are originally agricultural, the soils may contain high levels of nutrients and may be unsuitable for some types of habitat. There may be ways in which subsoils and topsoils can be used differently to achieve results. Soils may be important sources of seeds.

Land-use of adjacent land

Information is required to assess current management regimes and risk of activities off-site affecting the habitat creation scheme, eg fertiliser inputs, landfill sites, ongoing mineral extraction. Other possible constraints, such as potential damage to neighbouring land by creation objectives, should also be identified. Constraints are possible, for example sites designed to attract large amounts of birds, eg wildfowl, should not be situated within eight miles of civilian or military airfields – contact the Ministry of Defence (MOD) or the Civil Aviation Authority (CAA) if necessary.

Hydrology

Hydrology is especially important during wetland creation, eg open water, reedbed, wet grassland and wet heathland. Expert advice is best sought on the level of detail required. Most investigations involve gathering information on:

- local climate (seasonal rainfall variation and evapotranspiration) to allow water budgets to be put together
- site watercourses (type, distribution, slope and degree of functioning). Aerial photographs are useful in tracing old drains and watercourses
- site water outputs – allowing site water losses to be gauged
- soil hydraulic conductivity and seepage flows
- distribution and stability of open water
- availability of water – likelihood of obtaining abstraction licence (if necessary – any abstraction over 20 m^3 will require one).

It should be noted that when creating large waterbodies (eg during gravel and chalk extraction there can be problems estimating the final water level, which leads to design problems regarding features such as marginal profiles and islands (Box 2.2).

Box 2.2 College Lake, Buckinghamshire

College Lake resulted from a chalk quarry operated by Castle Cement from the late 1960s until 1991. The original restoration plans to agriculture were subsequently changed to a nature reserve with mainly wetland and grassland habitats, extending to 100 acres (now 210 acres). Since 1985 over 160 bird and 450 plant species have been recorded. Waders such as lapwings and redshanks have bred and the site is an important refuge for wintering waterbirds. The site is currently managed by the Berkshire, Buckinghamshire and Oxfordshire Wildlife Trust (BBOWT) (Plate 2.2).

Water levels presented a problem at the end of the active quarrying phase in 1991. They rose over the maximum suggested by a hydrologist. Carefully constructed islands, bank profiles and planted trees were flooded. Rafts have been constructed, but the effect was a loss of breeding bird interest. Since then temporary solutions have included the creation of a large new island and some bunding to protect shallow scrapes and grazing marsh. A regime of pumping excess water out of the pit into the adjacent canal has provided a short-term answer, but long-term solutions are being explored such as re-landscaping the whole site to accommodate higher water levels.

The site has also been managed as an important arable weed reserve. Following the discovery of a rich seed source in topsoil stockpiled in the 1950s, a small area of land has been managed on a three course rotation producing wheat and root crops and an accompanying show of cornfield flowers including many national and county rarities. Following a recent extension of the reserve this project will be increased in area.

G J White

Plate 2.2 College Lake – a redundant chalk quarry, now a BBOWT nature reserve.

Water quality
Chemical properties of groundwater profoundly affect vegetation types that can be supported (Table 2.3).

Palaeoecological interest
On peat sites the palaeoecological record within the substrate may be important. Any important areas affected by extraction or restoration need to be properly recorded before work is carried out

Archaeological and geological interest
The UK has a particularly rich and varied geological heritage, which records changing climates, environments and landscapes in considerable detail. In general mineral extraction has played a positive role in conserving this geological record through exposures created and managed within the context of mineral extraction, and opportunities should be sought to maintain important exposures during restoration. However poorly planned extraction and inappropriate restoration can damage or destroy important rocks, fossils, minerals and landforms. Recently published guidance, *Geodiverstiy and minerals, a guide to planning, operating, restoring and managing mineral sites for geological conservation* (English Nature, 2002), provides detailed information on identifying sites of importance, management considerations, and opportunities for support, promotion and enhancement (Plate 2.3).

Contact should also be made with the county archaeologist who can advise on potential importance and management.

Potential for control of fire
This is especially important to assess on peatland, moorland and heathland sites. Access, potential firebreaks and water availability are all issues.

Plate 2.3 Important geological exposures should be maintained where possible – Barkway Chalk Pit nature reserve.

G J White

Table 2.3 The trophic states of water. (after RSPB, EN and ITE, 1997)

Nutrient status	mg/litre of nutrients			pH	Other characteristics
	Total phosphorus	Inorganic nitrogen (NO_3-N)	Calcium carbonate		
Oligotrophic to Mesotrophic	0.005–0.01	0.2–0.4	10–30	c 6	Moderate productivity. Slightly green algal colouration in summer.
Mesotrophic to Eutrophic	0.01–0.03	0.3–0.65	c 30	6–7	High productivity for algae and macrophytes. Often discoloured by algae.
Eutrophic to Hypertrophic	0.03–0.1	0.5–1.5	> 30	> 7	Discolouration noticeable due to high algal productivity. Macrophyte productivity variable.
Hypertrophic	> 0.1	> 1.5	> 30		Algal productivity extremely high. Few macrophyte species able to compete with algae.

Engineering requirements
This includes assessing the works required, properties and availability of on-site materials and the condition of existing structures.

Safety
This specifically includes physical and chemical hazards to workers.

Access for livestock and machinery
This is necessary to allow long-term management of the habitat (Plate 2.4).

Landscape
Occasionally there are conflicts between landscape and wildlife interest eg the Post-Enclosure landscape in 'planned countryside' contains many hedgerows, which although important for some species, reduce the suitability of habitat for breeding wading birds.

Existing site use
Existing site use by local people has the potential for beneficial community involvement or negative impacts, eg vandalism.

G J White

Plate 2.4 Shetland ponies in a reedbed/grazing marsh complex.

2.1.2 Scoping of habitat creation possibilities

The choice of target habitat is guided by ecological appropriateness and by strategic planning documents. It is then confirmed by a detailed feasibility study involving baseline ecological survey and examination of the site's use by people. Land-use is dictated by strategic development plans, which balance the requirements of different interests. Biodiversity planning must be incorporated into this process. Mineral planning is becoming more strategic with an increasing emphasis on an after-use-led approach (Coppin and Box, 1998). It is important that mineral extractors ensure that their restoration proposals fit into wider strategies and MPAs ensure that Local Mineral Plans are backed by coherent habitat creation strategies. At this stage a range of habitat creation possibilities can be drawn up. This will be based on strategic planning information and details collected relating to the site.

2.1.3 Feasibility study

In many situations it is worth conducting a feasibility study to look at the practicalities of a range of specific objectives. Feasibility studies narrow down the choice of objectives by:

- assessing practical and financial feasibility. Incomes may be lower from a nature conservation end-use than for agricultural restoration, although this depends on the habitat created and whether agri-environment grants are likely to be available, eg the Waterside Land category of the Countryside Stewardship scheme
- identifying the position of the site in planning context, ie habitat and development planning strategies
- identifying techniques for retaining the existing wildlife value
- identifying techniques for creating desired habitats/communities. There are four basic strategies that can be adopted (adapted from Jones, 1990):
    - 'hands off' approach leaving vegetation to develop as a result of natural processes. This can be particularly effective where there is a nearby semi-natural habitat as a source of colonising material (Plate 2.5)
    - allowing natural development as above, but with management input or change. For example the development of grassland vegetation by natural colonisation, followed by regular mowing or livestock grazing, or alternatively, allowing regular disturbance to maintain a pioneer community typical of active or recently abandoned mineral workings
    - an initial intervention and then allowing natural, unmanaged habitat development eg floodplain woodland creation (Plate 2.6)
    - full intervention and management to produce target community eg heathland creation

G J White

Plate 2.5 Natural regeneration in a quarry.

G J White

Plate 2.6 Floodplain woodland developing on a mineral extraction site.

- considering other possible roles for the site, including education, research and public access
- an assessment of the potential cost of the various options.

This process should also include consultation with relevant specialists and agencies and engage local communities in dialogue (section 2.3.2).

Costs

Costs are site-specific and are likely to be linked to size, availability of restoration material and technical difficulty. Costs associated with creation projects come under the following headings:

- land costs
- staff time – a full-time site restoration manager is often necessary on large schemes, especially during the major earth-moving and habitat manipulation phases of the operation
- specialists – are required to undertake surveys, eg topography, hydrology, biological etc, and to assist in the creation planning and implementation. This can be expensive; consultancy fees vary from £200–£1,000 per day. The need for such work should be carefully thought through
- creation operations – these largely depend on the size, extent and nature of the project. Specialist machinery, usually with low ground pressure, is often required for creation work, although it may be available 'in-house'
- long-term management costs – such as vegetation management, grazing cost/revenue, requirement for infrastructure
- monitoring costs – for example surveyors, fieldwork and results analysis.

2.2 Formulating a restoration plan

2.2.1 Consultation and consensus building

Early and continued consultation with a wide range of agencies and individuals is essential throughout the planning phase, especially in relation to the selection of appropriate objectives and techniques. The local community should be included at the consultation stage (Plate 2.7). Key consultees and other relevant bodies are listed in Table 2.1. It is important that the consultation process is open and informs local people of the overall aims. Consensus building with stakeholders and user groups should be undertaken at various stages in the process and should build from the non-contentious (site information) to more potentially controversial issues (management objectives and prescriptions). All those taking part should be aware of the way in which comments received during this process are included in the decision-making. Confrontational situations should be avoided (eg panels of specialists on platforms facing the audience of stakeholders). Instead, informal gatherings where site staff can mingle with people to discuss the issues may provide a better format for consensus building.

Where local opposition exists to outline plans for a site, it is necessary to resolve these before writing the plan. This is partly aided by the management planning process itself, but where issues are complex then information dissemination and awareness raising programmes are important (section 5.1). Management plans can be drafted with input from different user groups and the result edited together. This approach can achieve a high level of ownership among stakeholders and solves confrontation through the necessary search for common goals and co-operation.

2.2.2 Choosing an appropriate habitat to create

The first stage is to short-list viable habitat options. This stage considers possibilities in terms of the feasibility study and selects options which are achievable. It is important to prepare options so that all the information is readily available for the consultation process.

Guidance on the requirements of a range of BAP habitats can be found in section 4 of this handbook. Options depend on a number of factors:

A Cooper

Plate 2.7 Consultation at an early stage is essential in any project.

- previous site history – what existed prior to extraction or before a previous intensive use. This indicates which habitats could be suitable under the local climate
- suitability and position within the ecological unit – contact should be made with the relevant statutory government conservation agency, county ecologists and the local conservation organisations to ascertain what habitats and species should be considered in creation plans. Attention should be paid to strategic plans such as Local Biodiversity Action Plans and English Nature's Natural Areas approach (Plate 2.8). Where extraction sites exist alongside semi-natural habitats, restoration can be used to create habitats that act as buffers or corridors between sites
- soil – what is possible on soils and soil-forming material present on the site?
- hydrology – the hydrology of the restored site dictates what is feasible to a large extent when creating both terrestrial and aquatic habitats
- the value of existing and potential pioneer communities that would develop on the site with no/minimum intervention or regular disturbance
- the potential for appropriate long-term management.

Plate 2.8
A local BAP.

On larger workings, variability within the site will allow a mosaic of related habitats to be considered (see Table 4.1), for example a range of wetland habitats depending on the wetness and substrate. Such mosaics of habitat can be extremely valuable. Climate change is also likely to influence the suitability of sites for particular habitats in the long-term. The potential impacts of climate change need to be considered when selecting which habitats to create.

2.2.3 Setting the objectives

Defining objectives is the first stage of detailed project planning. Objectives should be prioritised. They act as a guide during the planning stage and will eventually be used to gauge the project's success. Chosen objectives should form part of a comprehensive Project Plan. Objectives for nature conservation are either habitat based, the most important, or species based. Habitat based objectives can be general, for example provision of a ditch network, or highly specific, for instance creation of a desired NVC community. Species based projects aim to provide suitable habitat for target species, eg reedbeds for bitterns. Projects may also include objectives dealing with amenity, education, research and mitigation.

Setting the objectives at the start of the project ensures that:

- aims are not changed in a haphazard way during the project, although an element of flexibility should be provided
- continuity is maintained if staff changes occur (especially if a diary of events is maintained).

2.2.4 Project planning

Project planning is a very important part of the process of creating habitats. Parker (1995) reviewed just over 100 habitat creation projects and reached a number of conclusions, finding that in many cases:

- habitat creation projects failed due to poor planning and the lack of precise objectives
- projects were too ambitious and objectives were not realistic in relation to short- and long-term resource availability
- too little attention was paid to soil type, structure and fertility

- project planning did not sufficiently address long-term management, ie site management until vegetation is successfully established, which may extend for an indefinite period and implies a long-term financial commitment
- site monitoring was inadequate and as a result it was often impossible to determine project effectiveness. Inadequate monitoring can mean failure to adapt management programmes in response to changes in vegetation or site conditions.

Therefore project planning is essential to:
- state clearly the aim and objectives of the creation proposal
- safeguard the existing conservation interest of the site, if any
- identify appropriate target habitat and communities
- identify appropriate techniques to achieve project objectives
- identify project constraints, eg legal problems, access difficulties
- design operational details and working plans which give precise details for extraction, restoration and long-term management phases. Restoration operational details should include timing, landforming, removal of unwanted rubbish, soil handling techniques, use of soil, soil-forming material and imported materials, soil cultivation and vegetation establishment. Long-term management specifications should detail timing of maintenance management and site monitoring
- ensure that progressive restoration operations are well co-ordinated
- detail monitoring and long-term management programmes
- plan for the site's long-term funding and management responsibilities.

To fulfil the above objectives project plans must include the following:
- an outline and details of the project's scope – consideration of the proposed extraction process; scope and scale, mineral production requirements, spoil disposal and storage, land take etc
- site survey and appraisal – existing site conditions should be assessed in detail to identify topographical features, land-use and classification, climate, soil type, water levels and movements, ownership boundaries, rights of way, existing vegetation and landscape value. It is especially important to identify any nature conservation interest at this point
- details of proposed after-use
- formulation of restoration objectives which should identify, for example final landform and water levels, new positions of rights of way (Plate 2.9), planting details and management requirements of new vegetation, and treatment of unstable slopes.

G J White

Plate 2.9
The future use and interpretation of the site should be considered at an early stage.

The project planning process should ensure that:
- existing habitats and species protected by law are safeguarded. This is the primary reason for IDO/Review of Old Mineral Permissions (ROMP) process in many cases
- features of earth science and industrial archaeology interest are safeguarded
- trial plots are used to test methods of vegetation establishment
- during mineral extraction and restoration, there is no detrimental effect to surrounding areas of nature conservation interest
- during extraction and restoration and long-term management phases, the need for infrastructure, eg gates and fences, is assessed.

2.3 Planning for long-term management

2.3.1 Working with nature conservation organisations

Habitat creation projects undertaken by mineral companies are often in partnership with a voluntary body that eventually takes on management of the site. This:
- allows professional management and expertise to be channelled into site management
- provides instant links to the local community and volunteer work parties
- puts the site into the hands of those best able to attract sources of funding.

Many mineral extractors have adopted the partnership approach with local nature conservation organisations, eg the Durham Wildlife Trust (DWT) has its headquarters and a reserve on Rainton Meadows, a former British Coal opencast site. DWT has been gifted the former site offices and has a 99 year lease of the land from the City of Sunderland Council. When the aftercare period finishes, the Trust will take over management of the area. The Warwickshire Wildlife Trust also has its headquarters on a former gravel pit site at Brandon Marsh (Plate 2.10). Here, again, the land is leased on a 99 year lease from the mineral company for a nominal fee. In such cases co-operation and active participation continues between the mineral extractors and nature conservation bodies long after the sites have ceased working.

Other alternative means of ensuring beneficial management include the Great Linford approach. The Game Conservancy used this site for 20 years for research, before it was handed over to Milton Keynes Council as an environmental education resource. Working successfully with nature conservation organisations is achieved by an appreciation of their aims and objectives. Site design must ensure that:
- the objectives of the proposed managing body are met
- the proposed area will be valuable in some way
- a source of funds will be available through some mechanism to ensure appropriate management of the site.

Likely managing organisations include:
- The Royal Society for the Protection of Birds (The RSPB)
  The RSPB is the charity that takes action for wild birds and the environment. It is Europe's largest voluntary wildlife

Warwickshire Wildlife Trust

Plate 2.10 Warwickshire Wildlife Trust HQ, located on a former gravel pit at Brandon Marsh.

P Benstead

Plate 2.11
Many former mineral extraction sites are now managed as nature reserves.

conservation body, with more than one million members. The RSPB manages over 175 nature reserves covering over 121,000 ha.

- The Wildlife Trusts
  There are 46 County Wildlife Trusts and 52 Urban Trusts. Together they are responsible for the management of 2,300 reserves. Many of these sites are on former mineral workings. In Nottinghamshire, for example, 17% of the County Wildlife Trusts sites are on former mineral workings. The respective county and urban trusts are co-ordinated under a central body called The Wildlife Trusts.

- Groundwork Trusts
  A network of non-profit-making trusts backed by a national organisation, The Groundwork Foundation. Their aim is to improve urban and urban-fringe environments.

- The Woodland Trust
  The Trust is heavily involved in planting new woodlands and acquiring land. It has considerable expertise in managing urban woodlands and promoting community involvement and management.

- Single-site interest groups
  Some sites may be adopted by a local community group or trust, eg Sevenoaks nature reserve (Box 2.6, Plate 2.11). Details about how to set up a trust such as this are given in section 2.3.3.

2.3.2 Community involvement

Active community involvement in habitat creation projects is desirable from the outset of any planned extraction. Once the potential to create habitats has been realised at the planning stage then public meetings, events, walks and talks, door-to-door canvassing and discussions should be held to promote the idea. It is important to identify the local community's composition; it may be the people of the neighbouring village but could equally be a collection of local geological societies. Community involvement at every stage is important as it:

- formalises community ownership
- promotes active citizenship
- encourages an appreciation and understanding of nature through direct involvement
- enables new skills to be learned.

There are different degrees of community involvement, from projects initiated by local people and therefore directly linked to their needs, to projects initiated by an outside agency with more gradual involvement of the community. Community use of a site restored with ecological objectives is not necessarily incompatible and can bring many benefits.

Community liaison staff may be required to reach out to the community and involve them in planning and discussion, undertake market research and provide interpretation. Involvement can be sustained after extraction and restoration by community management, management in partnership by volunteering, having community representatives on advisory and management committees, starting 'friends' support groups and by using voluntary wardens.

One possibility is to invite volunteers to participate in the site's management

A Hay (rspb-images.com)

Plate 2.12 Volunteers can be crucial for maintaining habitats.

(Plate 2.12). When working with volunteers in this way it is important to:

- pick the right people
- look at health and safety issues
- check liability and insurance
- ensure adequate supervision and training
- communicate with and involve volunteers
- consider costs eg payment of expenses.

In many cases mineral site operators themselves could make greater use of voluntary help. Many birdwatchers, for example, can help with bird recording and monitoring and may even be able to provide species protection and habitat creation advice. Contact the RSPB, the local Wildlife Trust, the BTO or consult the annually published *Birdwatchers' Yearbook and Diary* (Buckingham Press), which lists the addresses of local bird clubs and groups that may be able to help.

The involvement of local volunteers with a mineral extraction company at Little Paxton, Cambridgeshire, has led to the creation of an interesting nature reserve – a valuable local resource. At Waterford Heath, Hertfordshire, a local community steering group helped restore a dry sand quarry with invertebrate and botanical importance (Plate 2.13). The site now provides a popular, local, open space and helps achieve local BAP targets. Similar community involvement is behind many successful projects. Involving the community also has the advantage of opening up more funding channels to the managing body (section 2.6).

2.3.3 Setting up a voluntary organisation

Types of voluntary organisation

When setting up a voluntary body there is no legal requirement to produce a formal framework and written constitution, but doing so can be helpful. A formal framework provides an identity, emphasising direction, allowing continuity and enhancing credibility when dealing with potential funding bodies. Voluntary bodies can take three forms, all of which can acquire charitable status if they meet the relevant criteria.

Unincorporated associations

These are cheap and simple legal structures, ideal for groups with a common aim that draws its committees from its membership. Trustees must hold any land and members are liable for any debts incurred. Unincorporated associations are not really suitable where large sums of money are involved.

Trusts

This is a good structure for an organisation wishing to hold land and/or property, employ staff and raise funds. Voluntary trusts must also be charities for technical and legal reasons. Trustees are liable for any losses. An example is the trust established to manage Sevenoaks nature reserve (Box 2.6).

Groundwork Hertfordshire

Plate 2.13
At Waterford Heath, Hertfordshire, the local community was fully involved in the site restoration.

Limited companies
Companies limited by guarantee are corporate with a separate legal arrangement from its membership. These are suitable for organisations that employ staff, own land and have large budgets. Such organisations tend to have more democratic processes and the risk of loss to members and staff is minimised. However it is complex to set up and legal assistance may be required on occasion.

Attaining charitable status
All the above types of organisation can become charities. To do so the organisation's purpose must be recognised as charitable and of benefit to the public or a section thereof. The organisation must then register with the Charity Commissioners. The advantages of becoming a charity include exemption from and recovery of some taxes, and relief on local authority business rates.

Land tenure and management agreements
Three main forms of tenure exist:

- freehold – outright purchase is sometimes possible, occasionally for a nominal fee
- lease – exclusive possession for a defined period. It is important that the length of the lease, its renewability, rent payments and the length of rent period are understood fully. There may be a liability to pay the rent for the whole period of the lease unless there is a let-out clause. Other clauses can be included to ensure that the lessee conserves natural values or to stipulate or deny specific management practices
- licence – limited rights to use a site for a stated period and purpose. There is no protection under tenancy legislation.

For nature conservation purposes leases and licences must be fairly long-term to be effective: generally greater than 25 years. Another method of securing appropriate management is by management agreement. Statutory agreements include:

- section 39 agreements (under the Wildlife and Countryside Act 1981), which permit local authorities to make agreements to conserve and enhance natural beauty and amenity. Such agreements can impose land-use restrictions, oblige owners to carry out works or empower the local authority to carry out necessary work. Normally s39 agreements are between the landowner, local authority and a wildlife body.

- section 15 agreements (under the Countryside Act 1968), which allow the statutory nature conservation bodies in England, Scotland and Wales to enter into management agreements with site managers on sites important for nature conservation (but not reserves) to safeguard the site's interest.

- a section 106 agreement (under the Town and Country Planning Act 1990), which can be drawn up during the planning stage by the applicant and the MPA. These can be used as detailed in section 1.4.6. Local authorities can make their wishes more permanent by entering into simultaneous section 33 agreements (under the Local Government (Misc Provisions) Act 1982).

2.3.4 Why produce a management plan?

Effective long-term management requires a realistic approach to planning. Aftercare requirements are set out for the operator (MPG7). Operators should submit outline aftercare strategies to the planning authorities and follow-up with a detailed, annual, long-term management programme following an agreed management plan. Ideally, progress of these schemes would be the subject of an annual review meeting attended by the operator, land manager and MPA. Whatever the proposals for a site, it is valuable if the background and reasons for any work are in writing. This can be a short project proposal or, where there are longer-term management implications, a comprehensive management plan. A management plan brings together information about a site enabling management objectives based on this information to be met through a prescribed work programme over a stated period.

The main functions of a site management plan are to:

- describe the site by collating all available physical and biological information.
  This is part of the creation planning process so should be in hand

- identify relationships between the site and site user groups and stakeholders, and identify stakeholders and resource users. *This allows stakeholders to be involved in the management planning process, and is vital in large complex sites with multiple uses*
- identify clear management objectives. *This ensures that all work is linked to objectives and allows the efficacy of management to be assessed during the review process. Part of the process of producing management objectives involves identifying constraints to ideal management and conflict resolution*
- identify and describe the management necessary to achieve the objectives. *All management prescriptions should relate directly to one or more of the stated objectives*
- identify the monitoring effort and methodology required. *Ensures that objectives are being met by the chosen management approach and provides a feedback mechanism whereby management can be altered according to results*
- ensure that project results are systematically recorded
- organise resources and funding. *Producing a management plan for a five-year period allows necessary work to be agreed with a funding agency*
- ensure continuity of management in the event of staff changes.

Plans should be prepared as soon as sites are established and require management. This will avoid unwitting damage to important features. A preliminary plan should be produced within six months. Preliminary plans should identify important features, management objectives and priorities and outline costs and other resource requirements. These plans are ideal documents to bid for funding and resources both internally and externally.

Completed management plans should be prepared within a year if possible. Large sites may take longer, especially where there is multiple resource use by local communities. Such sites will have to undergo programmes of information dissemination and consultation, before plans can be written. This is especially important where the levels of site protection are not very robust.

2.3.5 How to produce a management plan

Management plans should be written in consultation with site management staff, representatives of relevant government agencies and representatives of local user groups and communities. The management planning process logically follows the steps that are needed to deliver conservation on a site:

1 understanding the site
2 identifying goals or management objectives. Points to consider when setting management objectives are

Table 2.4 Points to consider when setting objectives for site management.

Evaluate status/ ownership	• Site designations and ownership • Existing and potential wildlife value • Past and current management • Scope for enhancement of wildlife value
Site characteristics	• Size • Proximity to existing semi-natural habitat • Surrounding land-use/management • Soil types • Hydrology • Potential problems with water excess, shortage or quality
Legal constraints	• Discuss any proposals with water, fisheries and conservation management agencies
Management constraints	• Availability of resources/labour/equipment/skills • Availability of grants

set out in Table 2.4
3 identifying the management required to achieve objectives (Boxes 2.3 and 2.4)
4 installing monitoring systems to ensure that management is effective in delivering conservation and allowing review and refinement of management objectives.

Box 2.3 An example of an operational objective with attendant outline prescriptions and projects

Operational Objective 5.1
To enhance floodplain wet grassland maintaining the internationally important population of breeding waders (350 pairs) and extend suitable habitat for nationally important wintering waterfowl population.

Outline prescriptions

5.1.1 Removal of encroaching scrub

Projects*
M/10/01 Manage wet grassland habitat by grazing
Graze grassland to prevent invasion by scrub
Compartments: 1, 2, 3
Graze grassland.

5.1.2 Minimise disturbance to wintering/breeding bird populations

Projects
P/10/01 Protect site/species patrol
Compartments: all
Patrol the reserve at least weekly to maintain a disturbance-free zone for feeding/roosting birds throughout the year.

5.1.3 Monitor breeding and wintering bird populations

Projects
R/10/01 Collect data on birds
Breeding bird monitoring
Compartments: all
Monitor numbers of breeding birds in the reserve using a standard methodology
Additionally record vegetation structure and height and hydrological information for each visit.

R/10/02 Collect data on birds
Winter waterfowl distribution survey
Compartments: all
Record the distribution of waterfowl within the reserve by compartment.

* Coding allows individual projects to be identified. A coding system should be developed to identify different categories of project, eg in this example M = physical management, P = protection and R = record information. A suitable coding system for the UK has been developed – see NCC (1988).

Box 2.4 Example of a work programme using the project examples from Box 2.3

Priority codes are: 1 = essential, action essential to safeguard species or biotopes, 2 = important task for the routine management of the reserve, missing task for one year will not immediately affect species or biotopes, 3 = desirable task if time and/or resources permit.

		Years active*				
	Project	99/00	00/01	01/02	02/03	03/04
M/10/01	Graze grassland to prevent invasion by scrub	2	2	2	2	2
P/10/01	Patrol the reserve	1	1	1	1	1
R/10/01	Breeding bird monitoring	2	2	2	2	2
R/10/02	Winter waterfowl distribution survey	2	3	2	3	2

* For ease of recording, management years run from April to March to take in an entire summer and winter season, as well as the entire financial year.

The steps in Figure 2.2 summarise the process of constructing a management plan.
For further details see Eurosite (1999).

2.3.6 Plan review

Management plans should be monitored every year by means of an annual report. For this purpose, it is necessary to record resource use and action taken for each project throughout the year. Reports should contain a summary of actions achieved against relevant objectives and follow the plan's format. Site management software is available to facilitate this task.

A larger review should be undertaken every five years. The starting point for this process is to compile information gathered during the period since the last plan was produced. The information to be reviewed should include:

- extent of important habitats and changes over the period of the plan
- population levels of key fauna during period of plan
- outline suggestions for revised management objectives and prescriptions.

The aim of the review is to assess how well the plan's management objectives have been met. Objectives, prescriptions and projects may have to be updated and a revised plan produced.

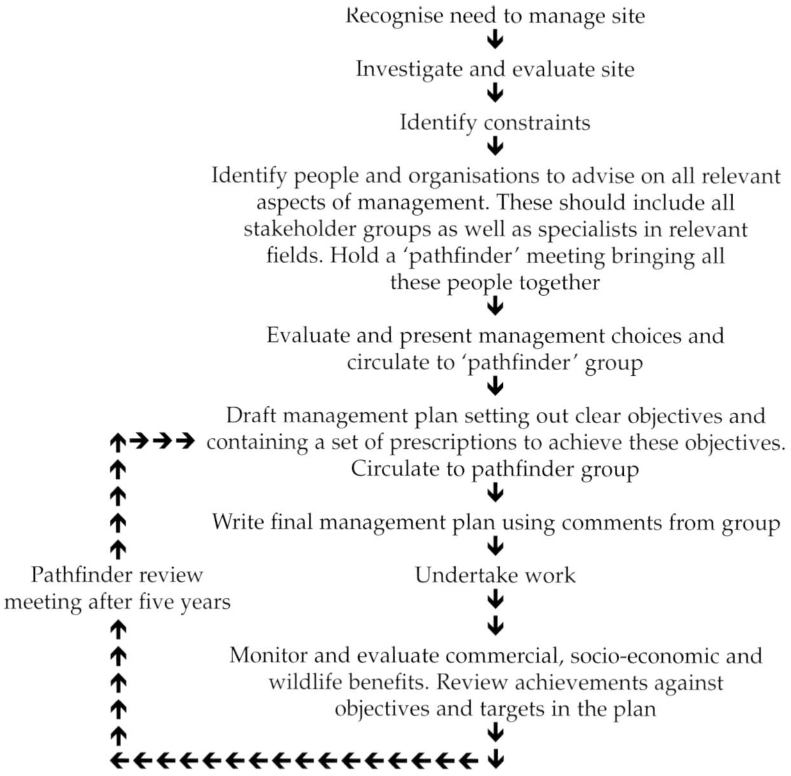

Figure 2.2
Essential steps in producing a management plan.

2.4 Monitoring and evaluation of habitat creation

Monitoring and evaluation are critical to ascertain whether a habitat creation scheme has been a success. Monitoring of soil and vegetation development and the site's colonisation by birds, invertebrates and mammals can be used to assess the site against its objectives (Plate 2.14). However, it is essential to undertake a baseline survey before restoration. This will also allow evaluation of the intrinsic wildlife value of the initial state of the site.

Currently only 54% of mineral operators maintain records of the nature conservation interest that has developed on mineral workings in their ownership (Box *et al*, 1996). Many lessons can be learned and shared from the evaluation of sites restored for nature conservation, especially where new techniques have been trialled. It is important to publish the results of any creation project, whether positive or negative, to inform others attempting similar work.

The monitoring programme needs to be tailored to the objectives of the site. For example, the creation of chalk grassland to attract butterflies would require a monitoring programme to record the establishment of the vegetation, probably using a network of permanent quadrats recorded every summer. Regular butterfly counts would also be required on warm dry days, and in the summer. Where wetland habitats have been created, monitoring of the birds using of the site should be undertaken alongside hydrological monitoring to ensure that the water regime is following the plan. An example of monitoring a reedbed habitat is shown in Box 2.5.

A method to analyse and evaluate the data collected during the monitoring programme should be laid down at the start. Commonly in the past data have been collected without knowing how they would be used or evaluated. This can lead to inefficiencies in data collection and

G J White

Plate 2.14 Monitoring will help evaluate the success of habitat creation.

should be avoided. The type and method of monitoring should be set out in the site management plan.

One strength of a good monitoring and evaluation programme is that it highlights good practice and illustrates areas where the management could be improved. This allows changes to be made to the management plan and ultimately should improve the value of the site for nature conservation. Advice on monitoring and evaluation can be found in *Ecological Census Techniques: A Handbook* (Sutherland, 1996).

Box 2.5 An example of a vegetation monitoring technique – reedbed monitoring (after Self, 1999)

Establishing reedbeds should be monitored annually at the end of the growing season (September). Samples should be taken using 1 m^2 quadrats, about 15 of which will be required for each compartment or area which differs significantly physically or chemically, eg different water regime, water chemistry, soil type etc.

Quadrat locations should be random, identified by generating random coordinates.

In each quadrat measure/count/estimate the following:
- percentage cover of each species (± 5%) when viewed from above (total can exceed 100%)
- total number of live and dead reed stems (you can count a quarter and multiply by four)
- the lengths of 10 randomly chosen reed stems
- water depth (to factor in the effect of water depth it is necessary to record water depth weekly in all compartments throughout the year).

In subsequent years use new sampling points. To measure the spread of reed from an established nucleus or an existing source, select a point along the edge by generating random figures and then run a belt transect, with quadrats every 2 m, outwards from the reedbed. Record the same information in the quadrats as above.

2.5 Feedback and reporting

It is important that there is feedback on habitat creation into the BAP process. A national database is being developed and contact with the Lead Partner or Agency for the habitat or species (section 1.2.2) is recommended. Currently, there are no formal mechanisms to share the information arising from habitat creation projects on mineral restoration sites. It is therefore difficult to find out which techniques have been the most successful and which should no longer be recommended. This problem has been addressed in other areas of habitat restoration. For example the River Restoration Centre holds a database of over 750 projects involving changes to river morphology. For each project there is a record of the objectives, the expertise used and the outcome. A similar model is being trialled by The Wildlife Trusts to record wetland restoration information. These databases have proved extremely valuable in sharing information and expertise and go part way to ensuring that different organisations do not make the same mistakes.

2.6 Funding

In terms of capital costs, the cheapest end-use for mineral sites is nature conservation (Land Use Consultants, 1992a), particularly those sites requiring little or no engineering. Subsequent management costs are also cheaper than some other after-uses, amenity for example. However, nature conservation after-uses, like informal recreation provision, rarely generate an income (Box 2.6) and therefore require sources of funding. Increasingly land is being passed onto other bodies for management. These bodies are often better able to apply for funding from government schemes such as Countryside Stewardship (Table 2.5). Other possible mechanisms to fund the management of mineral sites with nature conservation after-uses include:

- using a percentage of royalties to establish a trust fund to pay for the management
- selling land for a nominal fee to a nature conservation body and endowment of the funds required to restore site
- terms and conditions in subsequent lease to ensure nature conservation interest is maintained whoever manages a site
- introducing commercial agricultural use (appropriate for some habitats eg grasslands)
- cross-subsidy – an activity on part of the site pays for nature conservation on the remainder
- revenue generated from conservation activities – hay, biological material, reeds, short rotation coppice (Plate 2.15) and even gate receipts at sites with visitor facilities
- Heritage Lottery Fund
- Aggregates Levy Sustainability Fund.

G J White

Plate 2.15 Revenue may be generated from site management eg short rotation coppice.

Box 2.6 Sevenoaks nature reserve – an independent reserve run by a trust

Reserve management of this former gravel pit site started because an enthusiastic, small band of local volunteers, led by Dr Jeffrey Harrison, approached the mineral company and asked to help with habitat creation. The Trust was granted a 50-year lease for a nominal sum by the owners, Redland (now Lafarge), in 1980 and the first warden was appointed. The reserve now employs 2.5 staff. The trustees are mostly members of the Harrison family and provide direction to the management of the site. Talks are currently underway to extend the length of the lease and extend the area covered by the reserve.

One of the first gravel pit sites in the UK to be turned over to nature conservation, it consists of five main lakes and covers 55 ha (Plate 2.16). The site has a number of observation hides, trails and an impressive visitor centre. Current annual management revolves around coppicing, reedbed cutting, thinning back trees along pit margins, treating invasive New Zealand pigmy-weed and mink trapping.

The trust is a membership organisation offering access to the reserve, which is open six days a week to members and three days a week to non-members. The site is zoned with some areas strictly protected, some areas open to members only and remaining areas open to all. The trust has about 1,000 members and obtains additional funds by charging admission to the general public and from renting the angling rights to a fishing club. School parties also use the site, but charges for this service just the cover costs incurred. A lack of funding in most schools, for visits that involve transport, has caused a decline in the number of schoolchildren using the site.

This income, plus occasional grant aid, covers the reserve's running costs. The Environment Agency has grant-aided habitat work, the Countryside Commission (now Countryside Agency) gave money towards the building of the visitor centre, and English Nature has given small grants. Occasionally grant-giving bodies and neighbouring businesses give additional funds.

Plate 2.16 Sevenoaks nature reserve.

Table 2.5 Funding mechanisms available for the nature conservation of former mineral workings

Funding agency	Country	Grants and schemes
Countryside Agency	England	• landscape conservation grants • hedgerow incentive scheme • land acquisition grants • access grants • volunteer project grants
DEFRA	England and Wales	• Countryside Stewardship Scheme
English Nature	England	• up to 50% grants available for conservation work (under s134 of the Environmental Protection Act 1990) • Community Action for Wildlife • Reserve Enhancement Scheme • Wildlife Enhancement Scheme
Countryside Council for Wales	Wales	• land purchase grants • landscape and nature conservation grants • Tir Gofal
Scottish Natural Heritage	Scotland	• discretionary grants available to achieve aims of organisation
SEERAD	Scotland	• Rural Stewardship Scheme
DARD	N Ireland	• Countryside Management Scheme
Forestry Commission	England, Scotland and Wales	• Woodland Grant Scheme

Other sources include local authorities, grant-giving trusts and commercial sponsorship, Heritage Lottery Fund (HLF) and Aggregates Levy Sustainability Fund (ASLF).

3 MANAGING THE SITE DURING MINERAL EXTRACTION

This chapter deals with issues of management that are likely to arise during the period of mineral extraction. Restoration should be seen as a progressive action throughout the life of the quarry. Careful planning of the working method to minimise disturbance and manage existing or developing habitats, with the final restoration objectives in mind, will allow an early opportunity for species to colonise. Such early colonisers can be very important and care at this stage will often ensure a more successful restoration and avoid missed opportunities. The section is divided into two main areas; firstly managing soils and secondly managing the retained or colonising wildlife within the quarry.

3.1 Managing soils

Using a detailed soil strategy is an essential part of the habitat creation planning process. It will enable careful planning of the phasing and progressive restoration of a site. This section deals with the practical methods of site preparation that can overcome many of the problems in establishing vegetation on restored sites. It specifically deals with; soil movement and storage, ripping and subsoiling and soil fertility.

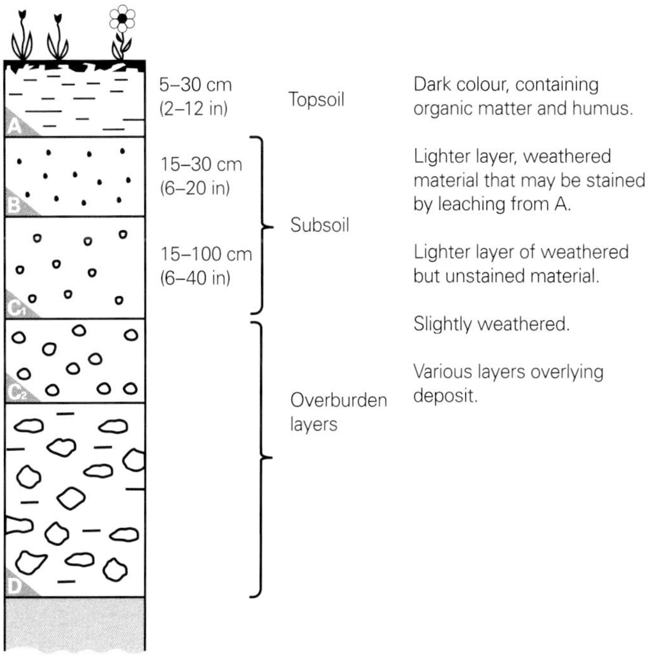

Figure 3.1
Soil horizons and overburden layers in a typical soil profile.

3.1.1 Soil movement and storage

General principles are:

- great care should be taken when moving soils to avoid compaction
- use clearly marked haul routes and avoid trafficking over replaced soils
- topsoils, subsoils and overburden should be stripped (and stored) separately
- storage times should be kept to a minimum, direct replacement should be used if possible (progressive restoration)
- use appropriate machinery eg back acter and dump truck
- to prevent damage and loss of structure, soils should never be moved when wet.

3.1.1.1 Soil movement

Removal of the fertile layers of soil (topsoil and subsoil, Figure 3.1) separately and their subsequent storage and replacement are requirements of successful restoration and are standard practice in the UK. Tracked excavators and wheeled earthscrapers are the cheapest method to use and can strip 100–300 mm of soil in good terrain (Plate 3.1 to Plate 3.4). Long-armed excavators are able to remove thinner layers with accuracy (50–100 mm) and are useful when trying to remove seed-rich upper layers of soil for the re-instatement of natural vegetation communities (Coppin and Bradshaw, 1982). However, in many cases, restoration to a nature conservation end-use may demand the return of a soil with reduced nutrient availability, eg when creating heathland it may be better to use a subsoil at the surface and bury or remove topsoil that has been artificially fertilised. In some situations, it is possible that the overburden, with a little improvement, will make a more appropriate soil. A full assessment of the soil-forming resources available should be undertaken at the outset.

A Hay (rspb-images.com)

A Hay (rspb-images.com)

Plate 3.1 (left) Stripping topsoil.

Plate 3.2 (right) Landscaping to achieve the correct profile for the desired habitat.

A Hay (rspb-images.com)

A Hay (rspb-images.com)

Plate 3.3 (left) Moving soils.

Plate 3.4 (right) Tipping and grading.

The following general principles should be applied when handling soil.

- Progressive restoration is beneficial, as it avoids double handling and storage of soils (Figure 3.2).
- Soil moisture content should be assessed before moving or handling soils. Moving soils that are wet can cause compaction and loss of structure, so avoid handling soil during winter and wet periods. It is very important to avoid operations likely to cause damage to the soil structure. It can be very costly and time-consuming to try and repair, and may jeopardise the habitat creation scheme. For example, compact soils may retain water on the surface when free-drainage is necessary for the desired habitat.
- Earthscraper's teeth should be fitted to the blade to break up soil as it enters the box during loading. Self-loading elevating scrapers are ideal as they break up soil while loading.
- Haulage roads should be well-defined and should not run over the surface of the topsoil or subsoil if possible.
- Tracked or wheeled loaders should only load from the base of stockpiles and storage heaps.
- To provide good contact between successive layers (and avoid lamination), the surface of each layer should be scarified to a depth of 50–150 mm before covering with the next layer.
- Heavily compacted layers should be ripped to a depth of about 500 mm

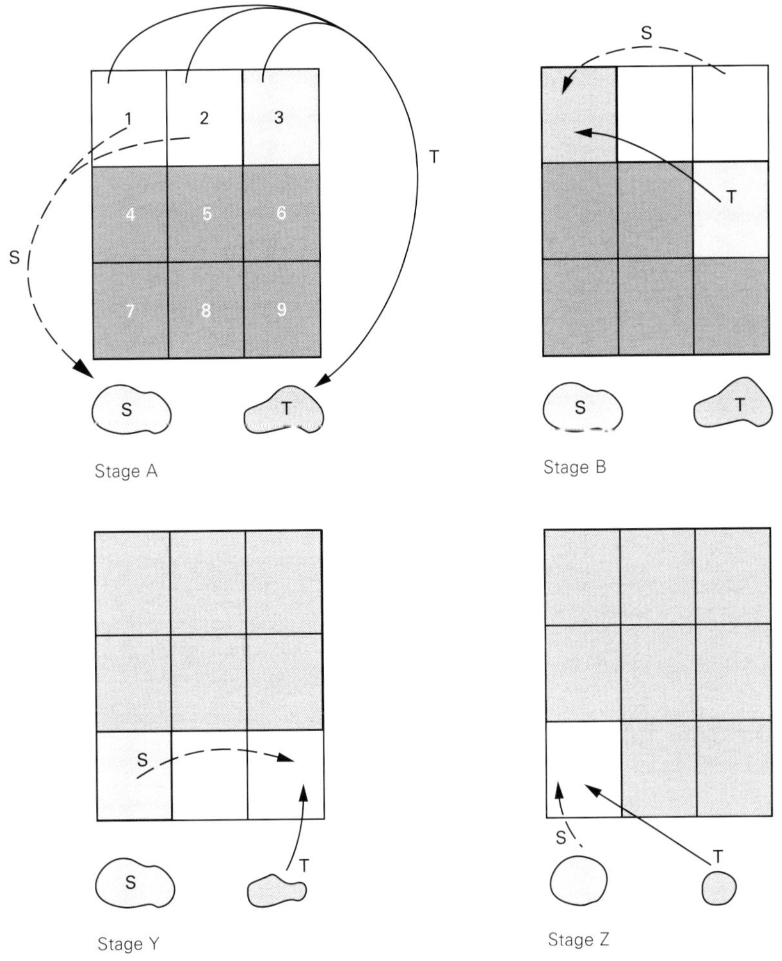

Figure 3.2
Soil movement regime allowing progressive restoration.
(after McRae, 1979)

(section 3.1.2). Ripping to depths greater than 750 mm may actually increase compaction.

- Create final landform features during soil placement operations to avoid trafficking on restored soils.
- Conveyor belts are ideal for moving and tipping soils and do not cause compaction problems. In fact consolidation may be required to prevent later settlement of the soils.

3.1.1.2 Soil storage

During mineral removal it is necessary to store some soils, although the majority may be immediately replaced in a progressive restoration programme. Soils should be stored carefully. Chemical changes occur in the soil

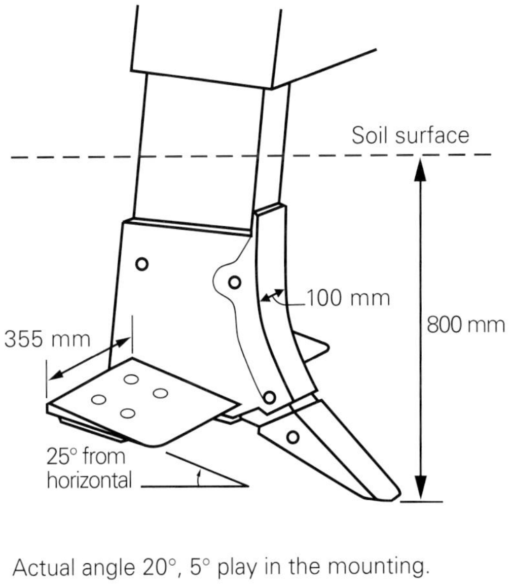

Figure 3.3
Subsoilers are often mounted on crawler tractors and the two outer tines are best fitted with winged blades for maximum disruption of the soil. The measurements given are indicative and may vary with the depth of subsoiling required.

G Spoor

Plate 3.5 **Very compacted soil.**

as microbial populations die, especially if the stored soil is compacted and anaerobic. This may lead to the build-up of toxic substances. Light, sandy soils are more resilient and harder to damage than heavy, clay soils. Peat soils stored at Plenmeller, Northumberland (section 5.2) showed a decline in the seedbank viability below 0.2 m after one to two years' storage. An increase in the concentration of ammonium ions below 0.5 m demonstrated that anaerobic conditions had been created in the soil storage mound, which was 2 m high. Soil pH, available phosphorus and potassium were also affected by storage.

Soil stored in heaps less than 1.5 m high suffer minimal damage for up to a year, after that structure and chemical composition gradually deteriorates. Preventing machinery running over the soil store also helps to maintain soil structure and prevent compaction. Soil heap management is important to control invasive weeds.

3.1.2 Ripping and subsoiling

Compacted soils may require cultivation to reduce adverse effects on plant growth (Plate 3.5). Some wetland habitats can develop on areas with impeded drainage, but most habitats will not develop well on compacted soils. Symptoms of compaction include ill or slow-growing trees, bare patches and poor surface drainage. All materials that have been compacted by more than 12% or have a bulk density greater than 1,400 kg/m^3 may benefit from ripping. Ripping has several effects, it:

- increases water infiltration into the soil, making water available to plants and reducing erosion
- reduces bulk density and resistance to root penetration, increasing root growth.

The exact effect depends on the implement used. Straight tines have limited effect and two passes with a conventional, three-shank ripper to 500 mm depth are usually required on compacted soils. Winged tines increase effectiveness requiring only one pass. A three-shank ripper with the two outer tines fitted with wings set at 20° to the horizontal is the best compromise between power needed to pull (usually by a crawler tractor), the best subsoil disruption and the protection of the wing mounting bolts from undue wear (Plate 3.6, Figure 3.3) (Coppin and Bradshaw,1982). Tines should be 1.0–1.2 m apart and have a maximum working depth of 500 mm. Ripping is best carried out before final site preparation, ie topsoil spreading. The direction of working during the final pass should take into account the likely effects on drainage. Ripping along contour lines will have the least effect.

G Spoor

Plate 3.6 **Subsoiler at work.**

Soil moisture conditions for ripping are similar to those for soil handling. Ripping in wet conditions can be very damaging. Suitable conditions for clay soils are when the soil is just drier than its lower plastic limit, ie when the soil cannot be rolled in the palm into a 'worm' about 3 mm in diameter without breaking. Usually conditions are suitable in late summer and early autumn.

3.1.3 Soil fertility

Soil nutrient concentrations found in semi-natural habitats tend to be lower than those found in soils formerly managed for intensive agricultural production. It is therefore likely that the topsoil present at a restoration site may not be suitable for the creation of many habitats. It is necessary to carry out tests of the nutrient availability in the soil and compare the results with the concentrations typically found in the target habitat for creation. Indications of the ranges of soil nutrient concentration for different habitats are given in section 4.

Where the topsoil contains high soil nutrient concentrations, there are several options:

- don't replace the topsoil, consider habitat creation directly onto the subsoil – the topsoil could be used for agricultural restoration elsewhere
- replace the topsoil below the subsoil, or mix the two together to create a more dilute soil – note that on some sites the soil resource needs preserving
- crop the soil for several years before attempting habitat creation – this is a very slow process and may not be feasible within the time constraints of a mineral restoration project.

The natural regeneration of vegetation on low fertility soils can produce very interesting results, as at Sandy Heath Quarry (section 5.12). The development of bare ground and bare rock habitat should also be considered. This produces conditions suitable for specialist invertebrate and plant species. In water-filled pits diverse aquatic plant communities are more likely to develop where nutrient input is minimised. In some circumstances, where a degree of agricultural use is planned, it may be necessary to use fertiliser to create suitable nutrient concentrations. In these cases, attention should be paid to the use of organic manures rather than artificial fertilisers to produce the necessary conditions.

Further reading

Bending, N A D and McRae, S G (1999) *Soil-forming materials: their use in land reclamation*. HMSO, London.

J Gilbert

Plate 3.7
The Eden Project.

Box 3.1 The Eden Project

The Eden Project (Plate 3.7) shows that it is possible, with experimentation, to create soils which have the correct balance of nutrients to be able to support plants growing in near-natural conditions. The Project is a ambitious scheme comprising a series of vast geodesic domes containing artificially created biomes together with extensive outdoor landscaping. It is designed to promote understanding and sustainable management of the relationship between plants, people and resources. Although the habitats created at the Eden Project are either non-native or highly artificial, the scale and ambition of works undertaken makes the site an interesting example of large scale restoration. The site has already attracted well over a million visitors, thereby demonstrating to an enormous number of people what can be achieved on a previously quarried site.

The Eden Project site is 50 ha; the domes themselves are situated within a 15 ha China clay extraction pit. This pit was a 60 m deep, inverted cone shape with little level ground. The pit was also prone to flooding, unstable and surrounded by heaps of waste spoil. In addition, there was no soil present to use as a growing medium. The site therefore presented a formidable engineering challenge to render it suitable for both large scale construction and habitat creation.

A key challenge was to provide large quantities of soil. Steeper slopes were spread with mushroom compost, whereas shallower slopes and level areas were spread with manufactured topsoil. Soil-forming materials were required in large quantities; 85,000 tonnes of soil were made from China clay waste, ball clay waste, green waste and bark waste over a two-year period. A variety of recipes were constructed to suit the needs of different plant communities. Some mixes were designed for maximum flexibility and productivity, others were designed to be low in resources to support diverse communities from regions such as the Fynbos or the North American prairies. The low fertility soil mix considered most appropriate for semi-natural habitat creation in the UK was composed of 60% graded sand, 30% composted bark and 10% clay.

Soil design focused on the primary physical characteristics needed by the different communities, particularly moisture holding and aeration characteristics. Chemical parameters were seen as easier to amend. Fertility reduction is harder than fertility accumulation; therefore all mixes were prepared initially without additional nutrition so that the appropriate nutrient load could be built up in each area.

Successful utilisation of wastes for soil manufacture requires a clear focus on performance specification. In the case of the Eden Project, only organic wastes with stable, lignin-rich composition were suitable. Using any locally available organic source would not have given the same control of soil behaviour.

3.2 Managing contractors and plant operators

Site restoration managers must be trained in habitat creation techniques, and be fully briefed on the project's aims and requirements. One of the most important tasks during restoration is the close supervision and management of plant operators undertaking creation work (Plate 3.8); paying insufficient attention can be costly. Close supervision is the only way to ensure that carefully laid designs are translated into the desired results. For example, seemingly minor changes in landform or gradient may significantly affect the success of establishing a particular habitat. It is beneficial to have an ecologist on-site at critical periods during the restoration. An integral part of the process is the production of detailed plans and clearly explained instructions, which should be incorporated into the contract with the contractor.

Plant operators inexperienced in habitat creation work have, for example, a tendency to create neat, smooth, uniform landforms, not an ecologically-desirable, rough topography. Many plant operators may have worked only on agricultural restoration projects, but will have to make a 'mental shift' when approaching habitat creation projects. They must abandon smooth lines in favour of the rough, haphazard, irregular landforms beneficial to species diversity.

It is often better to arrange the acquisition of biological material required for any project rather than leave it to the contractor to supply. This prevents accidents, errors and short cuts, and guarantees provenance of species introduced to sites. There are a number of sources where plants of local provenance could be sought. County Wildlife Trusts are a good point of initial contact, as well as Plantlife and Flora Locale. The latter have a list of suppliers on their website. This can be accessed through the Natural History Museum's plant finder database for lists of species local to the area at: www.nhm.ac.uk/science/projects/fff.

P Benstead

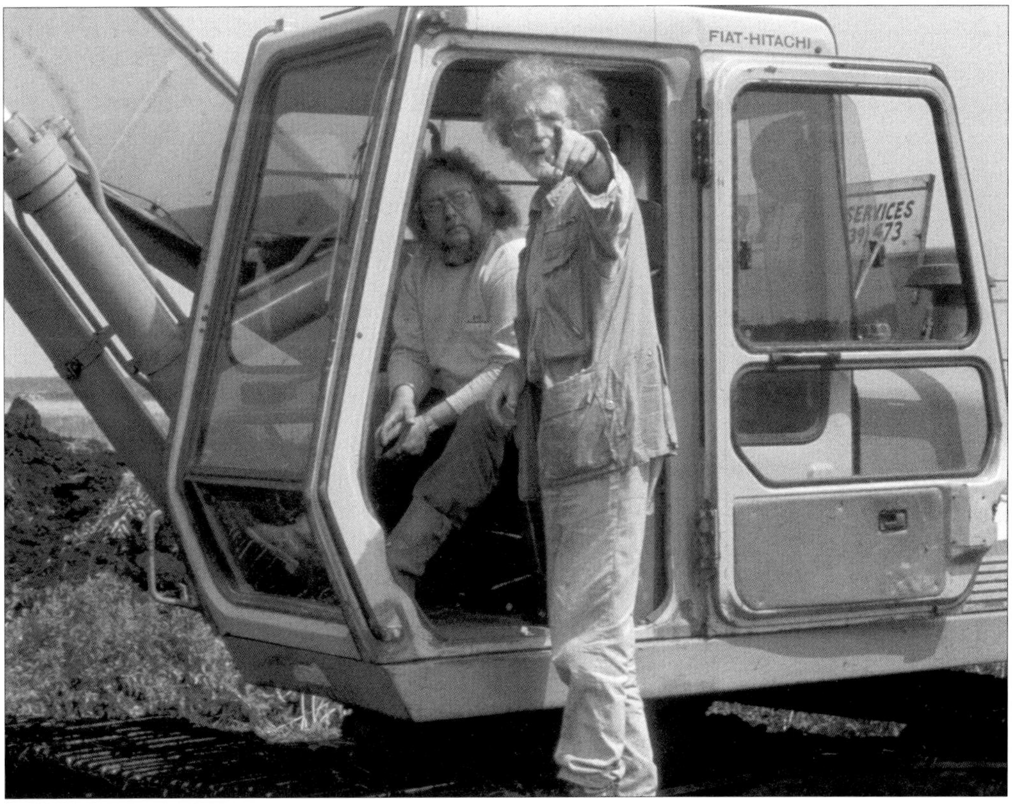

Plate 3.8
Close supervision of plant operators inexperienced in habitat restoration work is essential during landforming.

3.3 Managing wildlife

3.3.1 Animals associated with working quarries

A paradox of a disturbing process such as surface mineral extraction is that many species manage to survive and some even thrive during the working life of a quarry. During most operations a small percentage of the original landform/habitat is retained which helps by acting as a refuge (Box 3.2). Such refuge areas will most likely require management to retain their features of interest. In addition, some species regularly move into working quarries and may become a problem. This section deals with wildlife issues during the course of the extraction. The matter of protected species on sites that are subject to planning application is not dealt with; it is assumed that such issues will be resolved as part of the planning process.

Managing for wildlife during the operation of a quarry need not be an onerous activity for the site manager. Awareness of the site's wildlife locations and a flexible approach should enable the site to be managed without detriment to colonising flora and fauna. The colonisation process is critical to a successful restoration, and with a clear and ongoing approach to the chosen scheme, can be managed to provide maximum benefit.

With particular regard to the following mammal and bird species, close liaison with the relevant statutory Government Agencies, NGOs and local Wildlife Trusts should be sought.

Box 3.2 Wildlife using the site during extraction at East Chevington OCCS, Northumberland

Northumberland Wildlife Trust was involved in East Chevington opencast coal site (OCCS) from its inception, and undertook an inventory of wildlife using the site throughout the extraction. This revealed that a surprising amount of wildlife used the site during the working phase, including amphibians such as the great crested newt. It appeared that the mobile wildlife was largely able to survive the process.

About 5% of the original surface was retained during extraction and acted as a valuable refuge. The untouched coastal dunes fringing the site acted as a wildlife corridor. Some biological material was progressively translocated during the working phase. The cliff face produced by the deep extraction of coal from the void was colonised by fulmars and peregrines for several years before it was backfilled (Plate 3.9).

Plate 3.9 (below) Peregrines nested on the cliff faces at East Chevington during extraction.

Northumberland Wildlife Trust

3.3.1.1 Water voles

An inhabitant of well-vegetated rivers, ditches and ponds, the water vole is one of the UK's more threatened and declining mammals (Plate 3.10). Protected under Schedule 5 of the Wildlife and Countryside Act since 1998, it is an offence to damage, destroy or obstruct access to any structure or place used for shelter or protection, or to disturb a water vole while it occupies such a place. Licences are available from statutory agencies for research, but not to destroy water vole burrows for development or maintenance. Where development is proposed, planning authorities must ensure checks for the presence of water voles and apply conditions or appropriate mitigation to protect them. The statutory conservation agencies must be consulted for all work affecting water vole habitats.

rspb-images.com

Plate 3.10
The water vole may be found in well-vegetated rivers, ditches and ponds.

Where water voles are present or become established within a quarry, an essential first step is to seek conservation advice. A survey will usually be required and the following options may be available.

- The preferred course of action is to avoid damaging the occupied areas. Water voles are active mainly within two metres of the water and it may be possible to leave buffer strips of marginal aquatic vegetation along ditches, streams or ponds.
- If destruction of water vole habitats cannot be avoided, consider providing alternative habitat nearby. See section 4.6.2.3 for further information on habitat enhancement.
- 'Exclusion' is a technique that persuades water voles to abandon a stretch of water, allowing works to take place. The technique depends on the availability of alternative habitat and therefore applies mainly to small areas. It involves careful removal of vegetation in the affected area, allowing the voles to move into adjacent cover of their own accord, and fencing to prevent return. While exclusion provides for the conservation and welfare of the animal, it remains an unlawful act as the habitat is removed. It is therefore essential to liaise closely with the statutory agencies when considering any such action.
- As a last resort, there may be a need to trap and remove animals to a new area. Professional advice should be sought from the relevant body.

Further reading

Bennett, A, Watson, D and Hill, D (2001) Water Voles and development – a case study of mitigation techniques. *British Wildlife* 12: 167-172.

3.3.1.2 Otters

Following a significant decline during the 1960s and 1970s, when it was restricted to the north and west of the UK, the otter is gradually re-occupying sites in England. Otters may use quarries along or close to watercourses, especially as wetland habitats become established. Water-filled gravel pits in river valleys can provide excellent feeding opportunities and secluded locations for lying-up, especially where islands are present.

The otter has had full legal protection throughout England and Wales since 1978, in Northern Ireland since 1981 and in

Scotland since 1982. It is an offence to kill or injure an otter, damage or obstruct a holt, or disturb an otter in its resting place. Licences are required to carry out work that may disturb otters, such as the management of trees that are known to be used as resting places. Advice should be sought from the local Wildlife Trust or the relevant statutory nature conservation agency. Information on enhancing habitat for otters is given in section 4.6.2.2.

3.3.1.3 Badgers

The Protection of Badgers Act 1992 is based primarily on the need to protect badgers from baiting and deliberate harm. It is an offence to wilfully kill, injure, take, possess or cruelly ill-treat a badger. It is also illegal to interfere with a badger sett by damaging or destroying it, to obstruct access to a sett or to disturb a badger when it is occupying a sett. Care should be taken when carrying out any work near setts as offences can result from damage, disturbance or destruction.

The legislation recognises certain activities must be undertaken and allows licences to be granted for certain purposes, permitting work which would otherwise be illegal. The statutory nature conservation agencies are the licensing authority for sett interference resulting from land development.

Badgers may move into active quarries and have, for example, been known to excavate setts in soil heaps. It is important to confirm the presence of badgers by survey. It is not always easy to tell if a sett is occupied; surveys in the spring are most effective. Work that disturbs badgers is illegal without a licence. Guidelines are available on the type of activity that can be licensed, eg very heavy machinery within 30 m of a sett, lighter machinery within 20 m and hand digging or scrub clearance within 10 m. It is important to plan ahead if a licence for badger exclusion and sett removal is needed. Sett exclusion is nearly always restricted to the period from July to October. Advice should be sought from the statutory nature conservation agency as soon as possible.

3.3.1.4 Bats

All 16 species of bats in the UK are afforded full protection under the Wildlife and Countryside Act 1981 (section 1.4.7). In Northern Ireland, all bats are protected by the Wildlife (NI) Order 1985. This protection makes it an offence intentionally to kill, injure or take bats, or intentionally or recklessly (in England and Wales only) to damage, destroy or obstruct access to a bat roost. Under the Habitat Regulations 1994 it is an offence to damage or destroy a breeding site or resting place of any bat. Site managers who suspect the presence of bats should consult the statutory nature conservation agency (allowing time for a response) before undertaking any work. If bats are known to roost in a site other than a dwelling house, even if the bats are not present at the time, then a licence is required from the Government before any work can be undertaken.

All bat species in the UK are threatened or endangered. Declines are particularly hard to evaluate, as there is a lack of historical data on population sizes. Bats feed on insects, and woodlands, wetlands, old grasslands and, in particular, habitat mosaics, are important. In quarries, bats may make use of buildings, caves and fissures and, where retained, old trees with hollows. Information on creating special features for bats is given in section 4.6.2.1.

3.3.1.5 Reptiles and amphibians

Reptiles and amphibians are protected by the Wildlife and Countryside Act 1981, the Conservation (Natural Habitats &c) Regulations 1994 and the Wildlife (NI) Order 1985. Greatest protection is afforded to those species listed in European legislation (the great crested newt, natterjack toad, smooth snake and sand lizard), where both the animal and its habitat are protected. All reptiles are protected against killing or injuring (Plate 3.11). The most protected species are generally severely restricted in distribution, but great crested newts may be found over a wide area (Tables 4.30 and 4.31).

G J White

Plate 3.11
All reptiles are protected against killing or injuring – common lizard.

Some species may quickly colonise small pools or other features created during the extraction process. In general, the following guidelines should be adopted.

- Retain any feature important to amphibian or reptile populations.
- Avoid disturbing suitable pools during spring and summer.
- Where ponds or ditches have been specifically retained, it is vital to conserve a broad area of adjacent habitat.
- Fish should not be introduced to amphibian breeding ponds.
- It is important to retain important features during restoration, and schemes should include pond complexes wherever possible. See section 4.6.3 for information on creating features for reptiles and amphibians.
- Where the presence of specially protected species, such as the great crested newt, is suspected, advice should be sought from the local Wildlife Trust, amphibian and reptile group or the statutory nature conservation agency. A survey is usually essential.

3.3.1.6 Other wildlife

A wide variety of other wildlife, including colonising plants and invertebrates may become established during the working phase of a quarry (Table 3.1). Although it is unlikely that any will be legally protected, they may represent locally scarce species or vegetation communities. As a natural part of the colonisation process, these species are valuable to any future restoration.

Colonising flora can be diverse and include species with specialist niches. Low-nutrient pools can be important for stoneworts and other aquatic weeds, whereas the muddy margins of fluctuating waterbodies have a number of associated scarce species. Bare sandy, chalky or gravely soils will frequently be colonised by a diverse range of plants in a typically sparse sward with much bare and broken ground. Such areas can become rich in invertebrates remarkably quickly.

Many scarce invertebrates are associated with the habitats of a working quarry. These will include pioneer species, such as the scarce blue-tailed damselfly, and those associated with pioneer plants. The bare ground will favour various species of solitary bee and wasp as well as ground dwelling beetles, for example tiger beetles and seed-eating beetles. Shallow, warm, unvegetated or fluctuating waterbodies will quickly attract aquatic species, such as water beetles and water boatmen. Sparsely vegetated grassland will attract butterflies such as the grayling, common blue, brown argus, grizzled skipper (Plate 3.12), and maybe even specialist species such as the

G J White

Plate 3.12
Grizzled skipper butterflies favour herb-rich grassland in a sparse sward with associated bare ground.

Table 3.1 Wildlife (excluding birds) associated with working quarries: requirements and management.

Groups/species	Requirements	Necessary actions where present. It is appropriate to seek advice in most cases.
Pioneer plants	Low-nutrient, bare sandy, gravely, silty, chalky soils or shallow water.	Retain naturally regenerating communities. Avoid topsoiling or seeding such areas. Consider longer term management necessary to retain habitat, including periodic ground disturbance. Heavy grazing by rabbits may retain an open grassland.
Invertebrates Pioneer species, ground-dwelling insects and spiders, aquatic species associated with shallow, warm, unvegetated or fluctuating waterbodies, species of sparsely vegetated, herb-rich grassland.	Pools, seepages and bare ground attractive to a wide range of pioneer invertebrate species and their host plants.	Incorporate or design such features into eventual habitat creation scheme. Create or retain as wide a range of features as possible. The value of bare ground in the form of cliffs, shingles, muds, rocks, firm sand etc should not be underestimated.
Amphibians and reptiles	See Table 4.30 and Table 4.31.	Avoid disturbance to ponds, adjacent habitats and other key features. If the presence of specially protected species is suspected, seek advice.
Bats All species	Buildings, caves and fissures in quarries.	Bats and roosts are legally protected. Avoid disturbance. Retain or design in beneficial features (section 4.6.2.1). Enhance or protect hibernacula.
Water voles	Well-vegetated margins of rivers, streams and ponds.	Avoid disturbance.
Otters	Undisturbed resting and breeding sites: tree root cavities, scrub, logpiles, reedbeds, caves, holes in rockfalls.	Avoid disturbance. It is an offence to damage or obstruct a holt, or disturb an otter in its resting place. Artificial holts can be provided.

silver-studded blue, Adonis blue and small blue in appropriate areas. It is often the 'scruffy', haphazard nature of a working quarry that creates the range of micro features that benefits invertebrates and it is important that such features are valued and not 'tidied-up' in the restoration process.

Many sites will also have areas of retained habitat that may provide features of value in their own right and also a future source of colonists. A management regime for such areas should be established at the outset: it is all too easy for such areas to become degraded as traditional management ceases and ruderal species move in.

Both retained habitats and naturally colonising wildlife should be valued as an integral part of the final restoration. To benefit from these species it is essential to minimise disturbance by planning an appropriate working method and undertaking monitoring to ensure the correct management decisions are taken.

3.3.2 Nesting birds

The legislation protecting wild birds in England, Scotland and Wales is the Wildlife and Countryside Act 1981. It was recently amended in England and Wales by the Countryside and Rights of Way Act 2000. At the time of writing, new legislation is being consulted for Scotland and Northern Ireland. The principle of the Wildlife and Countryside Act is that all wild birds, their nests and eggs are protected by law, and some rare species are afforded special protection. It is an offence to intentionally take, damage or destroy the nest of any wild bird while it is in use or being built. It is an offence to intentionally (or recklessly, in England and Wales only) disturb any wild bird listed on Schedule 1 while it is nest-building or is at (or near) a nest with eggs or young, or to disturb the dependent young of such a bird.

Particular species associated with quarries are discussed below. A summary of nesting periods and possible management solutions that prevent loss of working time is presented in Table 3.2.

Table 3.2 Nesting details of bird species associated with working quarries.

Species	Nest site	Nesting period	Management
Peregrine*	Cliff ledge	Early March to mid-July	Create ideal nesting conditions away from working faces. Do not disturb during nesting period.
Raven	Cliff faces	Early February to mid-June	Create ideal nesting conditions away from working faces. Do not disturb during nesting period.
Chough*	Cliff faces with suitable cracks and fissures	Early April to mid-June	Create ideal nesting conditions away from working faces, retain loose rock, overhangs, caverns and old roofed buildings if possible. Do not disturb during nesting period.
Little ringed plover* Ringed plover Lapwing Redshank Oystercatcher	Nests on bare substrates	Beginning of April to mid-August	De-watered sand and gravel pits are a favourite with these species. Keep water levels high to prevent nesting in areas that cannot be kept dry during the breeding season. Do not flood sites that hold nesting birds until after the young have fledged.
Kingfisher*	Tunnel in vertical bank, usually by water	Beginning of April to end of August	Create suitable nesting banks away from working faces. Do not disturb during the nesting season (Andrews and Rebane, 1994).
Sand martin	Tunnel in vertical, sandy bank	Beginning of April to end of September	Often nests in working faces and stock-piles. Requires fresh, recently constructed nesting banks so can be managed with a little forethought. Banks should be 1.5 m above water and ideally 5+ m long. For more details of artificial bank creation see Andrews and Rebane, 1994.

* Specially protected species (Schedule 1 birds)

3.3.2.1 Peregrines and other cliff-nesting birds

The peregrine has undergone a remarkable recovery following the population crash linked to the effects of organochlorine insecticides. Although still commonest in the north and west of the UK, it is increasing in the south and east of England. The peregrine nests primarily on cliffs, with a tenth of the population nesting in quarries, many still worked. The nesting period is from early March to July. Where peregrines and other cliff-nesting birds, such as ravens or choughs (see below), are present, it is important to create ideal nesting conditions away from working faces and to avoid disturbance during the nesting period.

3.3.2.2 Choughs

The chough is one of our rarest breeding birds, restricted to west Wales, the islands of Islay, Colonsay and Jura, the Isle of Man and the Northern Ireland coast (Plate 3.13). Choughs have a long association with quarries and mines in Wales, with around a 10th of the population breeding in such sites and the old buildings associated with them, such as crusher buildings or explosive sheds. The main problems are the use of old shafts as rubbish dumps, the accessibility of some nest sites to egg collectors, the capping/grilling of disused shafts and particularly, modern quarrying techniques that favour blasting larger areas, potentially destroying a number of nest site opportunities. In active quarries:

- liaise closely with the RSPB about work schedules before any nesting behaviour begins (by late January)
- ensure sites are free from disturbance when in use (including within an hour of dusk at roosting sites)
- leave old roofed buildings, caverns and adits wherever possible, these provide good nest sites
- if possible, leave any loose rock, overhangs etc on worked quarry faces
- consider provision/creation of artificial nest sites
- undertake excavation near chough nest sites outside of the breeding season.

In disused quarries:

- do not use to dump rubbish
- do not cap or grille (if absolutely necessary seek to maintain access for birds)
- if fenced, do so in a way which allows stock to graze.

In north Wales there are many examples of good practice, with regular liaison and nest protection schemes. At Llechwedd, Blaenau Ffestiniog, a management plan has been drawn up with choughs in mind and at Penmaenmawr, chough feeding habitat has been created.

Plate 3.13
The chough feeds mainly on insects and other invertebrates that live in the soil.

A Hay (rspb-images.com)

R Wilmshurst (rspb-images.com)

Plate 3.14
Around 1,000 pairs of little ringed plovers nest in England and Wales, mainly in artificial sites.

3.3.2.3 Little ringed plovers and other wading birds

Little ringed plovers arrive on the breeding areas from late March until early May and generally leave in August, returning to their wintering grounds in Africa. They normally nest on predominantly bare sites, usually of gravel or sand. They tend to be early colonists of sand and gravel quarries, nesting on exposed gravels, on the floor of pumped workings or on islands, on silt lagoons and even in vehicle parks and stock-piling areas (Plate 3.14). They suffer high rates of nest failure, mostly due to bird and mammal predators. The total time between egg laying and young flying is 8-10 weeks. The eggs are laid on bare, gravely ground and are very well camouflaged. If little ringed plovers fail early, they will frequently re-lay. The plovers require shallow water edges for feeding.

- When birds are present from April onwards, breeding should be assumed and care taken to avoid disturbance.

- If possible, changes in water levels should be avoided during April to mid- August to avoid inundation of eggs.

- Major earth-moving should be timed for August onwards.

- If favoured breeding areas are known, inform site workers and, if appropriate,

- mark temporary exclusion areas, eg signs saying 'bird nesting areas'. Do not search for nests.

Several other wading birds may breed at extraction sites with extensive areas of shallow water and muddy fringes. Ringed plovers have very similar requirements to little ringed plovers. Lapwings may breed at extraction sites where there is a combination of very short grass, bare ground and shallow pools. Redshanks similarly favour shallow water margins to feed, but nest in longer, tussocky grassland. The same precautions as for little ringed plovers apply.

3.3.2.4 Sand martins

Sand martins nest in naturally eroding, vertical, sandy banks (Plate 3.15). They are a summer visitor to the UK, wintering in sub-Saharan Africa. They arrive from late March and breeding colonies establish wherever suitable banks occur. Traditionally found along rivers, they are increasingly restricted to active sand and gravel sites in some areas. Their habitat preference results in colonies in actively managed banks where there is at least a vein of fine sand. Colony size varies considerably, from a few pairs to several hundreds. Bank height and orientation is also variable, and preference depends more on the quality of the sand for burrowing. The burrow is up to a metre long and ends in a broader chamber. Nests are active from April through to July or August. Established sites may be used for number of years.

- Problems can arise in quarries where colonies establish in banks that are being actively worked. Where colonies become established every effort should be made to retain banks until after the breeding season.

- If suitable banks must be removed during the breeding season, pre-season work in February/March to make the site unsuitable may prevent any problems, for example by re-forming the top of bank to remove vertical aspect or by placing netting over the bank.

S Knell (rspb-images.com)

Plate 3.15 Sand martin colony in active quarry.

- At the same time, create habitat in an alternative area. This should be an undisturbed face of fine, vertical sand, preferably over 3 m high, with a clear, open aspect to the front.

- Avoid use of heavy vehicles above a sand face with an active colony.

3.3.2.5 Kingfishers

Kingfishers nest in vertical or very steep, bare, earth banks at least 1.5 m high, usually at the water's edge. They are resident in the UK, establishing nesting territories in March. Nest sites are active from April through to July/August. Issues are similar to sand martins and in addition fluctuating water levels may cause problems. Artificial nest sites have been constructed and can be very successful (Plate 3.16).

3.3.2.6 Plant machinery and nesting birds

A number of species habitually use machinery and buildings to nest in or on and cause problems, which need careful management. The most frequent are the robin, pied wagtail, stock dove, swallow and jackdaw. This list is not exhaustive, but the

RSPB

Plate 3.16 Artificial kingfisher bank, RSPB Rye Meads nature reserve.

same protection is afforded to the species as applies to those in 3.3.2 above. The majority of incidents relate to nests in machinery and every effort should be made in the spring to house or cover machinery overnight and at weekends, to prevent birds like robins and pied wagtails building a nest. Once nest construction starts that nest is legally protected against damage or disturbance and the machinery can potentially be grounded for at least six weeks or more.

In general, access to buildings with nests should not be a problem, so long as people are aware of the situation and avoid disturbing the birds. This can be done by minimising use of the area, not making any sudden noises or movements and not preventing access to the nest. Quarry buildings, particularly in south-east and eastern Britain, may attract a black redstart (Schedule 1). In such an event, specialist advice must be sought to manage the situation accordingly.

3.3.2.7 Rare birds

Local, regional or nationally rare birds are occasionally recorded at mineral restoration sites, particularly wetlands. If not managed carefully this can lead to frustration and conflict between all interested parties.

In most cases, locally and regionally rare birds are often less of an issue. The number of people interested in seeing the bird will probably be minimal and therefore managing access should not pose a problem. National rarities can cause much bigger problems and careful planning to manage access should such an event occur can save time and frustration. The occurrence of a rare bird, if managed properly, can bring a number of benefits. It can raise the profile of the site's management and in many cases has raised considerable sums of money for charities (not necessarily conservation).

It would be good strategy to discuss and plan a mutually agreeable strategy with the local county bird recorder or bird club before the event.

3.3.3 Water level drawdown in neighbouring areas

It is important to prevent damage to designated sites of nature conservation importance that exist close to extraction sites (Table 3.3). Neighbouring habitats can be threatened by de-watering of mineral sites especially in coastal and floodplain areas. Action to isolate the effects of lowering groundwater is required. Where possible, irreplaceable sites of nature conservation

Table 3.3 Measures to consider to avoid damage to neighbouring sites of nature conservation interest during mineral extraction (after Bate *et al*, 1998).

Habitat	Action required to prevent negative impact
Coastal and floodplain grazing marsh	Floodplain grazing marshes are traditionally one of the habitats most threatened by mineral extraction (especially sand and gravel). Special efforts should be made to avoid damage to neighbouring areas by ensuring that seasonal water level regimes are not affected by de-watering. If in doubt, isolate the working areas. Ensure no barriers are installed that prevent flooding, seasonal inundation and groundwater flows.
Purple moor-grass and rush pasture	Minimise disturbance to hydrological regimes of neighbouring sites.
Reedbed	Minimise disturbance to hydrological regimes of neighbouring sites.
Chalk river	Quarries active near chalk rivers should not be allowed to affect flows by lowering water-tables. The quarry site should be isolated and the river morphology unaffected.
Saline lagoon	Ensure that water-tables are not lowered near saline lagoons as this may cause freshwater incursion into saline systems.
Fen	Minimise disturbance to hydrological regimes of neighbouring sites.
Heathland	Ensure that sand and clay washings from workings and access routes do not enter the heathland.

importance on land held by mineral companies should not be subject to extraction.

The creation of large waterbodies can also have deleterious hydrological effects on neighbouring semi-natural habitats. This is not just restricted to the short-term effects of de-watering – the creation of lakes and their subsequent self-sealing (a natural process) can also be a problem. Such problems arose during the creation of the Cotswold Water Park (gravel extraction) where hydrological flows were significantly altered in some areas.

Recharge trenches and clay seals can be used to minimise the effect of drawdown in the water-table of the neighbouring area (section 5.1). A good understanding of the hydrological requirements of the neighbouring area is needed before the mitigation plans can be drawn up. It is important to ensure good water monitoring pre-application or pre-working.

3.3.4 Direct land-take from a habitat

Translocation of vegetation from the area due to be worked (donor site) to an area of restoration (recipient site) has been shown to have varied success. The restored vegetation rarely has the same species composition and vegetation structure as the original habitat and loses its historic and cultural context (Jefferson *et al*, 1999). This is often due to the inappropriate location of the translocated turves (especially with respect to soil and hydrological conditions), poor handling of the turves and lack of management of the vegetation in its new location. For these reasons, translocation should be regarded as a last resort when permission to work a site containing important vegetation cannot be prevented (Gault, 1997).

Translocation involves the transplantation of whole turves, which include lower plants and invertebrates. Although it cannot replace *in situ* conservation of important habitats, translocation can salvage some of biological material, which would otherwise be lost. It may provide the appropriate propagules for successful habitat creation.

Translocation of dry habitats, such as limestone grassland or heathland, tends to be more successful than wet habitats. Limestone grassland translocated at Thrislington Quarry NNR, County Durham, although differing in community composition from the donor site, still retains characteristics of limestone grassland.

Successful restoration of wet habitats relies on the creation of suitable hydrological conditions, which is theoretically possible but requires a detailed understanding of the donor and recipient sites' hydrology. The experimental translocation of wet heath has been attempted, in the context of the permitted extraction of ball clay near Wareham in Dorset. Here, a wet heath community was rescued and transformed into a mosaic of wet heath and mire vegetation, with great care being taken to construct a suitable hydrological regime (Hill and Box, 1999). Whole woodland translocation has been tried, but is at the experimental stage.

The scale of translocation varies with the level of mechanisation available, from small, spade-cut turves to turves several metres square cut by specialist machines. Costs vary from £20,000–£100,000/ha (Wilson, 1998). Where translocation is attempted, the following points should be borne in mind and close supervision by an ecologist or experienced restoration manager is essential.

- The best time to move turves is during winter months, preferably early winter at the start of soil wetting.
- Survey the donor sward prior to removal to provide the baseline information necessary to evaluate success.
- Clear scrub and trees before cutting turves.
- Cut turves at least 200 mm deep during damp but not wet conditions. Turves up to 500 mm deep may be required to include the tubers of some orchid species.
- Transport turves to the recipient site by the lifting plant or in single layers on flatbed trailers or dump trucks.
- Chose recipient sites for the physical and chemical similarity to the donor site. Recipient sites should not hold any species of biological interest. Remove a layer of soil equivalent to the depth of the turves from the recipient site.
- Lay turves as soon as possible after cutting; storage, even for a short time, is detrimental since shrinkage occurs.
- Ensure the soil surface of recipient sites is loose and scarified.
- Place turves carefully to ensure good contact between the turf and the underlying substrate and roll or trample to increase contact. Fill cracks and gaps between turves, especially on clay soils, to prevent drying out. Take care to ensure that the filling material is not nutrient-rich or contains a significant weed seedbank.
- On sloping ground, peg turves in strips along contours to reduce surface water run-off and improve stability.
- Water or irrigate turves in dry conditions.
- Finally, appropriately monitor and manage the recipient site to maintain the habitat following successful translocation. In particular, nutrients are mobilised by disturbance and weed control may be necessary. Ensure the cutting or grazing regime is similar to that before translocation.

It is also possible to inoculate bare areas with a small number of turves removed from a donor site. Species established in this way can then disperse into areas left to regenerate naturally or sparsely seeded swards. It may be feasible to remove a small number of turves from an existing sward without damage, although this needs to be checked experimentally before it could be recommended.

4 TECHNIQUES FOR CREATING BAP PRIORITY HABITATS

This section describes the general principles required to create five main habitat types. Additional detail is given under each of the BAP habitat types where they differ from the general principles. Table 4.1 is a guide to the possible choice of broad habitat type.

Landforming for specific habitats is dealt with in each sub-section in this section, there are however some general principles that should be adhered to.

- Ensure landforms are designed/engineered to provide diverse micro-topography by creating, for example, slopes of differing angles and aspects. Vary hydrology and microclimate by creating features such as hummocks and hollows for all terrestrial habitats. Consider leaving existing cliffs and rock exposures if this can be done safely.
- Ensure a mixture of water depths is produced when landforming aquatic habitats, generally shallow water dominates in most habitats. Maximise the edge to surface ratio by ensuring banks are sinuous and convoluted producing bays and peninsulas. Landforming should allow for extensive areas of marshy habitat between the aquatic and terrestrial habitats.
- Wherever possible, avoid hard engineering in favour of softer, more natural means to achieve the same result, eg at sites next to rivers that flood ensure 'soft' spillways are incorporated to prevent erosion when rivers over-top instead of installing sluices or concrete spillways.
- Take account of and, if possible, retain existing landscapes and features. Make features look as natural as possible.

Table 4.1 Guide to habitat selection based on site conditions.

		pH		
		Acidic	Neutral	Alkaline
Wetness	Freely draining	Native pine or birch woodland Dry heathland and scrub Acid grassland	Hay meadow and pasture Woodland Field margins	Calcareous grassland Woodland Scrub
	High water-table/impeded drainage	Wet heathland Poor fen Bog	Coastal and floodplain grazing marsh (wet grassland) Purple moor-grass and rush pasture Wet woodland Rich fen Bog	Purple moor-grass and rush pasture Marsh Rich fen
	Inundated	Open water Bog pools	Marsh/swamp Reedbed Open water	Open water
	Saline		Saline lagoon	

4.1 Grasslands

4.1.1 General principles

There is a diverse range of grassland communities that can be created on restored sites. The choice of community depends on the soil, and the climatic and hydrological conditions of the site, as well as the level of long-term management that can be achieved. The requirements of a wide range of grassland habitats are shown in Table 4.2. Grassland usually requires grazing, cutting, burning or a combination of these to maintain the habitat. It is important to ensure that suitable long-term management is attainable before embarking on grassland creation. However, grassland developed on mineral sites may need little management for some time. Species-rich grassland is generally confined to soils of low available nutrient concentration, particularly phosphorus (Figure 4.1). Topsoil should only be used if it does not contain a high concentration of available nutrients. This can be ascertained by simple laboratory tests. If the topsoil is unsuitable, then the habitat should be created directly on the subsoil.

4.1.2 Establishment techniques

4.1.2.1 Soil preparation

Soil preparation is required for many of the following methods. It can be undertaken using agricultural techniques with standard machinery on creation sites that are flat, ie slopes not more than 20%, and where the substrate is not too hard, sticky or stony. Special equipment is available to cultivate slopes steeper than 20%. Chisel ploughs may have to be used to break up compacted layers beneath the surface on stony soils, and for hard, compacted and deep soil layers subsoiling may be necessary (section 3.1.2). Most seedbeds can be prepared with disc harrows, although rotovators may be preferred for sandy soils. These machines are used to loosen compacted layers at the soil surface and prepare a seedbed for natural regeneration, hay strewing or broadcast seed. It should be noted that in some locations, compacted soils, where stress reduces productivity, may help create desirable habitat features, including bare ground and sparse grassland swards. Such areas should be identified and retained within a restoration scheme.

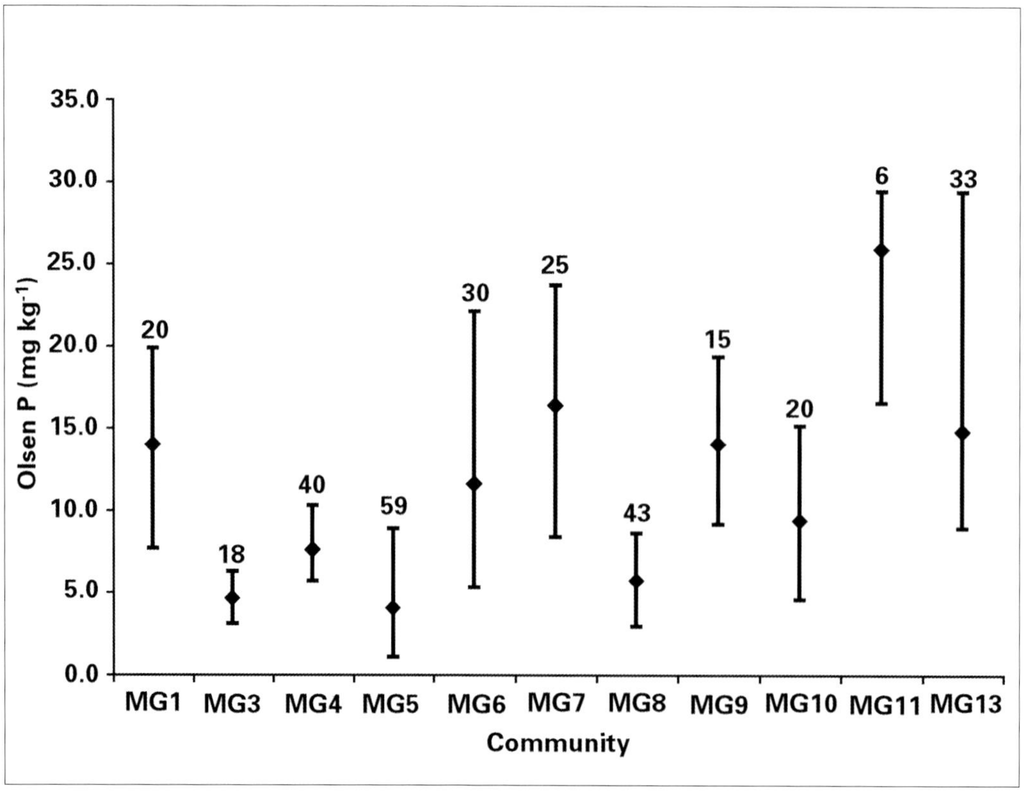

Figure 4.1 Soil P tolerance ranges of neutral grassland communities. Figure shows inter-quartile range and number of samples. (after Gilbert, 2000)

Table 4.2 Environmental requirements of grassland communities.
(after Gilbert *et al*, 1996 and Gilbert, 2000)

NVC community	pH	Fertility Olsen P (mgkg^{-1})	Wetness
Tall herb grassland False oat-grass grassland (MG1)	5.5–8	8–20	1–4
Flood meadow Meadow foxtail and great burnet grassland (MG4)	6–8	6–10	4–6
Ridge and furrow old meadow Crested dog's-tail and common knapweed grassland (MG5)	4.5–8	1–9	1–3
Rye grass pasture Rye grass and crested dog's-tail grassland (MG6)	5–8	5–22	1–3
Water meadow Crested dog's-tail and marsh marigold grassland (MG8)	5.5–7.5	3–9	5–6
Tussocky neutral grassland Yorkshire fog and tufted hair-grass grassland (MG9)	5.5–7.5	9–19	3–6
Rush pasture Yorkshire fog and soft rush grassland (MG10)	4–7.5	5–15	3–6
Wet alluvial meadow Creeping bent and marsh foxtail grassland (MG13)	5.5–7.5	9–29	4–6
Species-rich chalk grassland Sheep's fescue and meadow oat-grass grassland (CG2)	6.5–8	0–25	1–2
Brome chalk grassland Erect brome grassland (CG3)	7–8	6–25	1–2
Chalk grassland Tor grass grassland (CG4)	6.5–8	0–25	1–2
Limestone grassland Erect brome and tor grass grassland (CG5)	6.5–8	0–15	1–2
Chalk grassland Hairy oat-grass grassland (CG6)	6.5–9	6–25	1–2
Grass heath Sheep's fescue, common bent and sheep's sorrel grassland (U1)	3.5–6	0–15	1–2
Grass heath Wavy hair-grass grassland (U2)	3.5–6	6–15	1–3
Bracken community Bracken and heath bedstraw (U20)	4–6	6–25	1–2

Wetness class is taken from Hodgson (1976) where class 1 represents soils which are not wet within 0.7 m depth for more than 30 days per year, and class 6 represents soils which are wet within 0.4 m depth for more than 335 days per year.

N Symes

Plate 4.1 Natural regeneration of a sparse but species-rich grassland at Cavenham quarry, Suffolk.

4.1.2.2 Natural regeneration

Natural regeneration can produce a variety of interesting and species-rich habitats, and in many cases is underway before the formal restoration is undertaken. The value of natural regeneration should not be underestimated: by their very nature, naturally regenerated grasslands frequently look more natural than created examples (Plate 4.1). Where natural regeneration is underway, a careful survey should be undertaken prior to restoration work that may end up producing less pleasing results.

Natural regeneration is most likely to succeed where the soil contains a suitable seedbank or is adjacent to an existing grassland habitat similar to the target community. Colonisation from a neighbouring propagule source may be very slow since the dispersal range of many species is only a few metres. If the soil used in the restoration supported the target grassland community before it was lifted, then there is a possibility that the seedbank will contain a proportion of the species desired. This can be tested using the methodology described in Table 4.3. If the soil was previously cultivated for agriculture or had been stored for a long period, then it is less likely that there will be a suitable seedbank. Even soils supporting diverse vegetation do not necessarily contain a seedbank containing a full complement of species, as many perennial grassland species do not form persistent seedbanks. Seeds of annuals and prolific seeding species such as rushes, Juncaceae spp, are likely to form the bulk of the seedbank (McDonald *et al*, 1996). Annuals may produce a diverse but temporary flora of considerable value.

Natural colonisation must be coupled with management techniques to ensure that rank species do not dominate and suppress the establishment of new species. These techniques include hay-cutting, grazing and selective use of herbicides. Early introduction of grazing, especially during the spring, has been shown to be important in promoting species diversity in new grasslands (Gibson *et al*, 1987). Natural regeneration on nutrient-poor soils, which can produce sparse but diverse floras, may not require management for some time, especially if grazed by rabbits. Grazing by rabbits from first establishment of the vegetation can produce very good results in dry habitats.

Natural regeneration of limestone and chalk grassland has, in the past, created some excellent habitats eg Hopton Quarry,

Table 4.3 Seedbank testing methodology.
(Gilbert and Anderson, 1998)

- Collect several samples from the top 10–30 mm of soil.
- Spread samples thinly onto sterile, peat-free, compost in a seed tray.
- Label appropriately.
- Water and place inside a polythene bag to maintain humidity and prevent contamination.
- Keep the tray inside, in the sun but do not allow to dry out.
- Over three months count and pull out seedlings as they are identified, allowing the range of species and their relative abundance to be estimated.
- Record results.

Note: samples taken from the surface of soil heaps may not be representative as seedbanks can be destroyed if soil is not properly stored.

Derbyshire (section 5.9). It is likely that this process was assisted by nearby semi-natural habitats full of potential colonists – rarely the case nowadays. Also small scale workings, which were more common in the past, resulted in more heterogeneous working than modern practices. In general, if the soils and landform are suitable, natural regeneration will produce a good habitat. Any 'missing' species that may be expected in a target habitat may be selectively introduced if considered necessary.

4.1.2.3 Hay strewing

Hay collected from a local grassland of the desirable vegetation community can be used to introduce propagules to the restoration site (Plate 4.2). However, care should be taken to ensure that the process of collecting propagules does not damage the donor site. Grassland species mostly set their seeds between June and August. A hay-cut in early July should ensure that most of the seeds are still attached to the hay and are hence transferred to the restoration site. A second cut would also be desirable, timed to catch later seeding species. Precise timing of cuts will ultimately depend on location and species composition. Alternatively, a brush collector or forage harvester can be used to collect the seed. There is some evidence to show that seed loss may be greater from forage harvester-collected material compared with hay making, but the choice of method will depend on the availability of machinery and the time of year. The collected material should be spread at the restoration site as soon as possible after its collection to avoid the further loss of seed during storage or the loss of seed viability due to the onset of composting.

4.1.2.4 Seeding

Seeds may be collected from a local donor site using a brush harvester (Porter, 1994). The same precautions as hay collection need to be taken and the implications of damage to the donor site, seriously considered. If there is not a suitable local site then commercially available seeds can be used. However, care should be taken to ensure that the seeds are of native provenance and preferably from a local source. Flora Locale have developed a code of practice for use by seed merchants and purchasers, which sets out how seeds should be supplied and used in habitat creation schemes. Seed merchants have been encouraged to sign up to the code of practice and information regarding suitable seed merchants is given on Flora Locale's website (www.floralocale.org). A problem using commercial seeds is that only a restricted range of species is available. For instance, during The Wetland Centre project (section 5.6) species that made up 50% of the coverage of the inundation grassland community, MG13, were unavailable. Either

M Walker (FLPA)

Plate 4.2
Hay cutting at local sites may provide seed for restoration schemes.

the commercial seed mixture can be supplemented with seeds collected directly from existing habitats or, after successful sward establishment, the missing species can be introduced into the sward as pot-grown plants.

The choice of seed mixture composition depends entirely on the target habitat. Guidance can be obtained from the floristic tables in the NVC or from consulting a reputable seed merchant. The following method should be used to introduce seeds:

- create a moderately fine and firm seedbed (but be aware that even and efficient germination may not create valuable variation in vegetation structure)
- do not use fertiliser
- where perennial weeds dominate, allow the seedbank to germinate in the spring or late summer and spray off with glyphosate
- do not re-till the land, but sow seeds in September/October at 10–15 kg per ha. The rate required depends on the soil fertility and the speed at which green cover must be achieved
- sow in spring/early summer on winter waterlogged soils
- management during the first growing season is often critical. Light at ground level must be ensured by repeated cutting: this allows wild flower seedlings to develop and reduces competition from weed species. Three cuts may be necessary on the most fertile soils, less or none at all on the poorest. Any arisings should be removed.

4.1.2.4.1 Hand/machine broadcasting and hydroseeding

Broadcasting is a cheap and suitable technique to use where access or the nature of the substrate is a problem. Conventional tractor-mounted spreaders designed for both seed and fertiliser are widely available. Tractor machinery is limited to slopes shallower than 20%, but hand broadcasting can be used for small inaccessible areas. Broadcasting achieves variable seed distribution, so two passes, preferably at right angles, give better results. Seed hoppers should be agitated during broadcasting, as seeds of different sizes tend to separate out. Mixing with an inert material such as sand can prevent this.

Hydroseeding, where seeds and mulch are sprayed together, has been developed to enable seed to be delivered to areas that normal agricultural techniques cannot reach or onto unstable substrates. Hydroseeding requires expensive machinery and is usually left to specialist contractors (Box 4.1). However, this highly artificial approach is often inappropriate for a conservation restoration.

Box 4.1 Vegetating sand tips in the China clay workings of Cornwall

Hydroseeding is used on sand tips on English China clay holdings in Cornwall. Pre-liming the sand tips is essential, as the pH can be as low as 3.5. This is undertaken during the winter before seeding. A mixture containing a mulch of recycled wood fibre and paper waste, soluble fertiliser, red slag and lime is sprayed onto the tips. This is followed by a seed mix containing eight grasses, including red fescue, sheep's fescue, smooth meadow-grass and hard fescue, and some legumes, usually black medick and bird's-foot trefoil. These species help to stabilise the substrate so that more interesting vegetation communities develop.

The hydroseeding machinery consists of a lorry or trailer-mounted tank (700–14,000 litre capacity) fitted with a slurry pump and moveable water jet or hoses capable of moving solids of up to 20 mm in diameter. Paddles stir up the tank's contents to ensure even distribution of material. Small machines (700–1,000 litre) are suitable for seeding small areas (< 0.5 ha), while larger machines are capable of seeding up to 4 ha a day. Seeds are suspended in an aqueous mixture and can be sprayed over 60 m from the machine. Fertiliser, lime and mulch can be spread at the same time if necessary.

4.1.2.5 Using container-grown plants and plugs

The introduction of pot-grown plants or plugs is expensive but can have a very high success rate: 70% may be achieved. The technique is most useful to establish species that:

- do not grow easily from seed
- spread vegetatively
- flower only after a number of years, eg orchids, snake's-head fritillary.

When planting plugs, ensure they do not dry out, and water in after planting. Using a special dibber the same shape as the plugs increases success (Plate 4.3). Plugs should be introduced into areas where the sward has been removed and any long vegetation cut back. On bare sites this technique can be used in combination with seeding or as a process to speed up natural regeneration. It allows close control over composition and distribution of species. Planting should be carried out during September to mid-November or mid-February to early April.

Costs depend on the density of the planting; at three plugs/m² costs are likely to be in the order of £7,000/ha. For container-grown stock, costs are likely to increase threefold.

A Hay (rspb-images.com)

Plate 4.3
Planting plugs with a dibber.

G J White

Plate 4.4
Grazing marsh (wet grassland) in a river floodplain.

Planting density varies between two and 10 plants/m². Using 5–10 species at a density of 8–10 plants/m² in drifts covering 30-50% of an area quickly provides a natural effect if combined with seeding. Planting designs vary from planting in species groups to a mix characteristic of plant communities. Competitive species can be managed by cutting the sward above the height of the inserted plants and removing the cut material.

4.1.3 Coastal and floodplain grazing marsh

This habitat type is also known as wet grassland. Wet grasslands develop on land which is periodically flooded or waterlogged by fresh or brackish water and where management for agriculture – grazing, mowing or a combination of the two – promotes vegetation dominated by lower-growing grasses, sedges and rushes (Plate 4.4).

Many wet grasslands are the products of the drainage of large wetland complexes. They are therefore associated with networks of drainage channels, which may have outstanding nature conservation interest and support diverse aquatic floras and invertebrate faunas. Characteristic species of wet grassland are shown in Tables 4.4 and 4.5. The biological interest of wet grasslands is further increased if they form part of a matrix of other wetland habitats, such as reedbeds or saltmarshes (section 4.4). The design and management of wet grasslands has been described in a number of RSPB publications (eg RSPB, EN and ITE, 1997).

Table 4.4 Plant species suitable for sowing in wet grassland creation projects.

The list is not definitive. It is best to compare with a local grassland in a similar location in order to include local variation.

Grasses
Common bent, crested dog's-tail, meadow foxtail, red fescue, sweet vernal grass and tufted hair-grass.
Herbs
Betony, common knapweed, common sorrel, cowslip, creeping buttercup, devil's-bit scabious, meadowsweet, meadow buttercup, meadow vetchling, ox-eye daisy, pepper saxifrage, ragged robin, ribwort plantain, self-heal, tufted vetch, yarrow and yellow rattle.

Table 4.5 Characteristic species of wet grasslands.
For further details of scarcer, more restricted species, see RSPB, EN and ITE, 1997.

Plants	Plant communities of wet grasslands consist of grasses and wild flowers, rushes and sedges. Typical sites may be dominated by any one, or a combination, of 10-15 grasses, including red fescue, crested dog's-tail, creeping bent, rye grass, Yorkshire fog and sweet vernal grass. These occur with wild flowers such as white clover, sorrel, common mouse-ear, lady's smock, meadow vetchling and buttercups. Wetter areas may include marsh marigold and ragged robin. Drainage ditches support some 130 of Britain's 170 species of brackish and freshwater plants. These include submerged aquatics (such as water-milfoils, pondweeds and hornwort), floating species (duckweeds, frogbit and water-lilies) and emergents (such as bur-reed, reed sweet-grass, common reed and pond sedges).
Birds	Wet grassland provides breeding or wintering habitat particularly for waders and wildfowl. Characteristic species are the wigeon, shoveler, teal, garganey, whooper swan, Bewick's swan, wintering geese, snipe, lapwing, redshank, curlew, golden plover, black-tailed godwit, yellow wagtail and barn owl. More widespread species may also rely on wet grassland. Skylarks and meadow pipits may breed, while wintering flocks of starlings, thrushes, crows and gulls feed in large numbers on invertebrates linked with short-grass swards.
Invertebrates	Wet grassland supports large numbers of invertebrate species. Many, particularly some of the less common species, are associated with the drainage ditches and saturated ground rather than the grass sward. Wet grasslands are good at supporting the important range of invertebrates that are on the edge of both aquatic and terrestrial habitats. Characteristic species include dragonflies (including the hairy dragonfly, emperor dragonfly, ruddy darter and emerald damselfly), butterflies (the orange tip, skippers and rare marsh fritillary), beetles (especially water beetles, including the rare great silver water beetle, as well as ground and rove beetles), molluscs (notably aquatic species in the ditches) and flies (such as soldierflies, hoverflies, craneflies and snail-killing flies).
Mammals	Wet grassland with ditches is important for a small number of threatened mammals, notably the water vole, various species of bat and otters.
Amphibians	Drainage ditches and ponds support five of the six native species of amphibians, although only the introduced marsh frog has a particular association with wet grassland.

The ecological requirements of species associated with wet grassland are summarised in Table 4.6: for more detail consult RSPB, EN and ITE (1997). Landforming should create soil conditions where the water-table is close to the surface for most of the year and splash flooding or shallow flooding are possible during the winter months (Figure 4.2). Avoid flat field topography by creating a ridge-and-furrow effect or numerous small humps and hollows across each field. Varying micro-topography creates suitable conditions for very diverse swards to develop and benefits soil-dwelling invertebrates, which are food for birds including breeding waders (Plate 4.5). Avoid compaction when placing soil and especially when digging ditches; this can seriously affect the water movement through the soil. In permeable soils, the water-table may be controlled by adjusting the water level in the surrounding ditches and ensuring that ditches are fairly closely spaced. In less permeable soils, foot drains

Table 4.6 A quick guide to the ecological requirements of wet grassland flora and fauna.
For more details consult RSPB, EN and ITE, 1997.

Group	General requirements
Breeding waders	Require a high soil water-table between mid-March and the end of June, which ensures invertebrate prey are close to the surface. Chicks benefit from the provision of shallow, temporary pools and muddy margins to waterbodies. Vegetation structure is important in relation to nest site selection: it is best to provide a mosaic of sward heights to cater for different species.
Wintering waders	Feed on soil-dwelling invertebrates on unflooded fields with soft, damp soil, high water-tables and short (< 100 mm) swards. Shallow-flooded areas with islands are used for roosting.
Breeding wildfowl	Nest on the ground in tall vegetation, usually close to water. Ducklings feed themselves, mostly on small invertebrates in shallow waterbodies. Temporary pools are valuable for the high productivity, high biomass, pioneer communities that feed wader chicks and ducklings.
Wintering wildfowl	Provide a mosaic of flooded and unflooded grassland during the winter to cater for different guilds of wildfowl. Grazing wildfowl, eg wigeons, require a short, even sward (100–150 mm) comprising softer grass species such as creeping bent. Dabbling ducks, eg teals, are tied to shallow, open water and feed on plant matter, especially seeds, and invertebrates that they sieve from the water. Water depths for these species should be < 450 mm. Diving ducks, eg tufted ducks, require deeper water (1.5–2.0 m) with high densities of invertebrates.
Grassland invertebrates	Benefit from heterogenous vegetation structure, from areas of bare earth to tussocks. The presence of specific plant species, tall emergent plants, nectar sources, and hedges and bushes further diversifies the invertebrate fauna. Many species are dependent on exposed mud and litter. Summer flooding may be deleterious. See also Kirby (2001).
Aquatic invertebrates	Shallow, unshaded, vegetation-rich ditches with high water quality are important. Richest communities are found in ditches three to five years after management, but early and late stages of succession are important for specialist species. Temporary pools are valuable in supporting specialised aquatic and marginal species including scarce species of ground beetle.
Mammals	Otters require disturbance-free areas for holts, good water quality and high densities of fish. Artificial holts can be provided and are often successful (section 4.6.2.2). Water voles are likely to benefit from the provision of ditches and ponds within the wet grassland complex.
Aquatic flora	Ditch and waterbody profiles should create abundant shallow water for submerged macrophytes and emergent vegetation. Subsequent management should allow for a full range of seral succession, from open water to vegetation choked ditches. Species presence depends on water pH, salinity and trophic status.
Wet grassland flora	Soil type and water regime largely dictate the plant communities, although management is also important.

A Hay (rspb-images.com)

Plate 4.5
The snipe has declined significantly as wet grassland habitats have been lost.

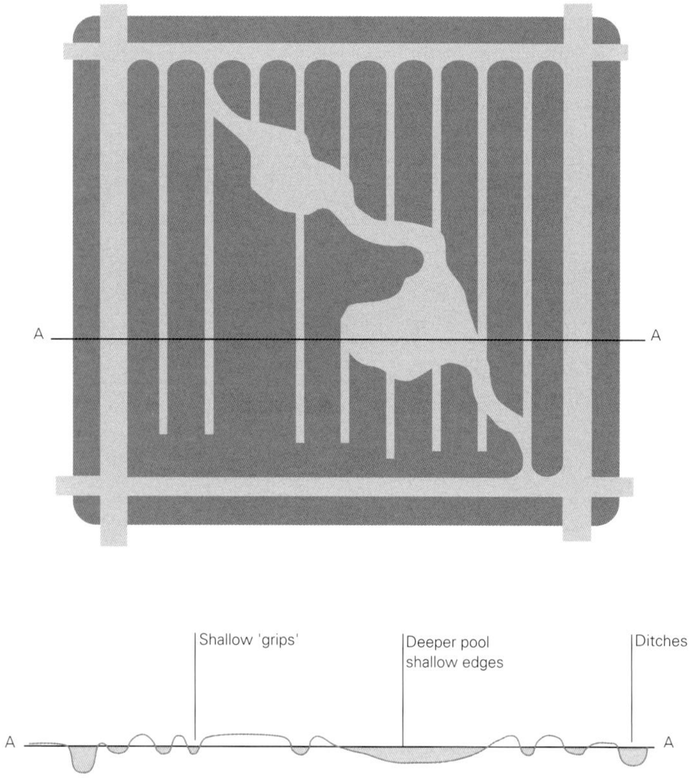

Figure 4.2
Suitable landform in relation to the water-table for the creation of wet grassland.

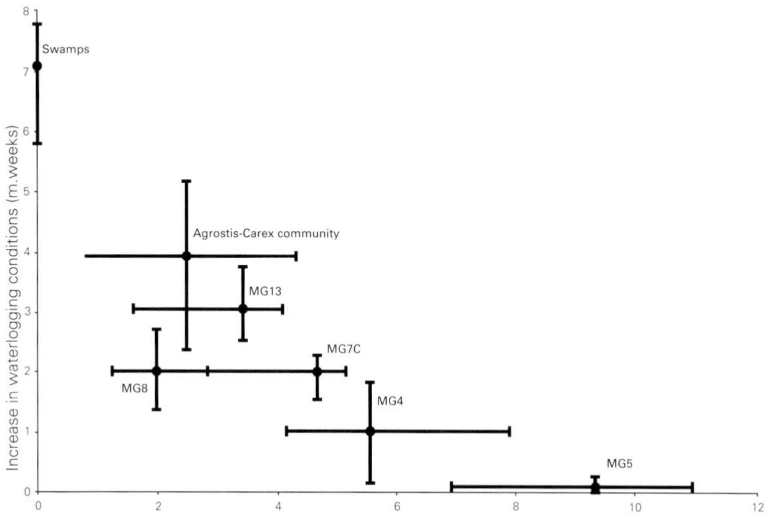

Figure 4.3
Water regime requirements of wet grassland vegetation communities.
(after Cranfield University, 2002)

and occasional surface inundation are necessary to manage the soil wetness. See section 4.4 for more detail on water-table control. Hydrological regime requirements vary between different types of wet grassland. Inundation grassland can tolerate flooding for long periods in the winter and occasionally in the spring and summer, whereas the more species-rich wet grasslands will not tolerate prolonged flooding, particularly in the late spring and summer (Figure 4.3).

Size is an important consideration when designing wet grassland for breeding and wintering birds. Both groups require large, open areas, devoid of overhead obstructions such as power lines. Larger areas allow colonies of breeding waders to establish, which collectively may be more able to deter predators. As a rule of thumb, sites greater than 100 ha are favoured. Such areas can also be managed more cost-effectively. Disturbance should be kept to a minimum as high levels can seriously reduce wet grassland use by wintering and breeding wildfowl. At least 10 ha of the site should be open ground, with no surrounding trees, tall shrubs and single trees, either within or on the edges of the area (Beaumont *et al*, 2001).

Some birds, eg whinchats, short-eared owls and hen harriers, small mammals and some invertebrates favour less intensively managed swards, preferring rank, wet grassland. These species can be encouraged by designing areas, perhaps river banks or boundary bunds, that are only cut, on rotation, every three years.

4.1.4 Hay meadow and pasture (lowland and upland)

Unimproved, semi-natural, neutral grasslands are rare. Only 3% of the area of this species-rich grassland found in the UK in the 1930s still remain (Fuller, 1987) (Plate 4.6). They are found on moist, low fertility, mineral soils with a pH of 5–7. Such substrates can support flower-rich grassland with the appropriate management: haying and aftermath grazing for hay meadows and grazing only for pasture. Suitable species for sowing are shown in Table 4.7.

Table 4.7 Suitable species for introducing during neutral grassland creation.

The list is not definitive. It is best to compare with a local grassland in a similar location in order to include local variation.

Grasses

Common bent, crested dog's-tail, crested hair-grass, flattened meadow-grass, meadow barley, meadow fescue, meadow foxtail, quaking-grass, red fescue, rough meadow-grass, smooth meadow-grass, soft brome, sweet vernal grass and yellow oat-grass.

Herbs

Agrimony, autumn hawkbit, betony, bulbous buttercup, burnet saxifrage, cat's-ear, common knapweed, common sorrel, cowslip, creeping buttercup, field scabious, goat's-beard, great burnet, hoary plantain, lady's bedstraw, meadow buttercup, meadow crane's-bill, meadow saxifrage, ox-eye daisy, perforate St John's-wort, ribwort plantain, rough hawkbit, self-heal, wild carrot, yarrow and yellow rattle (hay meadows).

Legumes

Bush vetch, medicks, bird's-foot trefoil and red clover.

4.1.5 Calcareous grassland (lowland and upland)

Calcareous grasslands occur on shallow, dry chalk or limestone soils (pH 6.5–8.5). High species diversity is encouraged by mineral nutrient stress and grazing, which prevents domination by a few aggressive species (Plate 4.7).

Chalk and/or limestone grassland is often a desired end-point for the restoration of chalk and limestone quarries. Interesting communities have developed by natural colonisation (Gilbert and Wathern, 1980; Dixon and Hambler, 1994). Chalk quarries often support interesting, early succession botanical communities. It may be desirable to maintain these by rotational scraping of the substrate in a small scale mosaic. The research undertaken at Twyford Down suggests that the best long-term management regime is mowing for years one and two while the plants are small, followed by a grazing regime in subsequent years. Alternatively, a hay-cut in late summer with cuttings removed may be tried.

4.1.6 Lowland dry acid grassland

Acid substrates can support interesting plant communities developed by natural colonisation. Typical substrates are podsols (pH < 5) overlying acid rocks. Management – grazing or cutting – is essential to maintain communities once they have established (Plate 4.8). Grazing must be controlled until the sward is established. Until they are ready to support grazing animals, young swards can be mowed and the cuttings removed. On some dry sites, growth may be very slow and not require significant cutting. After one year grazing can commence at low intensity. Supplementary feeding should be avoided to prevent nutrient levels increasing. An alternative management regime is to use the same system as hay

G J White

Plate 4.6
Traditional hay meadow with clovers, buttercups and yellow rattle.

G J White

Plate 4.7
Chalk grassland in an old quarry – Hexton Chalk Pit nature reserve, Hertfordshire.

G J White

Plate 4.8
Lowland acid grassland being grazed.

meadows – cutting in mid-July and grazing the aftermath until January. Cutting can be delayed in some years to allow late-flowering species to seed. Grazing by rabbits can produce excellent results but may be difficult to control.

4.1.7 Purple moor-grass and rush pasture

This species-rich habitat (Table 4.8) occurs in areas of high rainfall, mostly in south-west England, particularly in Devon, south Wales and south-west Scotland (Plate 4.9). It is found on poorly drained, usually peat or peaty mineral soils, which occur across a range of pH conditions and have low available nutrient concentrations. It is maintained by low intensity grazing or mowing. It is a priority habitat in the UK since its extent has been vastly reduced during the last hundred years. In Devon and Cornwall, where the habitat is known as culm grassland, only 8% of that present in 1900 remains (HMSO, 1995).

Attempts to re-create the habitat have largely centred on agricultural land, with no known use of mineral extraction sites. However, at sites within the habitat range where suitable conditions allow, re-creation of purple moor-grass and rush pasture should be considered. Importance should be placed on establishing suitable hydrological and soil conditions at the restoration site: generally a constant source of water and high water level in peaty soils. The Countryside Council for Wales is the lead partner for the national action plan.

4.1.8 Long-term management of grassland

Grasslands require a long-term management regime of cutting or grazing or a combination of both. The frequency and timing of these operations, in part, dictates the type of vegetation community that forms. Hay meadows should be closed up for several months in the spring and summer before taking a single hay-cut. This should then be followed up by aftermath grazing during the late summer and autumn. Chalk grassland habitats need to be grazed to ensure that the sward is kept short. This may be throughout most of the year or reduced during the flowering season and grazed harder from September to March. Wet grasslands require low intensity or no grazing until July, to ensure that breeding birds are not affected by nest trampling, followed by more intensive grazing in order to reach optimum sward heights for the next season. Where grass growth is particularly rapid, it may be necessary to introduce a low-level of grazing earlier in the year to maintain the community structure. Table 4.9 shows the typical management treatment of a range of grassland habitats.

Table 4.8 Characteristic species of purple moor-grass and rush pasture.

Plants	The vegetation has a distinct character, with purple moor-grass and sharp-flowered rush usually abundant. Associated plants vary with the location but may include tormentil, greater bird's-foot trefoil, devil's-bit scabious, marsh bedstraw, wavy St John's-wort, meadow thistle and cross-leaved heath. Rare species include butterfly orchids and whorled caraway.
Invertebrates	Characteristic, but rare, species include the marsh fritillary and brown hairstreak butterflies, and narrow-bordered bee hawk moth.
Birds	Typical birds include curlews, snipe and barn owls.

H Jessop

Plate 4.9 Purple moor-grass and rush pasture.

Further reading

Crofts, A and Jefferson, R G (eds) (1999) *The Lowland Grassland Management Handbook*. 2nd Edition. English Nature/The Wildlife Trusts, Peterborough.

Davis, B N K (ed) (1982a) *The ecology of quarries. The importance of natural vegetation*. Institute for Terrestrial Ecology, Cambridge.

Gilbert O L and Anderson, P (1998) *Habitat Creation and Repair*. Oxford University Press.

RSPB, EN and ITE (1997) *The wet grassland guide: managing floodplain and coastal wet grasslands for wildlife*. The RSPB, Sandy.

Walker, K J, Manchester, S J, Mountford, J O, Stevens, P A and Pywell, R F (2001) *Methodology for restoring and re-creating semi-natural lowland grassland. A review and quantitative model*. CCW Contract Science Report No 437.

Wells, T, Bell, S and Frost, A (1981) *Creating attractive grasslands using native species*. Nature Conservancy Council, Peterborough.

Table 4.9 Cutting and grazing requirements of a range of grassland habitats.
(after Crofts and Jefferson, 1999)

NVC grassland community	1	2	3	4	5	6
Tall herb grassland False oat-grass grassland (MG1)					√	
Tall herb grassland False oat-grass and meadowsweet grassland (MG2)					√	
Upland hay meadow Sweet vernal grass and meadow crane's-bill grassland (MG3)			√			
Flood meadow Meadow foxtail and great burnet grassland (MG4)		√				
Ridge and furrow old meadow Crested dog's-tail and common knapweed grassland (MG5)	√	√	√			
Water meadow Crested dog's-tail and marsh marigold grassland (MG8)	√	√	√			
Inundation grassland Red fescue, creeping bent and silverweed grassland (MG11)	√					
Wet alluvial meadow Creeping bent and marsh foxtail grassland (MG13)	√	(√)				
Limestone grassland Sheep's fescue and carline thistle grassland (CG1)	√				√	
Species-rich chalk grassland Sheep's fescue and meadow oat-grass grassland (CG2)	√					
Brome chalk grassland Erect brome grassland (CG3)	√				√	
Chalk grassland Tor grass grassland (CG4)	√				√	
Limestone grassland Erect brome and tor grass grassland (CG5)	√			√	√	
Chalk grassland Hairy oat-grass grassland (CG6)	√				√	
Rabbit grazed Breckland grassland Sheep's fescue, mouse-ear hawkweed, thyme grassland (CG7)	√				√	√
Magnesian limestone rough pasture Blue sesleria and small scabious grassland (CG8)	√					
Limestone hill pasture Blue sesleria and limestone bedstraw grassland (CG9)	√					
Upland calcareous grassland Sheep's fescue, common bent and thyme grassland (CG10)	√					
Grass heath Sheep's fescue, common bent and sheep's sorrel grassland (U1)	√					√
Grass heath Wavy hair-grass grassland (U2)	√					
Grass heath Bristle-leaved bent grassland (U3)	√			√		
Hill grassland Sheep's fescue, common bent, heath bedstraw grassland (U4)	√					

1 Livestock grazing
2 Mowing and aftermath grazing
3 Spring grazing, mowing and aftermath grazing
4 Burning and grazing
5 Unmanaged/sporadic management by grazing and/or mowing
6 Sporadic cultivation/ploughing/disturbance

4.2 Woodlands

4.2.1 General principles

The Biodiversity Action Plan lists seven types of woodland which require special attention: native pine, lowland beech and yew (Plate 4.10), lowland mixed deciduous, upland oakwood, upland birchwood (Scotland) (Plate 4.11), upland mixed ash, and wet woodland. Some of these habitats are currently threatened by mineral extraction, for example upland oakwood and mixed ash woodlands, and all should be protected from damage wherever possible.

C H Gomersall (rspb-images.com)

Plate 4.10 Beech woodland in autumn.

Woodland creation, as a discipline, has been subsumed under an avalanche of mediocre amenity planting schemes designed to green mineral extraction sites: in the past, inappropriate tree planting has reduced the wildlife potential of some areas. However, there are many opportunities to take a more ecological approach to planning woodland establishment. Woodland habitats can support multiple uses; they can accommodate recreation, forestry and nature conservation objectives. Woodlands are important for many groups of plants, birds, invertebrates and fungi that have a range of ecological requirements (Table 4.10). The establishment of woodlands may be appropriate for many locations, a summary of key guidelines is given in Table 4.11.

Rodwell and Patterson (1994) designed a methodology, based on the main woodland community types found in the NVC, for selecting appropriate woodland types based on soil and

J Andrews (RSPB)

Plate 4.11 Upland birch woodland.

Table 4.10 A quick guide to the ecological requirements of woodland and scrub fauna.

Group/species	General requirements
Mammals	In sites likely to hold dormice seek to maintain species-diverse inter-linked shrub habitat and a tree canopy that meets over rides to facilitate movement of this largely arboreal species. Bats depend on habitat mosaics and corridors of habitat that connect up roosting and feeding areas, so rides, glades, adjacent grasslands and linking hedgerows are all important. Roost sites within tree cavities are important. Bat boxes can be provided to encourage use where appropriate food supplies exist (section 4.6.2.1). Badgers can be encouraged onto newly created sites by providing artificial setts.
Birds	Avoid creating small, isolated woods. If woods are small try to cluster them in the landscape. Structure is very important. Young woods support species such as the turtle dove and tree pipit, while other species are favoured when the canopy closes. Likewise open scrub holds grasshopper warblers, linnets, yellowhammers and whinchats while closed scrub is more favourable to whitethroats and blackcaps. Mature woodland favours marsh tits, woodpeckers, nuthatches and treecreepers. Providing wide rides with scrub margins allows for both groups, assuming the wood is large enough. Ride width should be 1.5 times height of trees. A broad planting mix will encourage structural complexity. Nestboxes can be provided in new woodlands, but take care not to encourage birds to breed in sub-optimal habitat, which may lead to high chick mortality (Scullion, 1994). Monitoring nestbox productivity will be necessary to assess mortality rates.
Invertebrates	The richest fauna and the greatest concentrations of specialist and therefore scarce species are generally associated with long-standing, old woodlands with high structural diversity and abundant deadwood. The creation of new woodland cannot mitigate against the loss of ancient or semi-natural woodland. Rides must receive sun, be sheltered and have rich ground flora. Rides orientated east-west are best for summer sun. Nectar- and pollen-rich plants are important to many invertebrates. Ensure that open-structured plants are present eg umbellifers, composites and the rose family. Food plants, eg buckthorn and alder buckthorn for brimstone butterflies, prefer a mixture of structural and microclimate conditions, especially including sheltered, sunny conditions.

Table 4.11 Guidelines for woodland establishment.

- Don't plant trees if natural regeneration is likely to be successful (or at least only plant species that are poor at colonising).
- Aim to establish woodlands only on sites which would not develop into habitats of conservation value if left to natural recolonisation
- Design woodlands so that they blend with, and add to, the existing landscape. Build on what is already present
- Choose areas which are greater than 5ha if possible as these will support a greater variety of woodland species.
- Plant trees and shrubs appropriate to the local soils and representing the local woodland communities in terms of structural and floristic diversity.
- Planted trees in straight rows may make maintenance easier but resultant woodlands are structurally homogenous and lack variation.
- Plant at irregular spacing, remembering open ground is important.
- Retain open, treeless areas around water features as trees may deter waterfowl and will shade out the water margins that are important to invertebrates
- Patience and time are essential!

climatic conditions. Following this model ensures that communities are not created outside their natural ranges (Figure 4.4). It can be used to choose which trees to plant and in what relative proportions. Used carefully, the NVC can suggest:

- woodland types that would regenerate naturally on a given site, following a survey to identify soil type (including soil pH, nutrient levels and hydrology) and climate
- the frequency of appropriate species to plant in a given community
- appropriate management during the establishment and subsequent phases which will aid community development.

Large, new woods should include areas of open ground – about 20–30%. The desirability of this is recognised in the Woodland Grant Scheme (WGS), which allows 20% to remain unplanted. Structural diversity encourages high biodiversity.

When designing woodlands, size and proximity to other woodlands are important. Larger woodlands (sites should be greater than 5 ha if possible) are more likely to support and retain a wider variety of woodland species. Small woodland blocks could have scrub planted around their perimeters to reduce light levels in the interior (Usher *et al*, 1992). Adding to existing woods or creating new blocks close to existing woods increases the likelihood that species will colonise. Edges should be designed to maximise the ecotone between woodland and open ground, and managed accordingly (Figure 4.5).

Careful thought must given to the location of woodland creation projects. It is not appropriate:

- on sites with habitats of existing value, eg grasslands, open wetlands
- on sites with the potential to develop significant wildlife value in the absence of trees
- where woodlands will create barriers for wildlife movement between existing habitats eg wider areas of grassland.

Figure 4.4
Rodwell and Paterson (1994) used the NVC to identify areas of the UK where creation of different woodland communities, such as wet woodlands on alluvium, was appropriate.

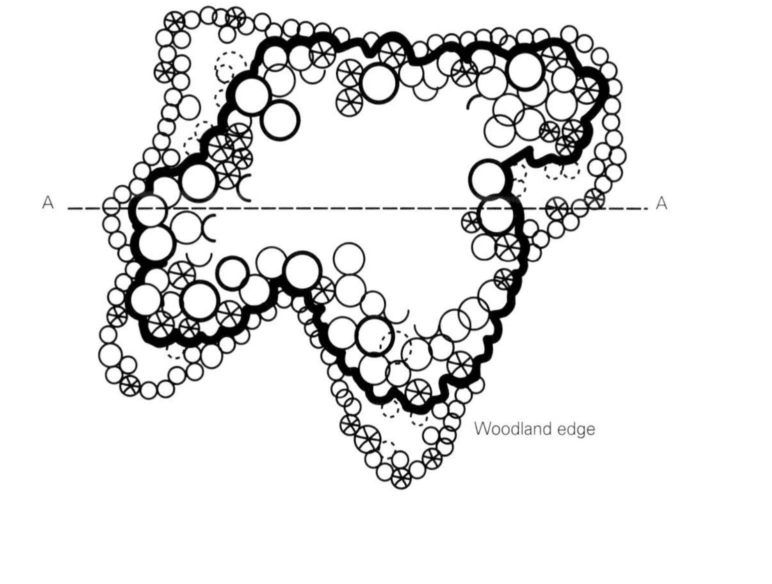

Figure 4.5
Woodland edges should be variable and have scrubby fringes.

G J White

Plate 4.12
Woodland natural regeneration in a sand quarry.

4.2.2 Establishment techniques

When considering the establishment of woodland or scrub, there are differing schools of thought, ranging from natural regeneration at one extreme, to close planting at the other. Each has merits and these are reviewed in Table 4.12. When deciding on what option to use, it is important to assess available resources, the local landscape and the site objectives.

4.2.2.1 Natural regeneration

Natural regeneration can be the best option on sites adjacent to existing semi-natural woodland (Plate 4.12). Regeneration can be encouraged by preparing a seedbed using agricultural techniques and, if necessary, removing highly fertile topsoil. Compaction and waterlogging severely affect tree growth, but under suitable conditions in most areas, a strong pioneer woodland

Table 4.12 Comparison of woodland and scrub establishment techniques.

Method	Advantages	Disadvantages	Example of use
Natural regeneration	• No material costs. • Natural selection of species of local provenance. • Variation in structure. • Natural spatial distribution and appearance of woodland/scrub. • Minimal maintenance.	• Slow process. • Poor species diversity in colonising sources will be reflected in the regeneration.	• Creation of woodland or scrub in an area with adjacent semi-natural woodland habitats.
Random wide distribution c 1 m centres shrubs; c 3.6 m centres trees	• 'Semi-natural appearance' with bushier trees. • Medium material costs. • Longer period before thinning.	• Longer maintenance period. • Longer period to reach canopy closure. • Difficult to source local plants.	• Creation of woodland where natural colonising sources are few but a 'natural' and cost-efficient result is required.
Regimental close distribution c 0.5 m centres shrubs; c 2 m centres trees	• Quick establishment and early canopy closure. • Easy maintenance between rows in establishment phase. • Shorter maintenance period.	• High material cost. • Early thinning required. • Lack of structure. • Hard to create a 'natural' appearance instead of a plantation of tall stems. • Difficult to source local plants.	• Creation of woodland shelter-belts, screens or scrub boundaries for instant cover.

community will develop in 30–40 years. Willows and sallows will colonise damp areas extremely quickly, forming dense thickets in less than 20 years. Other woodland species may have trouble displacing early pioneer species such as birch and willow during natural regeneration, especially where colonising material from trees of the desired species is scarce.

Benefits of natural regeneration are:

- low cost
- the natural appearance of woodlands created in this way
- species that colonise will be adapted to the conditions found on the site
- it promotes conservation of local biodiversity.

However, it can be a long process and may lead to habitats of low diversity if local communities are species-poor and the site is a long way from a seed source. If such a situation is likely, a combination of limited planting of slow colonisers, or those that can't reach the site, and allowing natural regeneration to fill the spaces, should be considered. Sowing tree seeds can also work well, and save time and money.

4.2.2.2 Tree and shrub planting

Whatever the planting method used it is important to ensure that:

- trees/shrubs are planted in 650–750 mm of loose friable soil to ensure adequate water storage
- rootstock is protected during planting to ensure there is no desiccation
- competitive, herbaceous plants are suppressed for the first 4–5 years (see below).

When preparing the soils it is important to avoid compaction (see 3.1.1). Sites with compact soils may need ripping (see 3.1.2), trees can be heeled in along these rips if desired. However, avoid planting in straight lines wherever possible as this leads to wind tunnelling and a homogenous structure.

There is a myth that trees require fertile soil. Work by Gough and Marrs (1990) on ancient woodland sites showed that the soils were infertile (especially deficient in phosphorus). The key issues for tree establishment are likely therefore to be root penetration and competition, not soil fertility. Woodlands established on poorer soils may well have reduced competition from ruderal herbaceous vegetation and be easier sites on which to establish a diverse ground flora.

Planting patterns and spacing have a major influence on the resulting woodland and have traditionally reflected organisational objectives, available management and financial resources (Plate 4.13, Plate 4.14). Even-spaced, dense planting in rows reflects forestry and aftercare objectives but not natural woodland. Wider spacing, for

G J White

Plate 4.13
An evenly spaced planting of few species – a dull future woodland.

G J White

Plate 4.14
This planting contained a wide mix of appropriate tree and shrub species in a random spacing, allowing natural regeneration of a herb-rich ground flora on the nutrient-poor soils.

example on average 3.6 m centres, is cheap as fewer plants are required per ha (772) and produces a bushy tree with the canopy slower to close. Maintenance costs during establishment are lower and any thinning is not required for several decades. Closer spacing, on average 2 m centres, results in taller trees and earlier canopy closure which requires thinning sooner. Such close planting may result in a woodland resembling a monotonous plantation of trunks. Spacing closer than 2 m should not be considered.

Spacing patterns and structure therefore require careful consideration. A more random spacing of planting, some areas denser, some wider, reflecting species and topography, may create a more natural-looking woodland. Planting should seek to establish self-sustaining mixtures of species appropriate to the soils and locality. On larger sites, planting schemes may include several sub-communities to match the variation in soils and slope within the site.

Planting mixes frequently undervalue shrubs and relegate them to the margins. An ideal ratio would be 40:60 trees to shrubs, with shrubs throughout the planting to generate structural diversity. Planting schemes should concentrate on creating a framework of slower-growing canopy trees, either singly or in very small clusters, at varying spacing of 2–10 metres. Structural diversity can be created by planting the gaps with shrubs and rapid-growing, short-lived trees, or allowing natural regeneration in larger open spaces. Shrubs should likewise be planted randomly, some in tight clusters forming thickets, others more widely spaced, some clusters of mixed species, others single species, depending on soils and topography. However, slow-growing species should not be planted in association with faster-growing, competitive species. Bramble frequently appears naturally and can be valuable as cover, as a source of food and nectar and may help to protect saplings.

Fast-growing but short-lived, nurse species are frequently used to:

- assist in soil formation
- provide a better microclimate for the growth of desired species
- green a site rapidly.

However, nurse trees can be competitive and follow-up management is essential as progressive removal of unwanted nurse species will be required after 5–7 years. It is therefore best to use limited numbers of nurse species that are desirable within the target woodland community. Suitable native nurse species include willow, birch and Scots pine. Native alder is good on wet sites but is poor at establishing from natural regeneration.

The same principles should be applied to existing plantations that require enhancement: diversifying trees and shrubs and introducing open spaces in the form of rides or glades. Group felling or coppicing will break up monotonous tree blocks (Plate 4.15). Dead wood should be retained.

Where nursery-grown trees are planted, whips (small, bare-rooted stock) generally out-perform standards. They can also be more cost effective, as prices range from just less than 50p to just under £1 each, depending on the species. Planting should be undertaken during the stocks' dormancy period – November to February – but avoiding frosty weather. The roots must not be allowed to dry out during the planting process. This can be achieved by reducing the transit and planting time and sealing roots in polythene bags. Unplanted stock should be heeled in until it can be planted out. One person can plant 800-1,500 whips a day by hand. On poor, stony soils trees can be heeled directly into the plough-line of a single tine subsoiler, although this encourages planting in lines.

Fencing or tree shelters are required to protect newly planted trees from grazing animals such as deer, hares, rabbits and domestic stock. Tree shelters are costly but increase survival rates and aid early growth. Fencing costs vary from £5/m for rabbit fencing to £10/m for deer fencing. Fencing should be removed after the canopy closes. Grazing pressure from deer is now extremely high in some areas. However, the use of deer fencing should be carefully considered. In certain locations, for example in uplands, fences can be very damaging to grouse by restricting movement as well as causing death by collision.

Plate 4.15 Group felling, natural regeneration and planting can increase the woodland structure of plantations.

Weed control is vital during the establishment phase to remove competitors for water and nutrients. Control of competing vegetation is especially important during April to September. Without weed control, tree planting schemes may fail (but some losses will create gaps and variety). In areas devoid of nature conservation interest, weeds can be controlled prior to planting using broad-spectrum herbicides. The aim throughout the establishment phase is to keep an area of 1 m^2 around the tree clear of vegetation. This can be achieved by using glyphosate once or twice a year during calm, dry days until the canopy closes. Bare ground between the trees may also provide a valuable habitat, especially for invertebrates. Cutting around trees can reduce the competition from weeds, although on grassy sites this may exacerbate the competition for water. Alternatively mulching can be effective in some situations, but is unlikely to be appropriate for the establishment of large woodlands and some aggressive weeds will grow through it. Mulching may increase soil moisture conditions and adds organic matter. Suitable mulching material can be either granular, eg compost, straw, bark, stone chippings, or sheet, eg geotextile, and should cover the area of 1 m^2 around the plant. Granular mulch should be laid to a depth of 50 mm.

4.2.2.3 Planting cuttings

Some tree and shrub species, eg willows and poplar, establish easily from cuttings. Cuttings, taken from one-year old material, should be 200–250 mm long with the top cut about 10 mm above a leaf bud and the bottom cut just below a bud. Cuttings should be heeled into loose, friable soil (to half the height) and protected from grazing and competitive plants, as above.

4.2.2.4 Ground flora establishment

True woodland ground flora species, such as wood anemone, dog's mercury, yellow archangel and wild garlic, colonise new sites very slowly. They are unlikely to reach some sites unless an existing source of potential colonists exists nearby. Introduction is required where colonising material is not available. Woodland topsoils can act as a good source of colonising material. During soil stripping, the top 75 mm should be stored separately for this purpose. Where there is no woodland topsoil, seeding can be undertaken. Species should be selected

Milton Keynes Parks Trust

Plate 4.16 Ground flora establishment by seeding, Milton Keynes. Primrose spreads quickly and gives a 'woodland' appearance to young plantations.

carefully for the site, avoiding competitive species.

On richer soils, it is necessary to wait for the trees and shrubs to establish before attempting to establish ground flora because the increase in shading reduces the dominance of some competitive species, such as stinging nettles. Experimental work in Milton Keynes (Francis *et al*, 1992; Francis and Street, 1993) showed that ground flora establishment was more successful on bare earth maintained under tree cover (Plate 4.16). Seeding took place during autumn to ensure vernalisation and reduce the risk of desiccation. Seeds were sown at a density of 3–5 kg/ha, which took 1.4 person days/ha and cost £600/ha (Gilbert and Anderson, 1998). Three categories of woodland herbs were identified (Table 4.13).

Species that do not establish well from seed may be introduced as pot plants. They should be planted in spring and arranged in single species clusters. In areas without bare ground, weeds can be suppressed by heavy mulching with wood bark and wood chips (Cohn and Packham, 1993; Cohn and Millett, 1995).

If woodland is established on poorer subsoils, ground flora may be established in the gaps between the trees at the time of planting, allowing for later spread when management around the tree base has ceased.

4.2.3 Scrub

Scrub is difficult to define, but is most often described as dominated by shrubs or bushes, which may include young or small trees. A robust definition has to include the characteristics of the vegetation itself and the thresholds that separate it from open habitats and woodland. In the JNCC report 308, *The Nature Conservation Value of Scrub in Britain*, Mortimer *et al* (2000) define scrub as including all stages from scattered bushes to the closed canopy, containing native or non-native shrubs and tree saplings usually less than 5m tall. The habitats included by this definition are carr, upland and lowland scrub (including wood edge), montane and coastal scrub. However, this excludes dwarf heath and gorse, planted stands and coppice regrowth.

Table 4.13 Woodland field layer species groups.
All three are required to create a complete woodland ground flora (after Gilbert and Anderson, 1998).

Category and sowing/planting density	Speed of establishment	Species (for neutral soil)
Woodland edge species (3 kg/ha)	Rapid	Garlic mustard, lords and ladies, smooth brome, false brome, foxglove, hedge bedstraw, wood avens, hairy St-John's-wort, wood millet, red campion, hedge woundwort, greater stitchwort and upright hedge-parsley.
Shade tolerant species introduced by seeding (10 kg/ha)	Slow	Ramsons, pignut, woodruff, bluebell, primrose and sweet violet.
Shade tolerant species introduced as pot plants (3–9/m^2)	Slow	Wood anemone, bugle, enchanter's nightshade, yellow archangel, dog's mercury, wood sorrel, wood sage and common dog-violet.

Historically, the conservation value of scrub has been undervalued. The invasive characteristics of some scrub types in certain situations have given it a bad press, and until recently, it has often been regarded as a problem in need of control with little consideration given to its nature conservation value. For example, only juniper and woolly willow have Species Action Plans (SAPs), while few SSSIs are designated specifically for their scrub interest, though the scrub component of SSSIs is identified where it is important. Of the current candidate SACs, 25% contain scrub habitats of conservation importance as described in Annex I of the EU Habitats Directive. The value of scrub communities for nature conservation has now been recognised and they are seen as an important feature of the countryside (Plate 4.17). Scrub often has a high value for wildlife, contributes to the natural beauty of the landscape, and is an important component of many UK BAP habitats and EU priority habitats, as well as being important for a number of bird and invertebrate species featured in SAPs.

4.2.3.1 Scrub management and creation

Scrub management (as opposed to eradication) and creation can deliver a balance of scrub and open habitat with a high conservation value. However, the critical factor is the ongoing need for management to maintain the desired balance. Successional changes in scrub habitats have corresponding changes in the associated flora and fauna. As the changes continue, different species make use of the available niches, be it with specific stages of growth and shrub species or even clearance. Most scrub eventually develops into woodland but if dense, this process can take many decades (Gilbert and Anderson, 1998). Dense scrub is also of least value ecologically. It is the early stages of scrub colonisation that are generally most important botanically and ornithologically. However, ancient scrub can be essential for some species, for example black hairstreak butterflies. Seasonal variation is also a contributing factor to the number and variety of species that occur in scrub.

G J White

Plate 4.17 Chalk scrub in the Chilterns.

Structural variation within scrub influences the communities and life cycles of the mammals, birds and insects that use the habitat. Many species have refined requirements: maintaining a mosaic of large shrubs with a range of age, structure and spatial distribution helps to provide as many niches as possible, encouraging a greater diversity of species. A diverse structural variation means there are more places in which the different species can feed and breed, as well as find shelter from predators, to roost and overwinter. The surrounding habitats are also important, especially the interface between, for example, grassland, scrub and woodland, which provides warmth and shelter for many species.

Where possible, stands of existing scrub should be maintained within the restoration scheme and incorporated into the management plan. Management should aim to diversify the structure, through rotational cutting and thinning, and encourage natural regeneration to extend, enhance and create new stands. Natural regeneration of scrub will allow a balanced age structure, spatial distribution and species diversity to develop. Where possible, and where establishment time is not a constraint, natural regeneration should be the favoured option.

Figure 4.6 Scrub planting patterns should encourage a varied structure and open areas of grassland within the scrub.

However, in some cases, instant cover is needed and this requires planting. It is important to use only native species appropriate to the local soil conditions and of local provenance. Scrub should be planted using the same techniques as for trees (see above). Planting patterns should be designed to give a varied and complex structure taking into account species, height, canopy shape and spacing with plenty of glades and open areas and a high boundary:area ratio (Figure 4.6). If possible, glades between stands should be orientated east-west. The stands should be planted with sinuous edges that have a southerly aspect, in order to trap more heat, provide better flowering and fruiting potential and therefore more feeding opportunities for different fauna. It is important that valuable vegetation develops on the scrub edge: introducing species that provide berries, nectar or act as larval foodplants could be considered. These marginal zones can become important for many sun-loving invertebrates where the large growth-forms of grassland plants occur (Hopkins 1996). Scrub in lowland valleys (often created as a result of mineral extraction) is now an important, and perhaps more 'natural', habitat for nightingales, largely replacing the losses of its former favoured habitat, coppiced woodland.

Plate 4.18 Wet woodland.

G J White

4.2.4 Wet woodland

Interest in floodplain forest restoration has been slow in the UK. However, floodplain forest is now being recognised as a missing component of the landscape. Woodlands are an important part of the habitat mosaic that makes up natural floodplains (Plate 4.18). The BAP process recognises wet woodland and the need to extend its coverage, but does not emphasise the rare and extremely fragmented nature of floodplain woodland. In fact the conservation emphasis in the UK is so focused on traditionally managed, semi-natural floodplain habitats – reedbed and wet grassland – that the presence of forest in floodplains is no longer considered natural (Peterken and Hughes, 1998).

Examination of floodplain woodland fragments reveals that most fall into the W1-W7 NVC categories. Alder-tussock sedge (W5) and alder-stinging nettle (W6) woodlands are explicitly associated with floodplain mires and winter inundation (Peterken and Hughes, 1998). Black poplar, together with various willows, once occupied areas of recently deposited mineral soil close to major river channels: a habitat that has declined to the point where this community is not recognised in the NVC. The black poplar now survives only along lowland streams and rivers and has declined since 1800: just a few thousand trees remain (Milne-Redhead, 1990).

The benefits of the re-creation of floodplain woodland may include:

- biodiversity conservation (Plate 4.19)
- timber production – hardwoods and short rotation coppice

LVRPA

Plate 4.19
The musk beetle is a scarce inhabitant of wet woodland, the larvae living within willow branches.

- water quality improvement
- flood control through wooded washlands
- landscape value.

4.2.4.1 Design

Hydrological conditions need to be suitable for the creation of wet woodland. The principles described in section 4.4 need to be applied, taking account of the habitat's water requirements, the potential supply of water and the possibility of water storage on the site.

Important criteria are:
- channel movement. Natural floodplains have a distinctive disturbance regime with the river constantly re-shaping, undercutting banks and moving sediment around
- regular inundation. Floods cut scour channels between trees and re-fill former channels and pools. Accumulated woody debris may hold water in shallow lakes and swampy areas
- size. Any floodplain woodland creation ideally would be integral to wider floodplain restoration
- planting schemes. These should match the topography, with alder-sallow on the lowest land to oak-ash on the highest. Open areas of swamp and shallow water are important.

The majority of floodplain woodlands that now exist are recently developed stands around flooded gravel pits and those in suburban areas. However, there are plans to incorporate wet woodland in some of the large wetland restoration schemes currently being proposed. Milton Keynes Parks Trust is proposing to create a floodplain woodland on a site they own on the River Ouse through the process of gravel extraction (Box 4.2).

Box 4.2 Manor Farm, Milton Keynes – proposed floodplain woodland creation

Creation of floodplain woodland within the land-holdings of the Milton Keynes Parks Trust (MKPT) at Manor Farm is important to add richness and diversity to the local and regional ecology. The Manor Farm site covers 50 ha in the Great Ouse valley, a wide and shallow valley through which the river meanders gently. The proposed project aims to establish wet woodland in the valley floor. To achieve this MKPT intends to remove shallow gravel deposits allowing the desired landform to be created (Figure 4.7) and provide ring-fenced funds, through royalty payments, for site infrastructure and future management.

The extraction process will retain existing river and channel features and create new, multiple-braided river channels, pools, islands, marshes, reedbeds, sandbanks etc. As many floodplain forest species are pioneers that have good mechanisms of seed dispersal and readily colonise disturbed ground, natural regeneration will be encouraged. Species that are slower to colonise will be seeded or planted to create a mosaic of diverse woodland types mixed with wetland habitats. After five years, grazing by a small herd of a suitable, hardy animals will be introduced (one animal per six hectares). Existing public access will be retained and enhanced by providing a trail.

An additional benefit of the proposal is the reduction of peak flood flows downstream in Newport Pagnell, which occasionally floods.

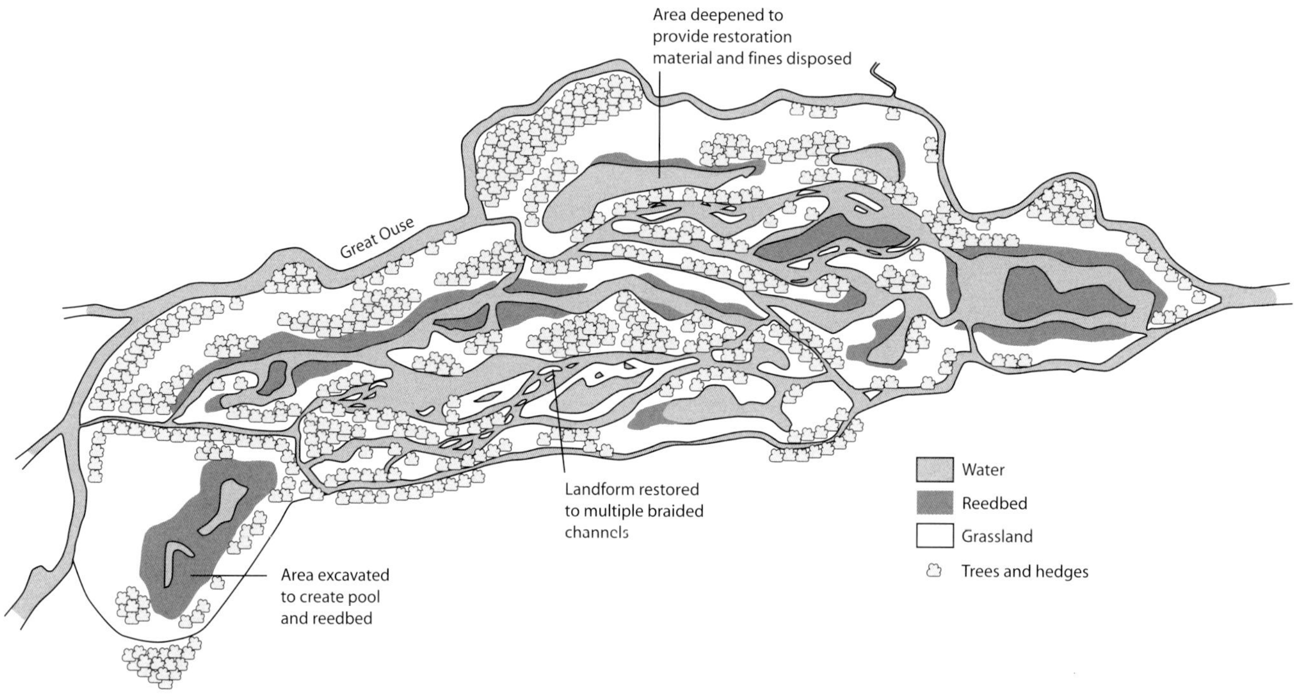

Figure 4.7 Proposed design of the natural floodplain site at Manor Farm Milton Keynes.

4.2.5 Native pine woodland

Caledonian pinewoods cover just 1% of their historical range and support a range of threatened bird species and many insects. Within the range, there is very little mineral extraction and therefore the industry's role in the creating this habitat is very limited. Creation guidelines exist in Rodwell and Patterson (1994).

4.2.6 Long-term management of woodland

Long-term management may include the removal of nurse species, and thinning and coppicing of pioneer species to allow the next stage of succession to 'get a toehold'. It may not be necessary to fill in gaps where plantings have failed. Subsequently, long-term rotational management may be required (Forestry Commission, 1994b). Regular management of woodland rides is important to retain open areas, which maximise benefits to wildlife such as butterflies. The retention of both standing and fallen dead wood is important. Litter piles can be created and should be stacked and bound for maximum benefit to wildlife. Coppicing, heathland and grassland management may all be necessary to maintain the wildlife interest of a woodland site (Plate 4.20). See Peterken (1993) for more details of woodland management for wildlife.

Further reading

Buckley, G P and Knight, D J (1989) The feasibility of woodland reconstruction. In G P Buckley (ed) *Biological Habitat Reconstruction*, pp 171-88. Bellhaven Press.

Francis, J L, Morton, A J and Boorman, L A (1992) The establishment of ground flora species in recently planted woodland. *Aspects of Applied Biology* 29: 171-78.

Hodge, S J (1995) *Creating and managing woodlands around towns*. Forestry Commission Handbook 11. HMSO, London.

Holmes, N T H (1998) Floodplain restoration. In R G Bailey, P V José and B R Sherwood (eds) *UK floodplains*, pp 331-348. Westbury Academic and Scientific Publishing, Otley.

G J White

Plate 4.20 **Maintaining diversity within a woodland by ride management and coppicing.**

Hopkins, J J (1996) Scrub ecology and conservation. *British Wildlife* 8(1): 28-36.

Moffat, A and McNeill, J (1994) *Reclaiming disturbed land for forestry*. Forestry Commission Bulletin 110. HMSO, London.

Peterken, G F (1993) *Woodland conservation and management*. Second Edition. Chapman and Hall, London.

Peterken, G F and Hughes, F M R (1998) Limitations and opportunities for restoring floodplain forest in Britain. In R G Bailey, P V José and B R Sherwood (eds) *UK floodplains*, pp 423-436. Westbury Academic and Scientific Publishing, Otley.

Rodwell, J S and Patterson, G S (1994) *Creating new native woodland*. Forestry Commission Bulletin 112. HMSO, London.

4.3 Heathlands

A Hay (rspb-images.com)

Plate 4.21
Lowland heath.

4.3.1 General principles

'Lowland heathland' and 'upland heathland' (moorland) are treated together here, as creation techniques for both are very similar. Both habitats are open, relatively tree-less landscapes dominated by dwarf shrubs, usually heathers (Table 4.14). Moorland occurs on upland areas, which tend to be wetter and where thin organic soils predominate. Lowland heathland is found below 300 m altitude, and tends to occur on sandy soils, which, although they are usually more free-draining than moorland soils contain botanically important mires or valley bogs (Plate 4.21). The distinction between lowland heathland and mire communities and moorland becomes blurred in the west of Britain where climatic and soil conditions allow heathland vegetation to occur at low altitude on older rocks. Here the communities tend to be lowland in character, but the dynamics that maintain the habitat are upland: high rainfall and organic soils. The ecological requirements of heathland species are summarised in Tables 4.15 and 4.16.

Table 4.14 Characteristic species of lowland and upland heaths.

Plants	Typical species include heather, bell heather, cross-leaved heath, gorses, broom, purple moor-grass, wavy hair-grass and bristle bent grass. Scarcer or localised plants include Dorset heath, sundews, marsh gentian and bog orchid.
Reptiles and amphibians	Lowland heathland supports all six of the UK's native reptiles (Plate 4.22). Though less important for amphibians, it is still very valuable for natterjack toads.
Birds	Lowland heath is internationally significant for four species: the stone-curlew, nightjar, Dartford warbler and woodlark. Upland species include the red grouse, black grouse and golden plover. Other birds at least partly dependent on heathland include the hen harrier, merlin, pipits, wheatear, whinchat, stonechat and linnet. The chough is locally dependent (mainly in Wales) on coastal heath.
Invertebrates	Heathland is very important for invertebrates, supporting many species at the edge of their European range and 50% or more of the UK total of some groups, such as spiders, dragonflies and true bugs. The most important sites are in southern England. The soils of heaths are ideally structured for a wide range of ground-dwelling and burrowing species such as tiger beetles, potter wasps, bee flies, mottled grasshopper and grayling butterfly. Shrub specialists include silver-studded blue and green hairstreak butterflies, crab spiders and heather beetle. Decaying materials attract dor and minotaur beetles. Pools and other open waters attract dragonflies, diving beetles and the raft spider.

Table 4.15 A quick guide to the ecological requirements of lowland heathland flora and fauna.

Plants	Heathland plant communities are often dominated by a few species that are adapted to impoverished soil conditions, either dry or waterlogged. Heather is widely distributed but limited by soil characteristics and climate. With only a relatively low frost and drought tolerance, it is most abundant in oceanic climates. It is a slow-growing shrub, tolerant of low pH, has a low demand for nutrients and a very large seed production. Gorse is at its most robust on free-draining soils where it will form compact, impenetrable bushes. Where these grow through mature heather, they are of real value to nesting birds and invertebrates. The sundews are a group of insectivorous plants that occupy bare, wet peat. The waterlogged soil is infertile and these plants derive a small amount of nutrient from the insects caught on their sticky leaves
Invertebrates	All of the heathland communities and the successional processes that take place provide opportunities for a range of invertebrates. Bare ground, either sand or peat, pioneer and mature dwarf shrub, grasses and herbs, rank grasses, degenerate stands of heather, and scrub and pioneer woodland all have value. The variety of niches that exist on heathland means that the numbers of invertebrate species using heathland can be relatively high. Many species prey on or parasitise others and many are specialists adapted to exploit the conditions. Where sandy soils are exposed, they provide excellent opportunities for tunnelling invertebrates. The hot microclimates, especially those associated with bare ground and short turf, allow species with a more southerly range to exist. Many of the specialist heathland invertebrates have very specific habitat requirements, so it is important to ensure that all features of lowland heathland are represented
Reptiles	Lowland heathland is the only habitat that supports all six of the UK's native reptiles, so is critically important for this group. See Table 4.30 for more detail.
Birds	Stone-curlews nest on free-draining, stony soils, which are characterised by sparse, short vegetation. Suitable conditions occur on chalk downland and grassy heathland, as well as on spring cultivated, arable land. Woodlarks occur in open woodland, heathland, sparse grassland and light cultivations, where the common factor is well-drained, light soils. In the nesting season woodlarks feed on terrestrial invertebrates, foraging by searching bare ground or through very short, sparse heather or grasses. In winter they feed on seeds and invertebrates. They use scattered trees or woodland edge trees as song posts and lookout posts. The Dartford warbler is limited to dwarf shrub communities of lowland heathland. As a wholly insectivorous and non-migratory bird, in Britain the Dartford warbler is vulnerable to cold, winter weather and particularly to prolonged snow cover; the limits of its distribution and its population density are influenced by climate Nest sites are low above the ground in deep, dense heather or compact European or western gorse. They feed on invertebrates found in foliage and on the ground, foraging in gorse species, the dwarf shrub canopy, low tree scrub and among leaf litter.

C Carver (rspb-images.com)

Plate 4.22 Smooth snakes are restricted to southern heathlands.

Table 4.16 A quick guide to the ecological requirements of upland heathland flora and fauna.
(from Backshall *et al*, 1998)

Plants	Both wet and dry heaths exist in the uplands, all characterised by the presence of dwarf, ericaceous shrubs, such as heather. Dry heaths tend to occur on mineral soils with thin accumulations of peat and at lower altitudes. Wet heaths tend to occur at higher altitudes (and higher rainfall) and on a peat soil, which isolates the plant roots from the underlying mineral soil and rocks.
Birds	Many species nest in heather and rough grazing while feeding in boggy patches, next to water or in agriculturally improved grassland near the moor, eg waterlogged areas with pools and mossy hollows of *Sphagnum* are important feeding grounds for birds such as dunlins and redshanks. Heather is an important food for red grouse and to a lesser extent black grouse. Moorland areas provide hunting grounds a well as nesting habitat for a number of rare raptors such as merlins and hen harriers.
Invertebrates	Moorlands tend to have some elements of lowland heath fauna reaching their northern limits as well as montane species at their southern limit. On the whole the diversity is low when compared to lowland habitats, with the highest diversity being among spiders, moths, ground beetles, rove beetles and craneflies.
Mammals	Moorland provides the habitat of the mountain hare. Structurally diverse moorland, especially grass moorland, can provide high densities of small mammals, notably field voles and shrews. Moorlands provide valuable habitats where they are adjacent to woodland blocks. For example, rocky, undisturbed moorlands near woodland can support pine martens and wild cats. Open moorlands provide areas for foraging for deer. However, there is concern about overgrazing by deer, notably in adjacent woodland habitats.
Amphibians and reptiles	Large expanses of structurally diverse moorland, rich in both lizard and mammal prey, are important for adders. Two lizard species occur, the common lizard and slow-worm. For details of requirements see Table 4.30. Amphibians use may be restricted by the occurrence of suitable breeding ponds. Moorland ponds are sometimes too acidic due to surrounding peat.

Lowland heathland in particular has suffered massive losses since the 19th century, and the Lowland Heathland BAP sets a target of recreating 6,000 ha of habitat in the UK. The BAP steering group has recommended that, in appropriate areas, there should be a presumption of re-establishing this habitat following mineral extraction. Priority should be given to rejoining fragments and expanding existing sites to a size where viable populations of species can be maintained.

4.3.2 Establishment techniques

Extensive practical research has been undertaken on heathland creation and management. To date much of this work has concentrated on re-instating heather cover on bare substrates, rather than re-creating identifiable heathland or moorland communities. Large scale field trials have been undertaken on both upland moorland and lowland heath. Restoration of wet heath, including reconstruction of the hydrological regime, has also been attempted (Hill and Box, 1999).

When establishing heathland it is important to bear in mind that success depends on meeting a number of physical criteria.

- Soil fertility has to be very low; do not attempt restoration on soils that have not been tested for and achieve low nutrients. The availability of soil phosphorous (P) is critical for weeds to compete and should be less than 10 mg/kg.
- Lowland heath creation is only viable on acidic soils with a pH 3–5.
- The natural characteristic of heathland, especially plant species composition, varies geographically, so it is very important to establish heathland that is appropriate to the local area. Otherwise the wrong species may be introduced and corrupt existing heathland – this could be illegal if it affects designated sites. Seeds and turves should be sourced carefully and should be from the same vegetation communities as the target community.
- Landforming determines the distribution of heath communities within the site (Plate 4.23). Wet heath only establishes in areas with seasonal waterlogging with base-poor water. Mire vegetation will only occur where waterlogging is permanent. It is therefore important to

create topography that mirrors the natural heathland landform, with variations in slope and aspect, and retains bare ground features where possible.

The most appropriate method of creating heathland habitats depends on local circumstances, eg availability of local seed material. A variety of methods are discussed here, but more detail should be sought from the literature listed in section 4.3.4. It is very important that *heathland* is established, not just *heather*. Indeed in some cases heather may be only a small part of the typical community. In the past, there has been a tendency to sow heather with a nurse grass mix. However, this only creates a field of heather, which takes many years, if ever, to develop into a heathland. Nurse crops should be used with care (see below).

4.3.2.1 Natural regeneration

Natural colonisation of true heathland requires very nutrient-poor soils, an adjacent seed source and plenty of time. Seeds blown from adjacent heathland will be very slow to establish. Ericaceous seeds are not adapted for wind blown dispersal, but individual seeds may move several hundred metres by this means.

Natural colonisation is a potentially successful means of establishing heathland, as long as weed species (birch/pine seedlings, bracken, rough grasses) are kept at low thresholds and if enough time is allowed. Heathland is a habitat with a slow growth dynamic – up to 50 years may be required. Where only scattered ericaceous plants have become established in the first few years, heathland may still develop so long as competition is kept low, as these plants will flower and seed within the first three to five years of life.

Although natural regeneration is a slow process, the mosaic of acid grassland, bare ground and incipient heathland habitats can provide substantial benefits to wildlife during the process as they develop naturally to suit the local conditions. Bare ground is especially valuable for specialist species that occupy the early stages in the development of the habitat. Such areas can develop interesting plant communities and support important populations of invertebrates (section 5.12). However, bare ground habitat should also be planned in the design for the long-term.

P Benstead

Plate 4.23
It is important to create a varied landform in order to achieve a diverse heathland habitat.

4.3.2.2 Topsoil and turf application

Topsoil or turf are not often readily available because until recently they have been a product of heathland destruction. However, there are considerable benefits in removing turf and accumulated litter as part of restoring under-managed heathland, so material can become more available. On an appropriate scale, scraping or the cutting of turves is effective in removing accumulated organic litter, so reducing available soil nutrients.

The appropriate statutory conservation agency must be consulted before turfing or scraping on a designated nature conservation site: as should the county archaeologist to ensure that archaeological interest on the donor site is not damaged. A search for reptiles should be carried out before considering topsoil removal (section 3.3.1). Avoid removing soil when birds and other wildlife may be breeding. Careful assessment of the site's important feature will be required to determine the least damaging time, late summer or autumn may be best. Small turves were traditionally gathered using alternate (chequer board) spacing carried out over a long rotation.

Taking turves to re-establish heathland vegetation

- Where the soil profile is undisturbed, the seedbank will be present in the organic horizon immediately below the fresh litter and in the top five centimetres of the mineral soil.

- Turves need to be dug deep enough to avoid damage to the roots which are close to the surface – a 10–20 cm depth should be sufficient, but ideally research this on site.

- Smaller turves will have the advantage of being easier to transport and will spread farther: a scatter of turves will supply seeds into spaces between. Larger turves may be less likely to desiccate and less prone to damage on site but can be difficult to transport. The turves can be widespread, as there is no real need for complete colonisation of heathland in the short term.

- Laying turves in a block to establish a total heathland cover can be done and achieves instant heathland, but it is unlikely that sufficient donor turves will be available to cover any but a small site. It is better to spread the turves across the site and allow the plants on them to seed into the gaps, creating a structural diversity in the plant community.

- Turves need to be lifted, transported and laid before desiccation of the rootstock occurs.

- Turves should be lifted in the autumn/winter, when plants are dormant and there is less risk of desiccation.

- Turves need to be dug into the ground flush with the surface; this avoids desiccation of the rootstock.

Using topsoil to relocate the seed material from a donor area.

- Standing vegetation should be removed prior to soil removal as fresh organic matter will heat up/compost when stored and risk killing the seeds. Cut material can be spread on the receptor site as a seed source. Cut heather in the autumn (post-flowering) and collect the material with suitable machinery (double chop forage harvester or hi-tip type mower), as this contains seeds that can be used during restoration (see below).

- When removing the topsoil, use a machine that strips material to a determinable depth. The organic horizon and the seed-bearing soil should be taken together with an extra few centimetres to ensure that the maximum number of seeds is gathered.

- Ideally topsoil should be lifted, transported and laid in one operation. But if storage is unavoidable, it should be done with care to avoid the organic material composting and heating, which if above 50 °C will kill ericaceous seeds. To prevent heating, heaps should be kept shallow, < 1.5 m high, on free-draining ground, preferably a geotextile sheeting. Ericaceous seeds can remain viable for over 14 months in such storage conditions, but vegetative material of species such as purple moor-grass, bilberry and cotton-grass will be killed quickly and should be moved as turves.

- Heathland topsoil is spread relatively easily; a manure spreader is ideal because it is quick and cost effective. Any clods can be broken up with a light harrow. Alternatively piles of material could be dumped and spread using a hi-mac, or on small projects, by hand. If an even and complete cover of vegetation is required rapidly then spreading to a depth of 2.5 cm is ideal, but this requires extensive areas of donor heath. However, the material can be spread more thinly where even distribution across the site is not essential. Small gaps will infill later with seeds from established plants, creating a structural diversity in the plant community. On coarse, mineral substrates, eg gravels with low sand content, it is worth spreading a fine, sandy, mineral subsoil first to increase water retention and improve soil-plant nutrient exchange.

- Soil surface stabilisation – a nurse grass crop can be sown to provide soil stability and to create microclimates that protect germinating seedlings from desiccation.

Nurse species should be chosen with care. It is important that nurse species have a low nutrient demand, so there is no need for additional fertiliser, and short viability, so they die out after three or four years without the need for control. Nurse species should not form a dense sward, ie they must leave space for heathland species to develop. The nurse species can be sown by broadcasting onto the laid topsoil, and rolled in with a Cambridge roller. On steep slopes biodegradable geotextile netting may be needed to stabilise slopes and prevent erosion by water run-off. Note that in most situations, a nurse crop should be unnecessary and, if used, may compete with the desired vegetation (Gilbert and Anderson, 1998). Locations most likely to require soil stabilisation include higher altitude and deep peat sites.

- Timing – topsoil should be spread in late winter or early spring, when conditions are relatively dry. The first stages of germination take place relatively quickly and a full growing season is available to allow roots to develop as much as possible. Early autumn is also possible in the lowlands, but the advantage of establishing strong root systems will be lost. Spring or late summer/early autumn are the times to sow and establish a nurse crop.

4.3.2.3 Litter and brash transfer

Collecting viable seed material of a range of heathland plants from existing heathland for use elsewhere is a relatively cheap, non-destructive, repeatable method. Cutting and spreading involves the following.

- For the receptor site: a suitable seedbed can be relatively rough, with small clods or shallow furrows – this will shelter young plants from desiccating winds. A relatively compact soil structure will reduce desiccation. Sparse vegetation is beneficial as shelter for heather seedlings. A nurse crop may not be necessary on flatish ground as the chopped brash shelters the seedlings.

English Nature

Plate 4.24 Cutting and baling heather on a donor site.

- Cut mature heath on the donor area to ground level with a double chop forage harvester or other machinery that cuts and collects in one operation (Plate 4.24) – cutting then baling will cause too many seeds to be shed. Collect cuttings in a trailer for transport.

- Cut between late September and late November when ripe seeds are present (check capsules for seeds to achieve accurate timing). Small amounts of topsoil will inevitably be picked up during the cutting; this imports the heather's mycorrhizal fungal associate, which is thought to benefit establishment of ericaceous species.

- Transport the cut material to the receptor site and spread it immediately or store in low piles to prevent heating.

- Spread the donor material using a clean muck-spreader, a walking-floor spreader is probably the most efficient. Tease apart any clods either manually or with a light harrow. Roll with a Cambridge roller to press the seeds into the ground and promote better germination.

- To establish a dense cover of seedlings quickly, spread 1 cm deep; when cutting mature heath this will give a ratio of approximately one hectare of cut area for two hectares of spread. For lower densities spread more thinly and the material will go farther.

- The rate of heather germination is variable; some seeds germinate within six months, others take over two years – it is worth waiting to assess success. Note that a mature ericaceous shrub produces thousands of seeds per metre square, and new seedling ericaceous shrub plants are tiny so are easy to miss!

If the donor site comprises degenerate heath with a high proportion of very old or dying heather, it can be restored by removing the standing shrubs and the organic litter layer, which contains a mass of seeds. It would be beneficial to test the seedbank in advance to determine that sufficient viable seeds are present. This method will strip the donor site to mineral soil and regeneration will occur from remaining buried seedbank. The organic litter taken to the receptor site will contain a large number of seeds to establish heath on that site. The following procedure is recommended:

- use a grading blade with a very sensitive control to scrape the organic litter without digging into the mineral soil and lift into trailers, or
- loosen the litter with a harrow, allow it to dry and then vacuum into a trailer, or
- scrape the litter into piles and lift into a trailer
- transport and spread on the receptor site in the same way as heather cuttings.

4.3.2.4 Harvesting and sowing seed from donor sites

When cutting and collecting seeds is not possible, seeds can be harvested from standing heather plants (Plate 4.25). A number of machines are available to do the job: brushing the seeds from the plants and collecting them without damage to the vegetation. However, certain horticultural seed merchants can be contracted to collect, clean and heat treat heather seeds. While this may be expensive, any transport and spreading costs will be relatively low because of the low volume involved. Unlike the methods described above, this tends to produce uniform stands of heather without any species richness.

As ericaceous seeds are extremely small and light, a nurse crop of fine grasses may need to be established on a minority of sites, before heather seeds are introduced. This helps to shelter the seeds and maintain soil surface humidity. However, on most mineral soils it is better to use the double chop harvesting method to provide some mulch with the seed.

4.3.2.5 Sowing commercially available seed

Unless local progeny can be guaranteed, introducing genetically 'alien' heather into a

D Hosking (rspb-images.com)

Plate 4.25 Collecting litter/seed for heathland transfer.

local heathland community should be avoided. As with cleaned seed this will create a monoculture of heather, with low wildlife value in all but the very long-term.

4.3.2.6 Planting seedlings and plants

This is a very labour intensive and consequently expensive method. Seedlings have to be collected or grown from seed, grown on, then hardened off before transplanting. Once planted they need plenty of care, particularly to avoid drought and to suppress competition. Many thousands of plants are needed to cover even a small area. Planting at relatively wide spacings means fewer plants are required, and once the plants begin to flower they seed into, and therefore fill, the gaps. This method could be used to introduce 'missing' species after monitoring of early regeneration.

4.3.3 Long-term management of heathland

It is vitally important to keep establishing heathland free from competition from other plants, and to keep the soil fertility to a minimum. Any management must avoid introducing nutrients through incorporation of organic matter. Management options include:

- light spring and early summer grazing – controls the level of competition from grasses and palatable forbs as they are preferentially taken by the livestock (Plate 4.26). The timing of introduction of grazing is not critical, so it can be left until a problem with the level of competition is identified
- rabbit browsing – if intensive, this can inhibit the development of heather seedlings and the surviving heather can take on a prostrate growth form. Prostrate heather and open ground provides a very valuable pioneer community, dominated by ruderal plant species, and is beneficial to invertebrates. The heather eventually grows on to its normal growth form
- mowing and removing cuttings – can be used to reduce grass dominance; the heather will survive in a prostrate form
- rabbit-proof fencing – if rabbits are to be excluded then fencing may be necessary for about five years, thereafter the heather may be browsed but not killed
- herbicide – use to control bracken, gorse or birch weeds. A tractor-mounted weed-wipe avoids any collateral damage to heather or other plants (Plate 4.27). Glyphosate has been used successfully. When re-creating wet heath, rushes may become a problem. Possible control options include applying herbicide via weed-wipe or mowing.

Because 'heathland' comprises an array of species tolerant of impoverished acidic soil conditions, it is important not to regard non-ericaceous species as weeds: the aim is a balance of appropriate species.

D Woodfall (WWI)

English Nature

Plate 4.26 (above, top) Grazing of heathland.

Plate 4.27 (above, bottom) Weed-wiping.

Further reading

Box, J and Hill, A (1999) Mineral extraction and heathland restoration. *Mineral Planning* 80: 5-8.

Clarke, C T (1997) Role of soils in determining sites for lowland heathland reconstruction in England. *Restoration Ecology* 5: 256-264.

EAU (1988) *Heathland restoration: a handbook of techniques*. British Gas, Southampton.

Gilbert, O L and Anderson, P (1998) *Habitat Creation and Repair*. Oxford University Press, Oxford.

Gimingham, C H (1992) *The Lowland Heath Management Handbook*. English Nature, Peterborough.

Hill, A and Box, J (1999) Experimental translocation of wet heathland in Dorset, England: implications for restoration of mineral workings. In P E K Fuchs, M R Smith and M J Arthur (eds) *Mineral Planning in Europe*, pp 342-351. The Institute of Quarrying, Nottingham.

Larson, P (1999) Mineral development. A net contributor to heathland in the South-West. *Quarry Management* March: 39-44.

Putwain, P D (1992) The creation of heathland vegetation: theory and practice. *Aspects of Applied Biology* 29: 33-40.

Putwain, P D and Gillham, D A (1988) Restoration of heather moorland. *Landscape Design* 172: 51-56.

Pywell, R F, Putwain, P D, Webb, N R (1996) Establishment of heathland vegetation on mineral workings. *Aspects of Applied Biology* 44: 285-292.

Pywell, R F, Veitch, N and Webb, N R (1991) Locating and reconstructing former heathlands. *ITE Annual Report* 1991-1992, pp 66-69. Institute for Terrestrial Ecology, Monks Wood.

Pywell, R F, Webb, N R and Putwain, P D (1994) Soil fertility and its implications for the restoration of heathland on farmland in southern Britain. *Biological Conservation* 70: 169-181.

Pywell, R F, Webb, N R and Putwain, P D (1996) Harvested heather shoots as a resource for heathland restoration. *Biological Conservation* 75: 247-254.

Sansen, U, and Koedam, N (1996) Use of sod cutting for restoration of wet heathlands: revegetation and establishment of typical species in relation to soil conditions. *Journal of Vegetation Science* 7: 483-486.

Symes, N C and Day, J (2003) *A practical guide to managing and restoring lowland heathland*. The RSPB, Sandy.

Woodrow, W, Symes, N and Auld, M (1996) *RSPB Dorset Heathland Project 1989-1995: a management case study*. The RSPB, Sandy.

4.4 Wetlands

4.4.1 General principles

This section considers a wide range of wetland habitats including reedbed, open water, fens and bogs, and rivers and streams. Wet grassland and wet woodland have been addressed in the grassland and woodland sections respectively. The wetlands section is laid out slightly differently because the establishment and long-term management techniques vary greatly between wetland habitats. It also constitutes a large section of the handbook since wetland habitats are particularly well-suited for the restoration of the large number of sand and gravel extraction sites. Using appropriate techniques could greatly enhance the value of these sites for nature conservation.

All of these habitats have specific water regime requirements and a good understanding of the hydrological situation is needed to restore them successfully. The quantity of water required to support the wetlands must be calculated, then the method of supplying and managing the water levels must be planned.

The choice of wetland habitat to create depends largely on water availability and quality, as well as soil conditions. Fens and bogs require a peat substrate whereas all of the other habitats may occur on mineral soils. Where a site has variations in topography and hydrology, they should be carefully considered and compared with habitat requirements. Mosaics of wetland habitats can be especially valuable.

4.4.2 Calculating the water requirement

The water available at a site can be estimated using the following calculation:

Water available = rainfall – evapotranspiration (ET) – seepage losses + seepage inputs

The Met Office hold rainfall and ET information and can produce daily, weekly or monthly estimates for a specific location. However, seepage estimates have to be made considering the site conditions. Seepage depends on the ability of water to flow through soil (hydraulic conductivity), which varies according to soil type and soil structure. The hydraulic conductivity of soil can be severely reduced by compaction (section 3.1.2). Seepage also depends on the difference in the height of the water-table between one location and another (the hydraulic gradient). Where the water-table in a field is higher than the water level in an adjacent ditch, water will move towards the ditch at a rate dependent on the difference in heights and hydraulic conductivity.

When ET and seepage losses are greater than water inputs from rainfall and seepage inputs then the water-table falls. Each habitat type has a range of water-table depths that it can tolerate at different times of year. For some habitats, such as reedbed, it is possible to specify the optimum depth of water throughout the year to give maximum conservation benefit. Estimates of the maximum depth to which the water-table may fall yet still support different wetland habitats are shown in Table 4.17. These estimates should be used with care as they have been made based only on the best available information.

Where the quantity of water available is less than the wetland requires, it may be necessary to provide supplementary water either by storage of winter excess rainfall or by abstraction from rivers. Providing supplementary water is potentially unsustainable in the long-term, and should be carefully considered.

Climate change predictions suggest that the pattern of rainfall and ET is likely to change across the UK over the next 50 years. When estimating the water availability at a site, the predicted effects of climate change should be incorporated. Catchment Abstraction Management Strategies (being introduced across England and Wales) will be a good source of information about the likelihood of water being available for habitat creation.

Table 4.17 Maximum water-table depth tolerated by wetland habitats.
(from Souch *et al*, 2000)

NVC community	Water-table depth below ground surface (m)				
	May	June	July	Aug	Feb
Flood meadow Meadow foxtail and great burnet grassland (MG4)	-0.3	-0.6	-0.8	Dry	-0.1
Water meadow Crested dog's-tail and marsh marigold grassland (MG8)	-0.2	-0.4	-0.6	-0.8	-0.2
Tussocky neutral grassland Yorkshire fog and tufted hair-grass grassland (MG9)	-0.2	-0.8	Dry	Dry	0
Rush pasture Yorkshire fog and soft rush grassland (MG10)	-0.1	-0.5	-0.8	Dry	0
Wet alluvial meadow Creeping bent and marsh foxtail grassland (MG13)	0	-0.6	Dry	Dry	0
Reedbed Common reed swamp (S4)	0.2	0.1	0.05	0	0.3
Tall herb fen Common reed and hemp-agrimony fen (S25)	0	-0.4	-0.7	Dry	0
Alder carr Alder and tussock sedge woodland (W5)	-0.1	-0.6	-1	Dry	0

4.4.3 Water level control

Water levels on any site are controlled by the rate at which water enters and leaves. Control of water levels is important for managed wetland habitats such as reedbed and wet grassland as water drawdown is essential for management to take place. Installing water control infrastructure may adversely effect the movement of fish and other fauna. Careful consideration should be given to the potential effects of such construction. If it is possible to achieve target water regimes without these structures, the result will be wetlands with better circulation and no barriers to the movement of plants and animals.

The types of water control structure are described below.

Plate 4.28 Bunds allow winter water to be retained into the spring.

J Leece

4.4.3.1 Bunds

Bunds, or low earth banks, keyed into an impermeable substrate can be used on site to retain water above the water-table level in the surrounding land (Plate 4.28). Using bunds it is possible to create tiered wetlands that have constant flow, which is important for some wetlands such as reedbeds (Figure 4.8). Bunding also permits the retention of winter floodwater, thus reducing the flood risk in other areas and offsetting to a degree the summer moisture deficit. Construction follows the same general principles as dam construction (see below), but is less complicated and relatively cheap.

Bunds should be set well back from the edges of drainage channels to prevent slumping and reduce seepage. Creating mower-friendly profiles is advisable as bunds may be colonised by rank vegetation such as thistles if covered with nutrient-rich topsoils (Figure 4.9). Shallow profile bunds can also have a more natural appearance.

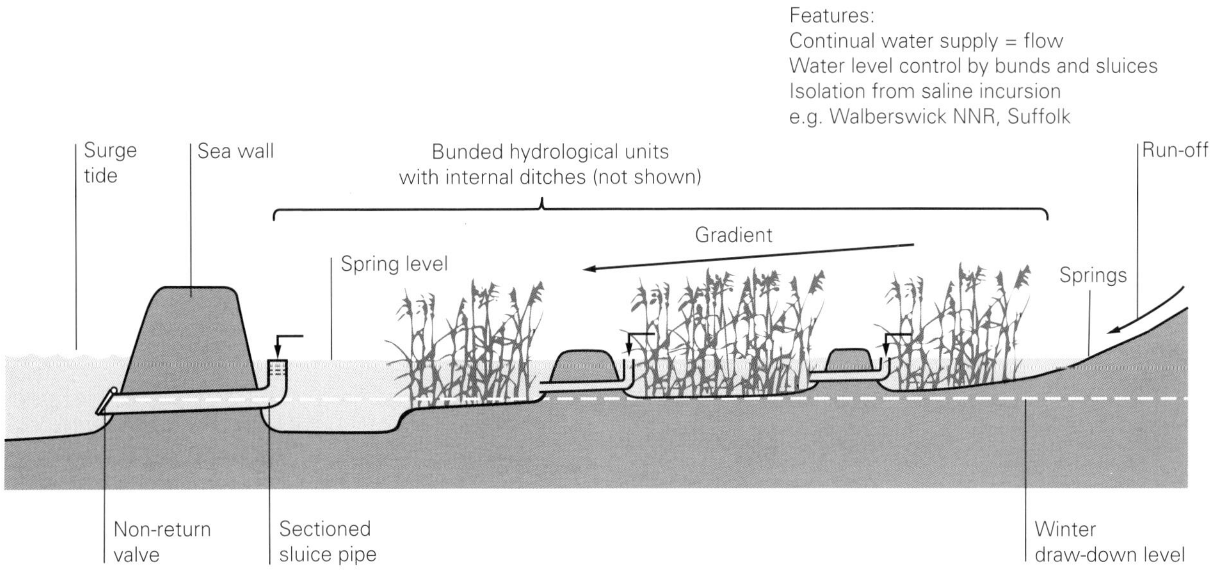

Figure 4.8 Reedbeds benefit from a terraced landform.

4.4.3.2 Dams

Dams are often constructed in drainage channels to retain water within isolated hydrological units. This is an important technique for the treatment of damaged peat bogs for example (section 4.4.7). Creating compartments with independent water level control allows great flexibility in managing sites. Dam construction is easier using clays and loams. Clay and loam dams can be used effectively across channels up to five metres wide. Peat will only make satisfactory dams if well compacted and even then the maximum width is less. In general the basal width of the dam should be five times its height. The top of the dam should be level and at least 500 mm above the normal water level (Table 4.18).

4.4.3.3 Sluices

Sluices can perform the same function as dams, but are designed to permit controlled through-flow so that water levels can be regulated if necessary. There are four main types.

- Flexi-pipe sluices – cheap, easy to install and are an effective method of precise water level control, but are only capable of moving low volumes of water. They consist of flexible, ribbed, plastic pipe, eg 300 mm single wall aquapipe, incorporated into an earth bund or dam (Figure 4.10, Plate 4.29).
- Dropboard sluices – simple structures comprising a series of boards that drop

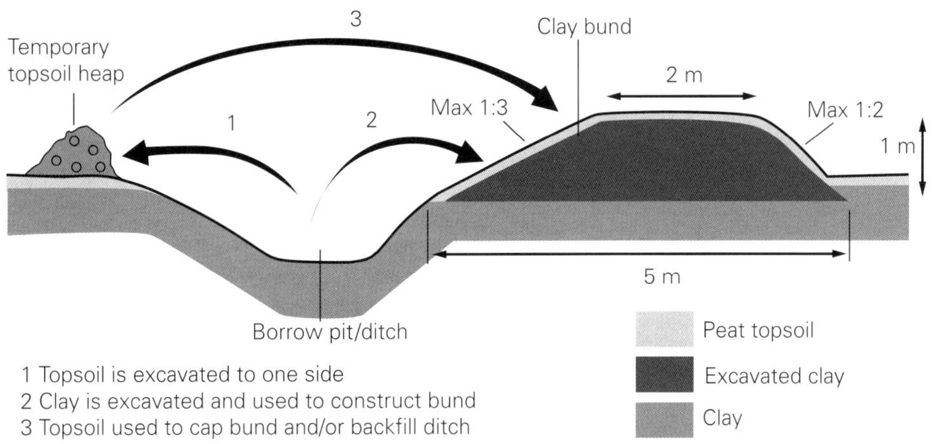

Figure 4.9 Ideal bund profile to enable mowing.

Table 4.18 Principles to be adopted when building dams.

- Construct dams during late summer when water levels are lower and rainfall less likely.
- Use temporary dams to block drainage channel on both sides and pump dry before constructing dam. Temporary cofferdams can be made using double rows of sandbags or wooden boards with a clay infill.
- Remove topsoil and scarify subsoil where the dam is to be built, this enhances keying and reduces seepage.
- Build the dam up slowly, eg in 150 mm layers, and compact. Allow extra material for settling – 10% for mechanical compaction and 20% for compaction by foot. Peat may settle by twice as much as silt.
- Topsoil can be replaced above normal water level and sown with a grass mix – ensure seed is of local, or at least UK, origin. This stabilises the surface and discourages deep-rooting plants.
- In areas grazed by livestock it will be necessary to fence dams to prevent trampling and subsequent erosion.

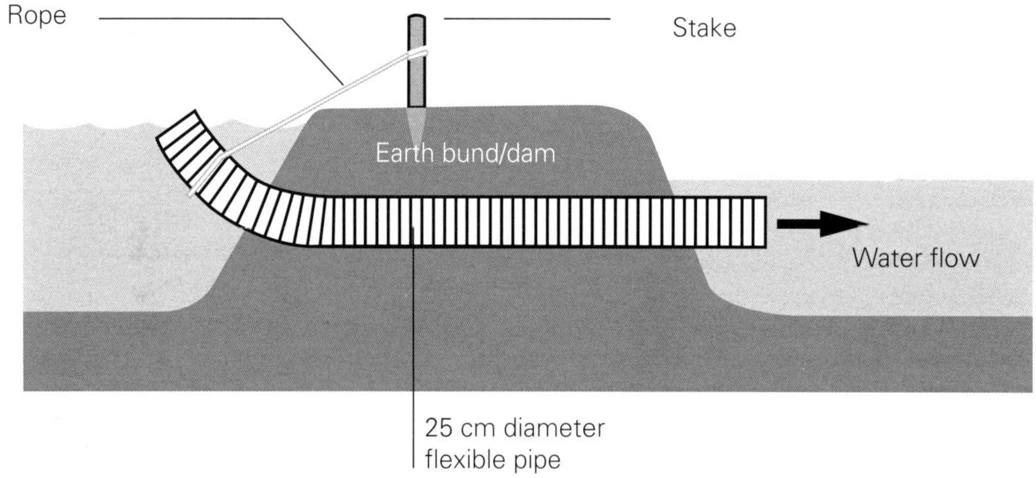

Figure 4.10
Flexi-pipe sluice design and operation.

RSPB

Plate 4.29
A simple pipe sluice with an angled 'turner' to give precise management of water levels.

into a grooved spillway. Water levels are adjusted by inserting or removing boards appropriately. For details of construction see Brooks and Agate (1997) and Figure 4.11.

- Lifting gate sluices – characteristic of old water meadows and are unpopular because precise water control is impossible. They work on an 'all or nothing' principle.

- Tilting weir or drawbridge sluices – very effective at precision water level control but are expensive.

Spillways to handle excess water and to prevent flooding should be incorporated into sluice and dam design where appropriate.

4.2.3.4 Drainage channels and ditches

Drainage channel networks can be important water distribution and control features; they can also be important for a range of aquatic plants and animals. The spacing between channels and the hydraulic conductivity of the soil determines how effective the water level in the channel is at controlling the water-table at the site. Close channel spacing and high hydraulic conductivity allow the best control.

Drainage channel design should incorporate features that will benefit wildlife (Figure 4.12). Profile and depth significantly influence the wildlife value of drainage channels. Some species depend on specific water depths. It is important to maintain a variety of depths grading to a shallow, wet marginal fringe. Maximising shallow water habitat creates conditions suitable for the majority of wetland plants and invertebrates. Winter water levels are less critical, but some water must be maintained year round. Clay sites benefit from the creation of foot drains, or small, shallow ditches that allow water onto field centres when drainage channel water levels are high. Conversely, they provide drainage to the site if the drainage channel water level is low.

The physical disturbance of creating new drainage channels can release soil nutrients and cause temporary eutrophication. Newly-created channels should not therefore be connected to existing ditches or waterbodies of nature conservation significance until their nutrient status has stabilised.

Drainage channels require regular management in rotation to ensure they remain clear and fulfil their primary purpose (Plate 4.30). Management should aim to provide every stage of succession from recently cleaned channels to those heavily choked with emergent vegetation. It is important to survey ditches prior to management to ensure that rare species will not be lost during the process. For details of best practice management see Hawke and José (1996) and RSPB, EN and ITE (1997).

4.4.3.5 Pumps

Pumps are required to move water against a hydraulic gradient, ie uphill. Wherever possible wetland systems should be designed to avoid using pumps. If pumps must be used then sustainable wind

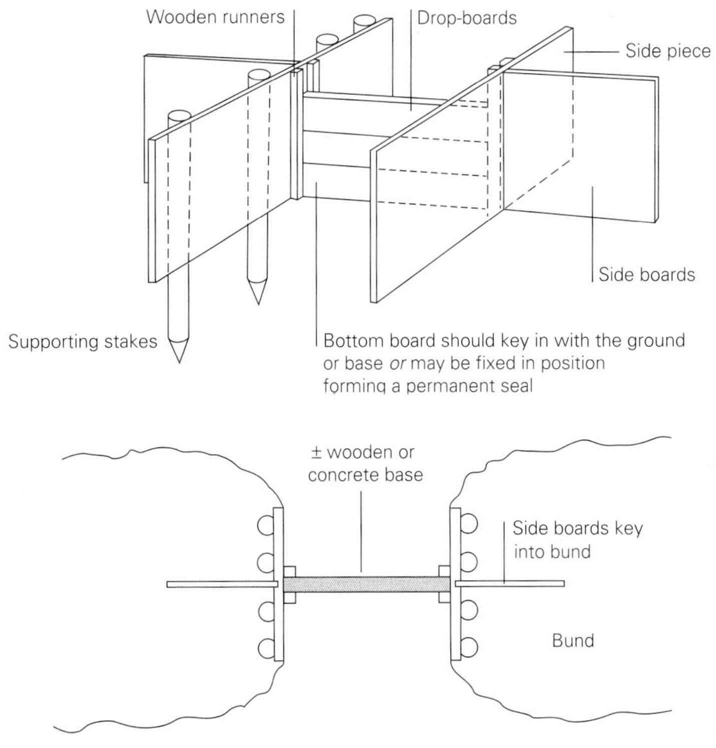

Figure 4.11
Design and operation of dropboard sluices
top: 3D view of structure
bottom: top view showing how side boards key into bund.

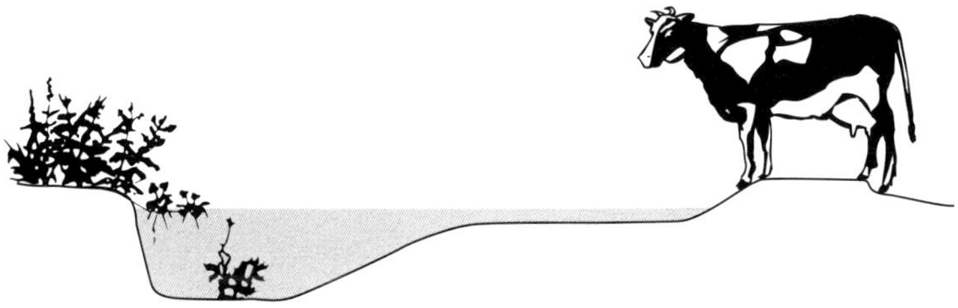

Ditch edge can be pulled back creating shallow water or exposed mud for feeding waders. Grazing is important to prevent invasion of emergent vegetation.

Both sides sloped to about 45°.

- Gently sloping banks allow greatest light penetration into ditch for plants
- Cattle can drink without falling in
- wading birds can feed on shallow edge

Figure 4.12
Profiles for stock-proof wet fences (drainage ditches) that maximise benefits to wildlife.

T Callaway

Plate 4.30
Drainage ditch management.

C H Gomersall (rspb-images.com)

Plate 4.31
A windmill design incorporating a centrifugal pump driven by a 4 m wind tower with a 4-sail 3 m diameter rotor.

A Hay (rspb-images.com)

Plate 4.32
Water storage at Otmoor.

pumps should be considered in preference to diesel or electric (Plate 4.31). Pump specifications must match the site water requirements and conditions. The following should be taken into account when considering a pumping operation and which type of pump to use:

- volume of water and delivery rate required
- the height of head – difference between input and output levels
- distance between intake and discharge points
- need for an abstraction licence or equivalent (section 1.4.8)
- proximity to electricity supply if an electric pump must be used.

4.4.3.6 Water storage

Where summer water supplies are unpredictable or insufficient, it may be possible to incorporate a water storage area into a wetland design (Plate 4.32). Such reservoirs greatly facilitate management of some habitats, for example reedbeds and wet grasslands. Reservoirs should be designed with wildlife requirements firmly in mind. The following features greatly enhance reservoirs (Orford, 1996):

- creation of a deep area in the reservoir bed to provide refuge for fish and invertebrates when water levels are low in the summer. Underwater shelter from rocks or dead trees will also enhance these areas
- creation of a marginal shelf, or gently sloping edge, for plants
- creation of islands, either shingle covered or planted with vegetation, for nesting birds (although be careful not to put nesting birds at risk when water levels are lowered).

Alternatively reedbed areas that act as reservoirs for other habitats such as wet grassland can be designed into a scheme. A maximum depth of one metre is recommended for a reedbed storage reservoir.

All water management operations should be carried out with regard to relevant water resource legislation (section 1.4.8). The impact of raising site water levels on neighbouring land also needs to be carefully assessed. Work on or adjacent to a main watercourse may require consent from the relevant water resource agency. Additionally impounding or abstracting water may require licences, and constructing any feature that holds water may come under the provisions of the Reservoirs Safety Provisions Act 1975 (Table 1.4).

4.4.4 Reedbed

Reedbeds are comprised largely of common reed, a tall, perennial, flood-tolerant grass. In the UK the most extensive reedbeds are found in river floodplains and low-lying coastal plains (Plate 4.33). Reedbed is a nationally scarce habitat and its dependent species have a similar status. Reedbeds support characteristic communities of uncommon birds and invertebrates, eg the bittern and reed leopard moth (Table 4.19). Requirements of some of the important species found in reedbeds are detailed in Table 4.20. This section aims merely to outline design considerations and appropriate techniques to create reedbed habitats, for more detail, especially on reedbed management, consult Hawke and José (1996).

4.4.4.1 Reedbed design

Reedbeds can be created anywhere there is:

- a reliable water supply, sufficient to maintain flow and up to 300 mm of water depth in spring
- a level or very shallow gradient
- an available, vigorous reed source
- access for management.

C H Gomersall (rspb-images.com)

Plate 4.33 Reedbeds were once extensive in the now arable fens of eastern England until the major drainage schemes of the 17th century.

Reedbeds of any size benefit wildlife. However, larger reedbeds tend to support more species and also provide habitat for birds that require extensive reedbeds, eg the bittern and marsh harrier (Figure 4.13). The value of a reedbed is further increased if it forms part of a larger wetland complex of swamp, marsh, open water or wet woodland; all have their associated species. A reedbed with a large area of edge habitat adjacent to open water will support more birds than the equivalent area just covered in reed, since more fish are able to penetrate the reedbed. Reedbeds require management

Table 4.19 Characteristic species of reedbeds.

Plants	Reedbeds are dominated by common reeds. However, other plants are always present, in wetter areas these include yellow iris, rushes and bur-reed, in drier reedbeds hemp-agrimony, hairy willow-herb and bittersweet are frequently found. Scarcer species of the habitat, with a restricted range, include cowbane, greater spearwort and greater water-parsnip	Birds	In the UK there are four species that are highly dependent on reedbeds: the reed warbler, bittern, marsh harrier and bearded tit; only the first is widespread. Species that use reedbeds and associated habitats include the reed bunting, sedge warbler, water rail and teal
		Mammals	Water voles, otters, water shrews and harvest mice all make use of reedbeds.
Invertebrates	At least 700 species of invertebrates are associated with UK reedbeds, 64 insects depend on reed to some extent. Moths are perhaps the best known associated group, notably the wainscot moths, but flies and beetles are also important. Rarer species include the reed leopard moth and Fenn's wainscot moth.	Fish	The fish found in the ditches and pools associated with reedbeds are those common to lowland rivers. These include pike, tench, roach, rudd, perch and eel.

Table 4.20 A quick guide to the ecological requirements of reedbed flora and fauna.

Group/species	General requirements
Breeding birds	Bitterns require clear water with abundant fish stocks. They hunt along the reed/open water interface in shallow water, so maximising edge habitat is important. Reedbeds should be > 20 ha, with 20% open water and at least 600 m of reed edge per hectare. These prescriptions favour all reedbed breeding birds. On sites trying to attract bearded tits consider constructing nesting 'wigwams' in new reedbeds.
Fish	Reed-fringed, shallow water and open water with abundant aquatic plants are important. Connectivity with rivers is often required to ensure recruitment of eels.
Invertebrates	All stages of reedbed succession support important invertebrate communities. Maximum diversity supported by reedbeds with damp, but not flooded, litter layer and an abundance of other reedbed herb species. Sparse reeds with other emergents in shallow water is good also.
Amphibians and reptiles	Amphibians require well-vegetated waterbodies within the reedbed. Grass snakes can be abundant in reedbeds, using piles of cut vegetation to lay their eggs.
Mammals	Reedbeds provide excellent refuge and lying-up sites for otters, which require abundant fish and amphibian stocks within the pools and channels. Water voles can also thrive within reedbeds, which may provide a refuge from predation by mink. Reedbeds should have higher areas above winter water levels to accommodate burrows and provide a winter diet of roots, rhizomes and bulbs. Reedbeds also provide habitat for the harvest mouse, which feeds on invertebrates in the summer and seeds during the winter. Water shrews may also be present.
Aquatic flora	Ditch and waterbody profiles should create abundant shallow water for submerged macrophytes and emergent vegetation. Subsequent management should allow for a full range of seral succession, from open water to vegetation choked ditches. Need areas of deeper water > 1.5 m to reduce the potential for reed dominance. Species presence depends on water pH, salinity and trophic status. Most aquatic plant species prefer mesotrophic-eutrophic conditions with a neutral to slightly acidic pH.

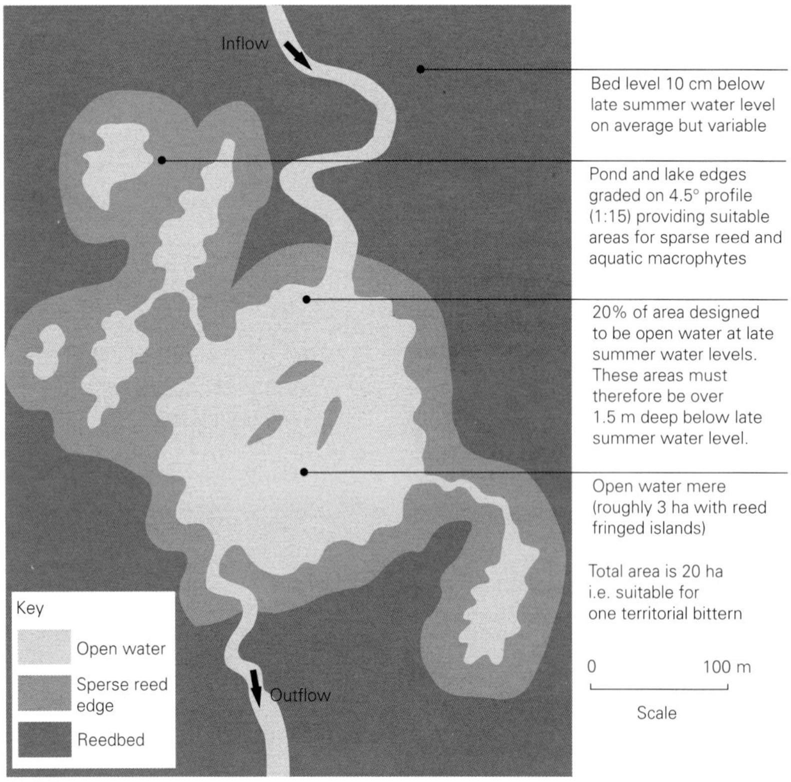

Figure 4.13
Reedbed design for bitterns.

to prevent succession. This can be achieved through sustainable commercial cutting in areas with demand for reed or biofuel. Clearly management should be considered in the design from the outset, eg to ensure machinery access if necessary.

Design considerations include ensuring an adequate water supply during the summer. Flooding in spring is necessary to control competing terrestrial weed species. Reedbeds also benefit from a variation in water levels. Dry periods allow management and also encourage the oxidation of litter build-up, making nutrients available and prolonging the reedbed's life. Dry areas in the reedbed allow litter build-up, which is valuable to invertebrates for food and cover.

An undulating landform giving a variety of water depths across the reedbed is ideal (Figure 4.14). Surplus soil required to create an uneven surface is often provided during the construction of ditches and the excavation of lakes and meres. Landform should be designed to complement water

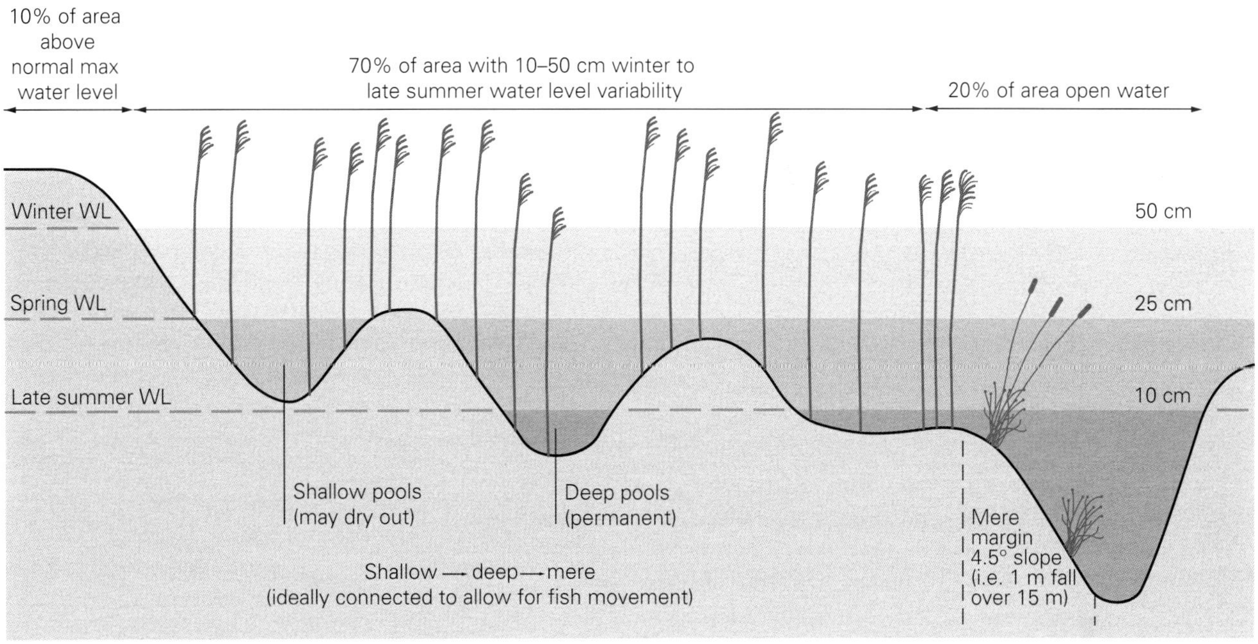

Figure 4.14 Ideal reedbed topography.

distribution and blend with the existing topography. Care should be taken with landforming operations in reedbeds where the aim is to provide commercial reed for harvesting. Too much variation in water depth leads to reed of variable quality and makes the reedbed difficult to harvest.

4.4.4.2 Bed preparation

Most reed establishment techniques require some form of bed preparation. The extent of bed preparation depends on the establishment technique, soil type and the condition of the bed. Reeds can be established on most soil types, though it is easier on finer soils such as clays and silts. Oxidised peat soils may require pre-flooding and drawdown before planting to de-acidify them. Bed preparation involves:

- Control of competing vegetation – this is a critical factor, failure to control unwanted plants effectively severely affects a project's success. Stripping vegetation and litter during landforming is simple and effective. Where landforming is not required, or possible, the use of herbicides, rotovation, ploughing or flooding is necessary. However, rotovation and ploughing can further expose weed seedbanks and can favour invasion by rushes. Reed should be introduced as soon as water levels are suitable.

- Control of water levels – water levels must be finely balanced in the early stages of establishment: low enough to promote establishment but high enough to discourage competition from other plants. Young reed plants are vulnerable to both dehydration and drowning. During sowing or planting, damp soil is required. After the reed shoots, water levels can be raised taking care to ensure that the top third of the plants are always above the surface. Managing water levels to reduce the extent of open water may also help restrict grazing of young reed by coots and geese.

4.4.4.3 Reed establishment

There are a variety of techniques to establish reeds. Whichever technique is employed, it is not necessary to plant up the whole site. Planting a nucleus of reeds in an area with good water level control creates a source of reeds that can spread out into appropriately managed areas. Expansion rates vary greatly from 1–10 m/year or faster in exceptional circumstances. Rate of expansion is likely to be affected by temperature and water depth. Where reeds are present in adjacent ditches natural colonisation can be rapid, especially if aided by turf transplant (see below).

4.4.4.4 Planting techniques

When planting, consider the source of the material – seeds, rhizomes and shoots. Ideally, material should come from the site itself: if this is not possible then from some other similar local site. Planting reeds taken from local sites with similar conditions will be more successful. Shallow flooding allows the site's lowest areas to be identified. These can be marked out using canes and planted following drawdown. The four most reliable techniques for establishing reed are described below (Plate 4.34 and Plate 4.35).

Plate 4.34 (Below top) Planting reed cuttings.

Plate 4.35 (Below bottom) Turf transplants can be very successful.

A Hay (rspb-images.com)

G J White

4.4.4.4.1 Sowing seed

Hand sowing is currently the only available practical option. Aerial seeding has been used effectively over large areas in the Netherlands, but is very expensive. The following factors need to be considered:

- seed viability should be tested before sowing (Self, 1999)
- sowing should take place in still wind conditions
- soil should be saturated but not flooded
- bed should be flat and free of vegetation
- sowing should take place in May/June, ensuring the daytime temperatures range from 10–25 °C and nights are frost free
- panicle fragments should be pressed gently into the seedbed to ensure good contact. Rollers are rarely suitable; instead compression boards or trampling should be used.

Seed density should be in the range 10–125 viable seeds/m^2 on bare, wet soil. In good conditions germination takes 3–4 days. The seedbed must be kept wet without over-topping seedlings. Rainfall during this period can wash seeds and seedlings away and is a risk. Once shoots have reached a height of 100–200 mm, the bed can be flooded to 50 mm (Parr, 1987). In the UK from Northumberland northwards, summer temperatures are too low to establish reed from seeds. All establishment techniques in cooler, more northerly areas may be slow, with the first year a period of consolidation before expansion from the second year onwards.

4.4.4.4.2 Planting seedlings

Planting out pot-grown seedlings of known origin is the most successful method of establishing reedbed. Planted out seedlings are more able to compete and survive adverse weather conditions. If the bed conditions are suitable, success rates are close to 100%. Buying nursery-grown material is expensive, although costs are reduced if buying in bulk for large scale projects. For large scale planting it may be more cost-effective to grow your own (Self, 1999).

Pot-grown material can be planted out by hand using a dibber to create a hole of sufficient size. Individual seedlings are usually planted at densities of 4/m^2. At this density planting time is approximately 540 person hours/ha. Mechanical planting is currently at an experimental stage. It is best to plant in June, as early as possible after the frosts have ceased. Planting any later leaves plants vulnerable to competition. Water levels should be at or just above the soil surface. An alternative to pot-grown seedlings is planting cuttings of existing reed stems. Typically a 0.9 m stem is cut and dibbed 0.6 m into the ground, leaving a small length of stem exposed (Plate 4.34).

Where good water level control exists, bed preparation is less important, as water levels can be used to discourage weed species. Seedlings less than a year old can tolerate water levels up to 200 mm below the topmost shoots. Species established in the first year of wetland creation tend to maintain their status in subsequent years. If reedmace or rushes gain ascendancy then they can be difficult to remove. However, under ideal conditions, reed is likely to out-compete in due course and some areas of mixed vegetation should be seen as beneficial.

Planting seedlings into a grass nurse crop has been successful at some sites. A grass crop, such as rye grass, is sown onto a dry seedbed and out-competes terrestrial competitors. Reed seedlings are planted into this sward and the water level is raised to the tops of the seedlings. This effectively drowns the grass, which rots down into a mulch preventing other species invading and supplying the growing reed with nutrients.

4.4.4.4.3 Spreading soil containing rhizomes

This is a basic technique involving the transfer of the top 300–500 mm of an existing reedbed to a prepared recipient site. Rhizome-rich soil is often excavated during the maintenance of drainage channels and can be used for this purpose. At Hauxley OCCS, Northumberland, small patches of reed were established by tipping loads of rhizome-rich soil into shallow bays.

The following points should be considered when using this technique:

- soil should be spread at least 250 mm deep and can be flooded up to 200 mm
- the soil must be moist and must not dry out
- soil manipulation should be minimised to avoid damaging rhizomes and the material should not be stored for long periods
- excavation and spreading should be carried out in the winter: November to February. Excavation should be to just below the rhizome level; the depth varies according to the site
- it may be necessary to pre-excavate the recipient site to achieve desired water levels.

This technique, together with turf transplant (see below), has the added advantage that litter and soil invertebrates are also introduced to the site together with plants that may be of conservation value. Spreading rhizome-rich soil in this way is only really practical over small areas, as 2,500 m^3 of material is required per hectare. Transportation costs over long distances are also prohibitive. Alternatively, loads of excavated rhizomes can be dumped at 10 m intervals, ie 100/ha across the proposed reedbed area.

4.4.4.4.4 Turf transplant

Actually cutting turves as complete rhizome mats decreases damage and reduces the volume of material to transport. This technique is very successful. On a small scale, turves can be cut by hand with a spade, but for large scale projects diggers with buckets capable of digging 1 m^2 turves are required. The same equipment is used to cut the recipient hole. Both hand and mechanical techniques have been used to good effect at Druridge Bay OCCS (Northumberland) restoration sites.

The spacing of planting depends on the size of the turves and the desired rate of spread. For commercial reedbeds full cover is often required as soon as possible, but for wildlife a slowly developing reedbed is more beneficial. Generally, the following points are important:

- larger turves contain more undamaged material and will establish a reedbed more quickly
- water levels may be from just below the surface to up to 500 mm deep providing turves have long, intact reed stems attached
- bed preparation is less critical, providing flooding is immediate to suppress competition

- when transported or stored, turves should not be stacked one on top of the other, as this damages aerial stems which supply oxygen to the rhizomes
- work is best carried out in winter during drawdown of water levels.

4.4.4.5 Protection of new growth

In the first year it is necessary to protect the establishing reedbed from competition with other plants and from grazing animals (Plate 4.36). Newly-sprouted reed is eaten by a variety of grazing animals, eg geese, coots, deer, rabbits and livestock, and this can seriously inhibit reed growth/expansion. Some form of fencing is essential. Plastic netting with tape stretched across the enclosure has been successful at some sites to protect new plantings from grazing, but needs to be combined with regular human disturbance of the site. Other possible solutions include: over-planting which may compensate for losses, but may prove expensive; minimising the area of open water; sowing strips of grass among the reed which will be grazed preferentially but can be removed by flooding later.

4.4.4.6 Long-term management of reedbeds

Rotational cutting and removal of reed in the winter, often commercially, is the commonest method of management and is used to:

- reduce the rate of litter accumulation
- stimulate the production of new buds
- provide temporary open, wet habitat
- control reed encroachment into other habitats.

Other management techniques include summer cutting, grazing and burning ensuring that only a proportion is managed each year to conserve invertebrate population. Old reedbeds may require lowering as litter levels build up. For full details of reedbed management consult Hawke and José (1996).

Plate 4.36 Reedbed protection.

G J White

C H Gomersall (rspb-images.com)

Plate 4.37 With appropriate restoration flooded sand and gravel workings can be important for wetland wildlife.

4.4.5 Open water

The sand and gravel extraction industry has already created some 20,000 ha of open water habitat (referred to as mesotrophic and eutrophic standing waters in the UK BAP) (Plate 4.37). This results in the creation of open water features in the landscape (in the absence of inert fill) as most gravel pits are situated in river floodplains. Many areas have become important for a wide range of wetland wildlife (Table 4.21). Other mineral industries, notably clay and chalk extraction, also create open water habitat. Chalk extraction below the water-table, eg at College Lake (Box 2.2), or gravel extraction in areas with chalk aquifers can result in the creation of marl lakes which support interesting stonewort communities. Opencast coal sites are often suitable for open water creation as the overburden may include considerable clay measures, which can be used effectively to create wetlands (Andrews, 1992).

The creation and management of such open water features, especially those arising from sand and gravel extraction, are discussed in several publications aimed at the practitioner (Street, 1989; Andrews and Kinsman, 1990; Giles, 1992; Merritt, 1994).

Table 4.21 Characteristic species of open water habitats.

Plants	Open waters may be classified according to their nutrient status, and characteristic plants will be associated with different nutrient levels. Typical aquatic weeds include duckweeds, stoneworts, pondweeds, water-milfoils and water-lilies.
Invertebrates	The invertebrate fauna is diverse and includes dragonflies, such as the ruddy darter and red-eyed damselfly, water beetles, aquatic snails, crustaceans and mayflies.
Amphibians	All three native newts, including the specially protected great crested newt, as well as the common frog and common toad.
Birds	Wintering and breeding waterbirds, including the great crested grebe, gadwall, shoveler, pochard and tufted duck. Common terns, little ringed plovers and sand martins particularly on gravel pits.
Fish	Largely coarse species such as the tench, roach, bream, perch, pike, rudd and eel.
Mammals	Wetland mammals include the water vole, water shrew, otter and bats.

G J White

Plate 4.38
Landforming should seek to create shallows, long shorelines and islands.

4.4.5.1 Large open waterbody design

Species requirements are summarised in Table 4.22. There are several general design principles for large open waterbodies:

- consider carefully soil handling and distribution during habitat creation as fertile topsoil can be detrimental in many circumstances
- create as much shallow water as possible (< 1.5 m depth), especially offshore beyond future overhanging trees
- maximise edge habitat by creating scalloped or sinuous margins (Plate 4.38)
- create low, wet islands that can be completely immersed to manage vegetation
- ensure conservation features are sheltered from the wind to reduce wave erosion
- create peripheral wetland habitats, eg ditches, ponds, reedbeds, marsh and wet grassland (Figure 4.15)

Table 4.22 A quick guide to the ecological requirements of the flora and fauna of open water.

Group	General requirements
Breeding waders	Secure, open nesting areas, usually islands, with plenty of shallow water habitat for feeding young.
Breeding wildfowl	Dense vegetation in which to nest, eg brambles and nettles, as well as abundant invertebrates for the ducklings to feed on. Waterfowl populations of newly created waterbodies are likely to decline after a number of years as the high biomass pioneer communities (largely comprising midge larvae) give way to other invertebrate communities (Danell and Sjöberg, 1982). The decline in midge larvae is often mirrored by an increase in benthic invertebrates, which favours diving ducks at the expense of dabbling duck populations.
Wintering wildfowl	Most dabbling ducks (such as teals) require large expanses of shallow water (< 500 mm). Diving ducks ideally require water 1.5–2.0 m deep, but can dive deeper. Grazing wildfowl require a grass sward 50 mm long close to the water.
Invertebrates	Variety in habitat is important, with each having its associated species. Bare marginal substrates and early successional habitat can be very important, supporting many scarce species. Irregular flooding and drawdown favour high biomass, pioneer communities and greater diversity. Shallow, open water areas with abundant emergent and submerged aquatic macrophytes generally support a diverse invertebrate fauna. Substrates are important, with mineral-bottomed and organic-bottomed waters having different faunas. Some species, eg the black-tailed skimmer dragonfly, favour gravel pits and have extended their ranges as more areas have been worked.
Fish	Warm, vegetation-filled shallows for spawning and sheltering fry. Variation in bed depth with some deeper areas for adult fish.
Mammals	Otters require disturbance-free areas for holts, good water quality and high densities of fish. Artificial holts can be provided and are often successful (section 4.6.2). Water voles are likely to benefit from the provision of ditches and ponds within the wetland complex.
Aquatic flora	Community development depends on good water quality and pH. Generally, clear water less than 1.5 m deep is best. Shallow, sloping banks with gradients of 1:5 to 1:15 will maximise floral diversity, by providing various inundation levels.

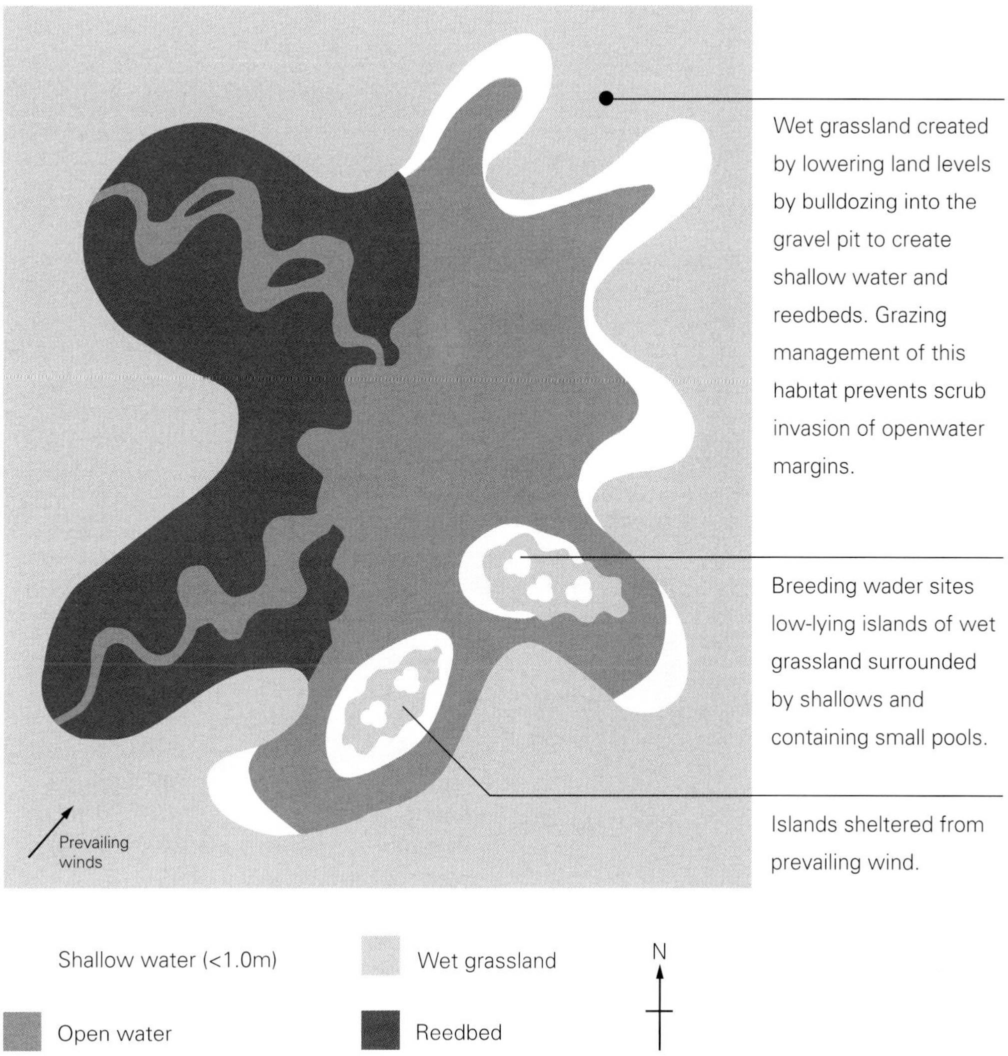

Figure 4.15 Ideally open water features should exist alongside other habitats, and include features such as islands and areas of shallow water.

- create gently sloping or flat beaches of exposed sediment to benefit predatory invertebrates such as ground beetles and wolf spiders.

4.4.5.2 Landform and island design

Landforming prior to flooding is the single most important aspect of open water habitat creation. Consider ways of reducing disturbance when designing landforms. Possible methods to reduce human disturbance include earth mounds and screens, security ditches and optimal siting of observation points.

The possible effects of wave and wind erosion must be considered and factored into design. However, limited wave erosion may not be a bad thing if it helps to form a beach rather than soil cliffs. Unstable sandy or silt margins of gravel pits have been found to support a rich invertebrate fauna in some locations. Tree plantings can act as wind shelters and reduce erosion but if they are effective, they are also likely to seriously detract from the open habitats favoured by waterbirds. In general, tree planting should be kept to a minimum and its location carefully considered.

Islands are valuable, providing disturbance-free breeding sites for ducks, waders and terns. They do, however, require annual management to maintain their breeding bird interest and this should be considered during design. To avoid erosion, islands should be located in the most sheltered area of the pit – in the UK this is usually the south-west 'corner'. Islands should be low in profile, with shallow gradients into the water. Ideally they should be situated in extensive shallows and incorporate small,

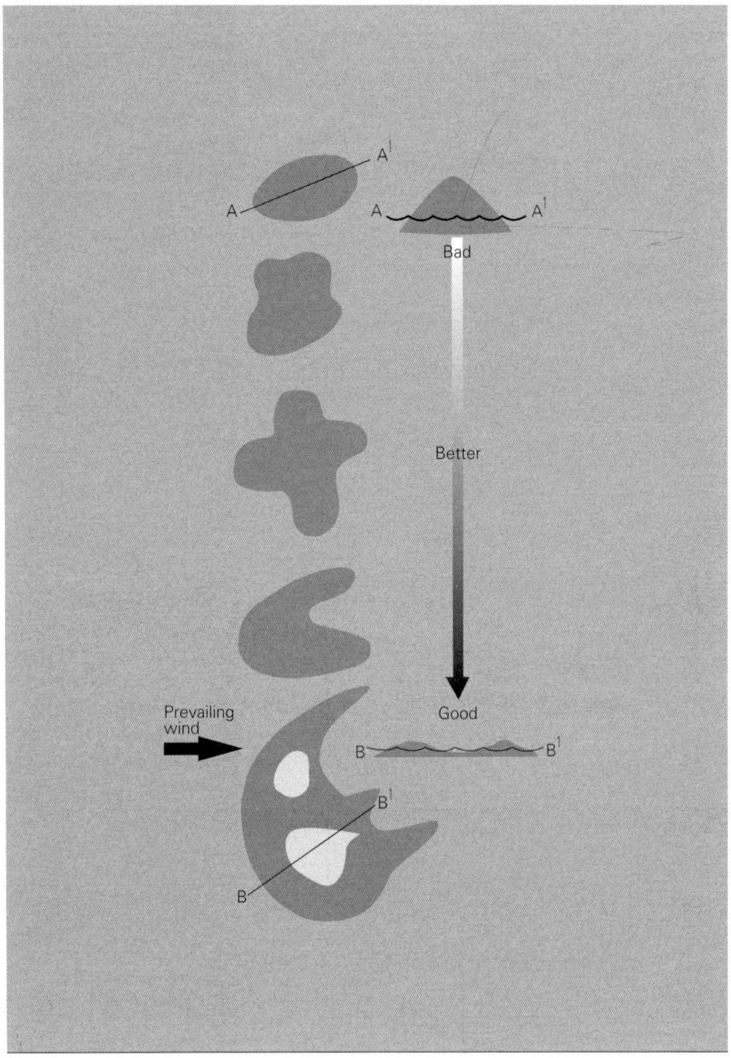

Figure 4.16
Island design suitable for breeding wet grassland birds.

Plate 4.39
Winter flooding can control terrestrial vegetation to create breeding areas for little ringed plovers and lapwings, Amwell Quarry, Hertfordshire.

shallow open waterbodies within them (Figure 4.16, Box 4.3, Plate 4.39). Naturally vegetated, clay-capped islands will attract wet grassland waders such as redshanks and lapwings. Topping with gravel will attract ringed plovers and common terns. Steep-sided islands, with naturally eroding faces, may be important for invertebrates and will provide nest sites for kingfishers and occasionally sand martins.

Box 4.3 Creating islands for breeding waders at Pumphouse Pit, Little Paxton, Cambridgeshire

An island complex at Pumphouse Pit (Bardon Aggregates, Little Paxton) was conceived as traditional shingle islands, including one horseshoe-shaped island surrounded by extensive shallows (Figure 4.17 and Plate 4.40). Water levels proved more variable and generally lower than expected, creating extensive, low-level wet grassland margins around the sand and gravel-capped island (total area c 1 ha). Inundated only at the highest water levels (c 10% of the year), the grassland has remained exposed during the breeding season and the shallow lagoon encompassed by the horseshoe island has proved to be permanent. The grassland areas have become regionally important for breeding redshanks and lapwings, while oystercatchers and ringed plovers breed on the raised gravel areas. Management consists of cutting the grass with a reciprocating scythe and raking into piles (to be left), and rotovating the sand and gravel areas. This is undertaken by volunteers and takes about eight person days each winter.

The results at Pumphouse Pit over a 10-year period have informed the design for similarly-sized new islands to be constructed on adjacent pits. To attract wet grassland waders to gravel pits, islands should be designed as low-level wet grassland, contoured a) to remain viable under a wide range of water level conditions and b) to facilitate unimpeded grass cutting by machine. This dictates a very shallow 'dome' profile overall. While control facilities to flood islands for extended periods during winter to control terrestrial plants is the ideal, this is not always possible with large waterbodies. Equally important, suitable conditions for feeding wader chicks must be created by maximising water margins and providing plenty of shallow pools and bays. Designs for the new islands at Paxton incorporate these features into a 'spread hand' shape (Figure 4.17).

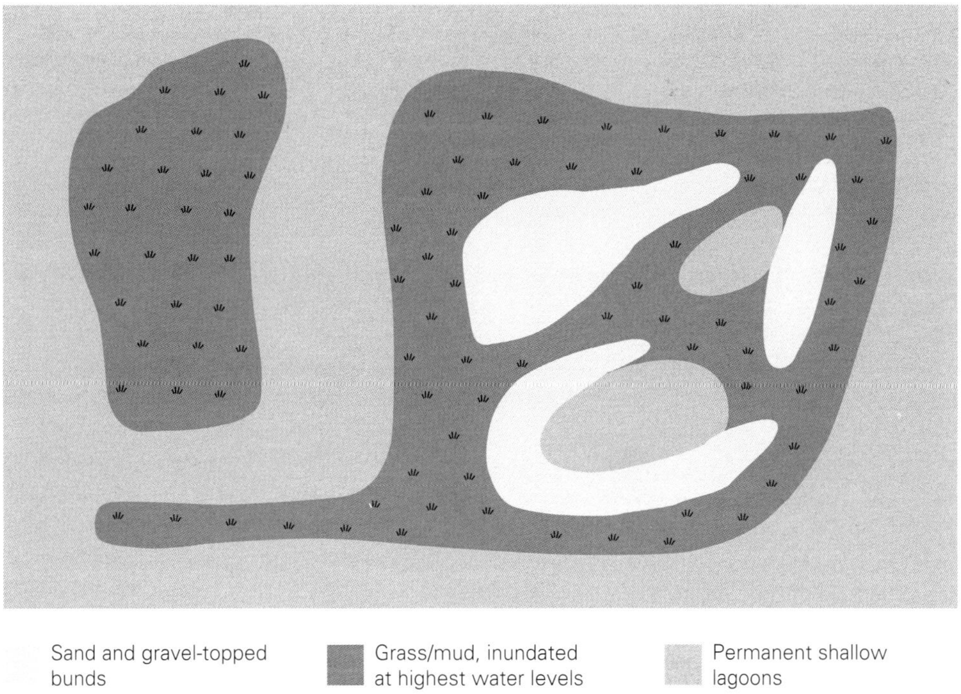

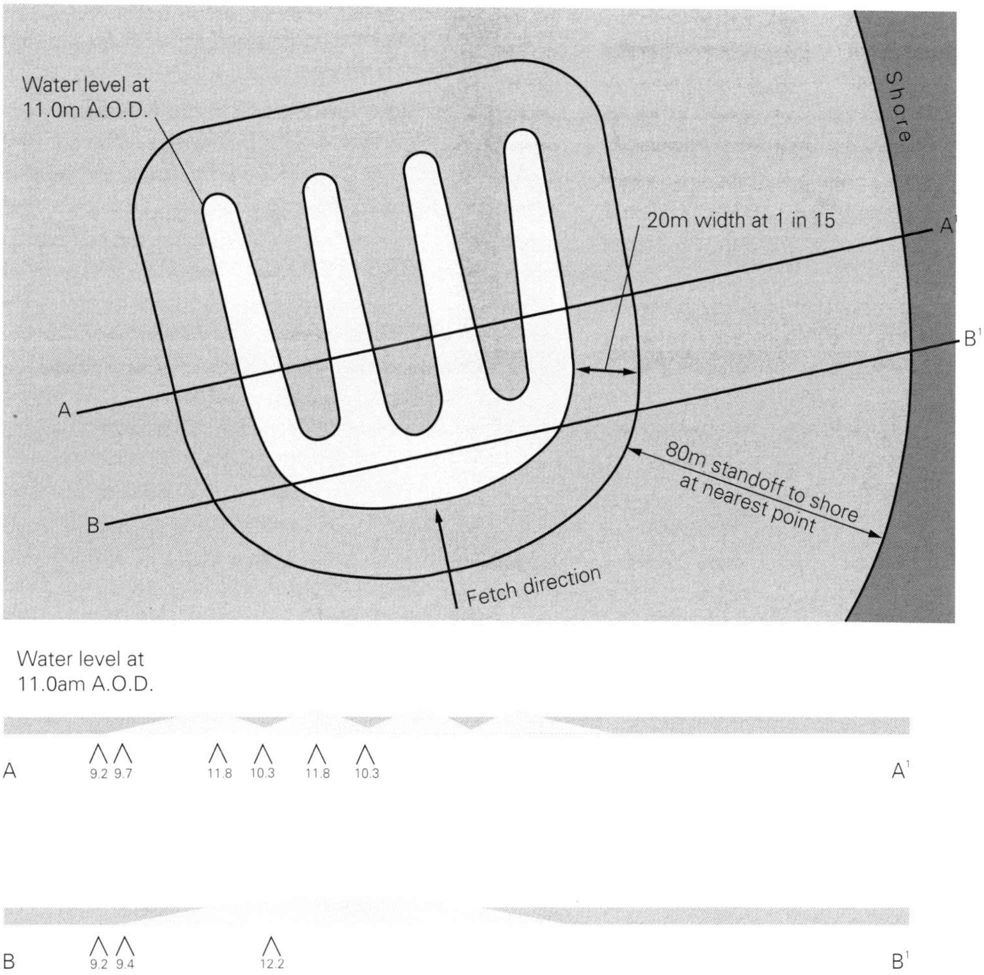

Figure 4.17 Island design at Pumphouse Pit a) traditional horseshoe-shaped shingle island surrounded by extensive shallows, b) 'spread hand' island surrounded by shallows.

R Matthews

Plate 4.40 Volunteers on a winter work party.

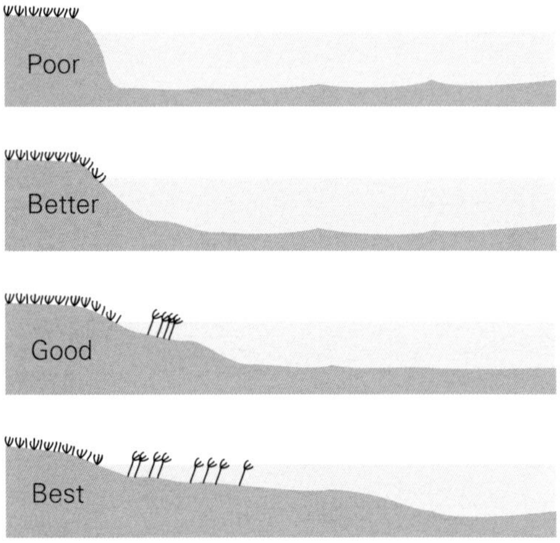

Figure 4.18 Bankside gradients and their suitability to wildlife.

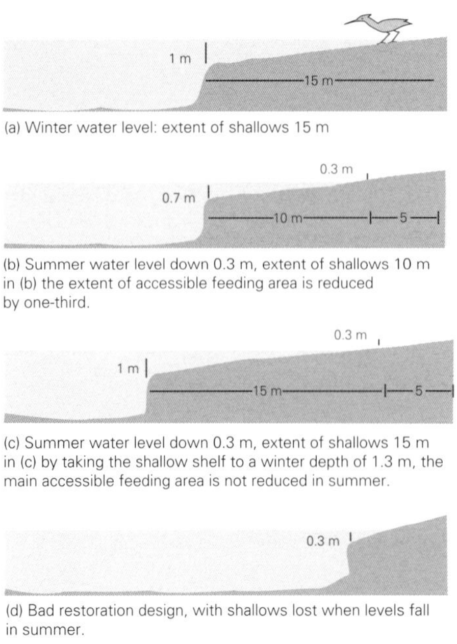

Figure 4.19 It is important to consider the effect of seasonal drawdown on the extent of shallow water provision and design shallows accordingly.

After working sand and gravel deposits, de-watered pits should not be bulldozed into flat basins prior to flooding. There is a tendency to fill in de-watering trenches and level piles of clay within the basin. These features, if left, provide a valuable varied topography that encourages diversity and may also provide a resource of wetland species to colonise the lake. Tidying basins in this way before flooding should not be a planning condition.

4.4.5.3 Creating shallow water and edge habitat

Shallow water is the most valuable for wildlife and therefore its extent should be maximised wherever possible. Doing so requires exact knowledge of eventual water levels and regimes in relation to the land being worked, as well as a supply of stock-piled fill material: topsoil, overburden and silt. If possible, edge habitat should be created that is gently sloping (1:20) and less than one metre deep (Figure 4.18). Where the eventual water level is known, it may be possible to create an edge with a micro-topography that creates a fringing strip rich in pools and shallow-flooded grassland. This may be made easier by undertaking the creation work in two phases (see below). Shelving margins should take into account the extent of summer drawdown (Figure 4.19).

Fill material may be overburden or silt. Topsoil generally has high nutrient concentrations and its use for spreading in shallow waters and edges is not recommended. Planting of aquatic vegetation is also unnecessary in most situations as natural regeneration, although slower, usually produces a better result. Diverse and valuable communities of aquatic vegetation, including for example stoneworts, are more likely to develop on nutrient-poor substrates. The nutrient boost given to a system by topsoil can eliminate important early successional stages. Bare, unshaded shores are often important for plants and invertebrates. The imaginative use of washery silt can also help create shallows on which marsh vegetation can develop, although willows seeding onto wet silt may require management (Box 4.4).

Box 4.4 Use of washery silt to create habitat

Waste water from the process of washing gravel is frequently pumped into lagoons or previously excavated pits in order to allow suspended particles to settle out. Such silt lagoons have the potential to develop into excellent wildlife habitats (Plate 4.41 and Plate 4.42).

The pumped silts tend to form a delta extending out into the lagoon. Heavier particles, such as sands, settle first, raising the land level around the discharge pipe. Finer silts settle out last, forming a gently sloping deposit down to the lagoon bed. Such material will consolidate and settle further over time. Key issues are the amount and location of discharge in relation to water levels and the subsequent management regime. By manipulating discharge pipes and the channels carrying the silty water, optimum levels and landforms can be created for a variety of habitats.

At Dungeness nature reserve silts were deposited around the margins of excavated lakes using a mobile, floating discharge head. The aim was to create shallow margins to benefit waterbirds. The margins of damp sand have subsequently been found important for invertebrate (notably a range of beetles) and plant communities. Colonising vegetation on these sandy margins is partly suppressed by the fluctuating water levels and by wind and wave erosion. However, it is recognised that natural succession will proceed and to maintain the open margins a variety of techniques are being trialled, including scrub control, winter grazing by sheep and rotational ground disturbance.

At Amwell Quarry in the Lee Valley (Herts/Essex) silts were discharged directly into the water-filled pit and have been manipulated, through varying the discharge pipe, to form habitat for breeding waders. Landform was created at winter water levels (and a suitable cutting regime maintained on colonising vegetation) as well as using silts to encircle shallow pools. Other, lower lying areas have been developed into reedbeds with ditches carefully excavated after several years of consolidation. A water control structure on the pit allows summer and winter water levels to be maintained at optimum levels. Where shallow water is retained over the deposit, important populations of breeding waterbirds develop.

Elsewhere in the Lee Valley silt lagoons have matured into interesting areas of grassland and woodland. Grassland areas have proved to be relatively species-rich, with several species of orchid colonising. They have also been found to be important for invertebrates, with for example, diverse populations of grasshoppers and bush crickets.

The wet silty material of active silt lagoons forms an ideal substrate for germinating willows: without management intervention most will quickly succeed to dense willow scrub. If left, this can develop into small, but excellent areas of wet woodland where high water levels are retained; in drier situations mixed woodland of birch and oak can develop.

G J White

G J White

Plate 4.41(left) Periodic movement of silt outlets can help create marshy shallows.

Plate 4.42 (right) Diverse grassland or wetland habitats can develop on carefully managed silt lagoons.

The potential to improve many open water habitats created by mineral extraction in the past is being recognised on sites managed by nature conservation bodies, eg Sevenoaks Nature Reserve, Kent (Box 4.5). Such improvements invariably rely on creating shallow water by backfilling with an inert fill. The pit complex at Great Linford benefited from the input of large volumes of inert fill made available during the construction of Milton Keynes. Such fill is only usually available in appropriate amounts in areas with heavy industry, power generation facilities or development (eg house building). When importing fill into sites of nature conservation value it is essential to check thoroughly the quality of every load brought onto the site. At Dungeness RSPB reserve two-phase creation has involved bulldozing new profiles along edges of old, deep, steep-sided pits to create shallow water fringes and ameliorate steep bank angles. This has significantly boosted wigeon numbers (Plate 4.43).

Box 4.5 Retrospective creation of shallow water and islands in an old sand and gravel pit at Sevenoaks Nature Reserve, Kent

At Sevenoaks Nature Reserve sand and gravel working between the 1930s and 1980s created five deep-flooded pits. To create more shallow water areas, as well as a series of 29 small, low islands, 150,000 tons of inert fill were imported and dumped into one of the pits. This retrospective habitat creation work was carried out during the winter (1997/98). The fill was tested rigorously at source. The work involved building a spit out into shallow water, two metres deep. There was a danger of slumping at the working end of the spit so lorries dumped material on consolidated ground and diggers put the material into the lake. This double-handling ensured quality of fill by allowing thorough examination. The spit was permitted to settle for two to three weeks before it was cut into islands and landscaped. The spit was divided into 29 islands (Figure 4.20). Each island was individually landscaped to give a variety of landforms and substrates. The islands are in the most sheltered corner of the lake and suffer little erosion. The pit has water level control, which allows ideal management of the created islands. All except six of the islands can be flooded in winter to a depth of at least 450 mm to control terrestrial plants. This control also allows manipulation of water levels to expose mud for migrating waders.

Before undertaking the work, only 10 islands existed on the whole reserve and these were mostly inappropriate for nesting birds: they were high and rounded in profile, not low and flat. Now migratory waders are a seasonal feature of the site and breeding wader populations have increased markedly.

4.4.5.4 Ponds and scrapes

Ponds are immensely important for the conservation of aquatic flora and fauna in the UK. Ponds support 65% of all UK wetland plants and animals (Williams *et al*, 1997), including some important species (Table 4.23). Studies have shown that new pond complexes (Plate 4.44) can quickly, within five years, become colonised by up to 20% of Britain's wetland plants and larger macro-invertebrates (Biggs *et al*, 1994). There is value in creating ponds within any of the habitats considered in this handbook. A pond's value is not limited to the aquatic flora and fauna inhabiting it, but also to a myriad of other species that use it for drinking, bathing and feeding. Where possible, ponds should be created in clusters of different depths and shape.

The requirements of many of the groups that utilise ponds are summarised in Table 4.24. Good semi-natural pond habitats can be created easily by following the key principles of pond design (Box 4.6).

The water supply of any pond complex (Figure 4.21) constructed should have good water quality. Those ponds fed by poor quality surface water may benefit from the creation of buffer zones. Buffer zones should be:

- > 20 m wide to avoid the effects of spray drift in areas under arable farming. Protection from spray is important

G J White

Plate 4.43
At Dungeness gently sloping profiles allow the exposure of muddy sandbanks and shallow pools.

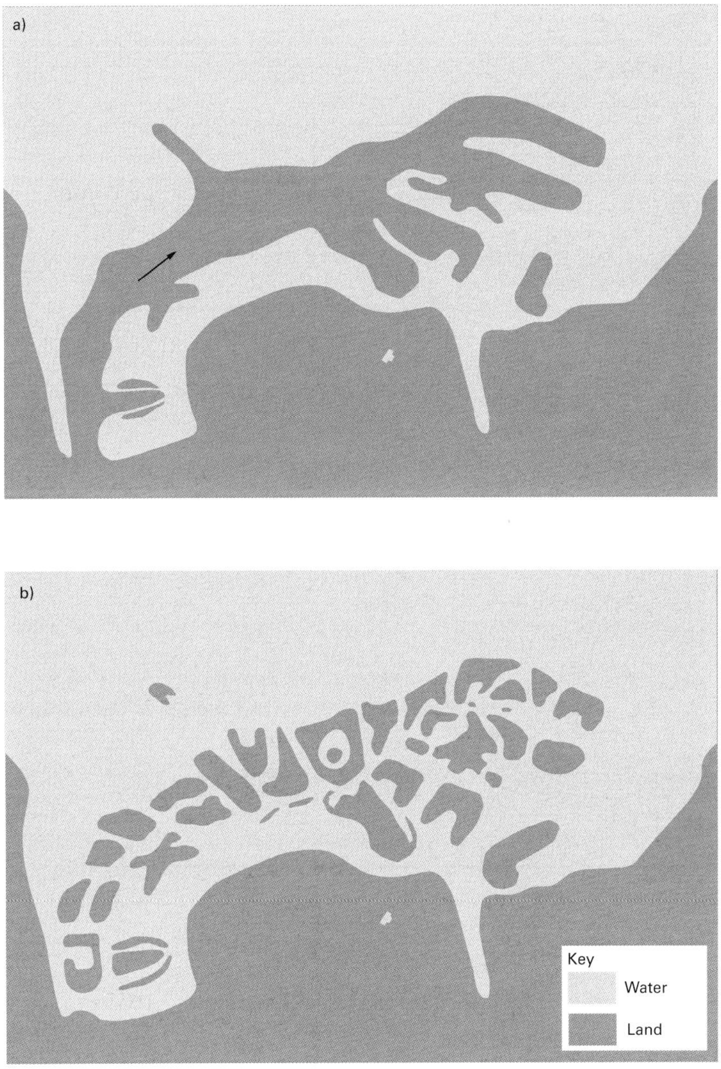

Figure 4.20
Retrospective habitat creation at Sevenoaks involved the use of inert fill to create islands in a two-stage process. Material was pushed out into the lake a), before being split into islands b).

(rspb-images.com)

Plate 4.44
The pond network at Dungeness is important for the medicinal leech and many other species.

Table 4.23 Characteristic species of ponds.

Plants	400 species of higher plants are associated with ponds. Typical species include ivy-leaved duckweed, water-plantain, yellow iris, broad-leaved pondweed, water-crowfoot. Rare species include adder's-tongue spearwort, starfruit and pennyroyal.	Invertebrates	Over 2,000 species associated with ponds, including dragonflies, water beetles and snails. Rare species include the scarce emerald damselfly and fairy shrimp.
		Birds	Moorhen, coot, reed bunting.
Amphibians and reptiles	All six native amphibians, including the common frog, great crested newt and natterjack toad. Also the grass snake.	Mammals	Water vole.

Table 4.24 A quick guide to the ecological requirements of pond flora and fauna.
(after Williams *et al*, 1997)

Group/Species	General requirements
Aquatic plants	Good water quality is important, as is proximity to sites holding potential colonists for uncommon species.
Emergent/ marginal plants	Extensive drawdown zones with variable micro-topography, giving variety in relation to waterlogging and depth of water. Water quality less important, although impoverished substrates promote diversity. Consult Grime et al (1988) and red data books for more information.
Bare mud specialist plants	Bare marginal mud is an important requirement; this habitat will have to be maintained by management such as grazing and trampling by livestock.
Invertebrates (general)	Mosaics of ponds, from pools as small as 1 m^2. Complex vegetation structure, varied substrates and good water quality are all important. Fish-free water can be important for all groups. Some species lay their eggs in the bare mud of drawdown areas. Consult Kirby (1992), Biggs *et al* (1994) and Freshwater Biological Association identification guides.
Dragonflies	Permanent waterbodies produce maximum diversity, although some species are linked to seasonally flooded ponds, eg the scarce emerald damselfly. Eggs and larvae are aquatic. Adults emerge to feed aerially on invertebrates, and require good feeding habitat close to water. Important features are abundant aquatic and emergent vegetation. Scarce species have more exacting requirements. Creating appropriate conditions for individual species may be possible. Consult Merritt *et al* (1996) for details.
Water beetles	High species-richness occurs in fish-free, shallow water. Some prefer the margins choked with low-growing grasses or mosses, others prefer open margins. A nearby source of potential colonists is important when creating habitat for scarce, non-mobile species. Consult Kirby (1992) for general guidance.
Semi-aquatic invertebrates	Many flies and ground beetles require an extensive, wet, muddy drawdown zone. Dense vegetation and scrub can also be important. Consult Kirby (1992) for general guidelines. For flies consult Stubbs and Chandler (1978) and Stubbs and Falk (1983).
Amphibians	See Table 4.31.
Mammals	Ponds, especially close to broadleaved woodland, are thought to be very important for feeding bats (Walsh and Harris, 1996). Otters may use ponds for hunting during their breeding season. Consult NRA (1993) for otter habitat management.

Box 4.6 Key principles of pond design (after Williams *et al*, 1999)

- When locating new ponds, avoid or minimise exposure to water pollution. If possible, create new ponds in areas where their catchments can be managed non-intensively.
- Dig trial holes before the pond is created to determine where water levels will be and what the substrate is like.
- Unless the pond is in a catchment with non-intensive land-use, avoid linking the pond to inflowing streams and ditches – these will create pollution problems in the long-term by bringing in polluted water and dumping polluted sediments.
- Where possible, create new ponds close to existing wetland areas but do not dig up existing wetlands to make new ponds.
- Design ponds with natural wetlands in mind: create pond mosaics and wetland complexes rather than single isolated waterbodies.
- Make particular effort to include very shallow pools with a depth of no more than 20 cm, and temporary ponds as well as semi-permanent and permanent ponds.
- Keep shallow and deep water pools separate – they can be as little as one to two metres apart, but should not all be permanently connected, except perhaps in high water conditions.
- Vary the size of waterbodies as much as possible.
- Focus on the edge habitats and maximise the extent of the drawdown zone in many areas.
- Most slopes at the pond's edge should be very shallow: a gentle slope is 2 cm every 1 m, ie 1:50.
- Create 'hummocks and hollows' in the drawdown zone to maximise the hydrological diversity of this rich area.
- Islands are valuable for birds, and where the margins of the pond are shaded, heavily trampled or grazed, they can provide a different kind of habitat for invertebrates and wetland plants.
- Planting up is rarely necessary for ecological reasons, as colonisation is usually rapid, especially when other wetland habitats are within one to two kilometres or less.
- Expect to take time – pond creation is often best considered as at least a two-phase process, with fine-tuning of the structure of the drawdown zone and margins one to two years after the first construction phase.
- Ensure that some effort is allotted to pond management during critical early colonising stages, to ensure that one or two plant species do not dominate the new site.

during the early colonising phase of a pond when muddy margins have a high proportion of annual plants and seedlings
- positioned to intercept flows from high ground
- checked to ensure they are not compromised by surface runnels.

Paradoxically annually flooded pools (Plate 4.45) are one of the most stable freshwater environments as they fill in very slowly owing to the oxidisation of organic matter during the dry phase. Today they are an exceptionally scarce habitat and support a suite of rare species (Bratton, 1990; Collinson *et al*, 1995). There is often a diverse group of terrestrial species dependent on the dry phase, notably ground and rove beetles, some semi-aquatic water snails, soldierflies, shoreflies and snail-killing flies. Seasonal pools are also exceptionally important for aquatic plants; 25% of the wetland plants protected under the Wildlife and Countryside Act 1981 are restricted to this habitat, eg grass-poly and

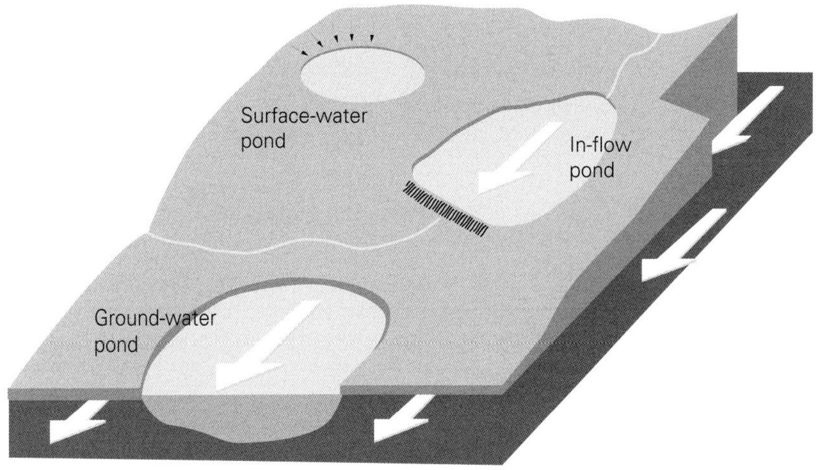

Figure 4.21
Potential water sources for ponds.
(after Williams *et al*, 1997)

J Day

Plate 4.45
Annually flooded pools that dry out in the summer can be a very important habitat.

R Wilmshurst (rspb-images.com)

Plate 4.46
Natterjack toads depend on temporary pools in heathland and dune habitats.

adder's-tongue spearwort (Collinson *et al*, 1995). Natterjack toads (Plate 4.46) also depend on temporary pools, largely because this environment lacks predatory fish. Frogs, newts and some dragonflies may also be more successful in pools which dry up seasonally.

Planting up ponds is not necessary and may be deleterious to the existing interest of the pond. Early phases of colonisation are often important for a suite of pioneer species that may not be present in later stages, eg the scarce blue-tailed damselfly, lesser water-plantain and rare beetles such as *Helophorus longitarsus* (Biggs *et al*, 1994). Planting may also increase the risk of spreading non-native species transported as fragments among other vegetation.

4.4.5.5 Long-term management

Generally, the best long-term management is to allow gradual, natural succession, excavating new ponds as the old ones become overgrown (Williams *et al*, 1999). Many ponds when left alone will fill with sediment, become shallower and have gradually changing communities. It is important to allow this process to occur as there are a number of specialist invertebrates that thrive at different stages of succession.

However, where individual plant species dominate the pond, removing a proportion of the invasive plant may promote species diversity. Also, if alien species have colonised a pond, such as New Zealand swamp stonecrop or water fern, then they should be removed completely as soon as possible.

4.4.6 Saline lagoons

Saline lagoons are bodies of brackish to hyper-saline water that are partially separated from the nearby sea, often by barriers of sand or sediment. Some exchange of sea water takes place either by the sea over-topping an impermeable barrier, or by percolation of sea water through the sediment. Tidal range is greatly reduced or non-existent and there is often little exposure of bed sediment. Most saline lagoons are formed in low-lying, soft sediment coastlines, so geographically they are most prevalent in south and east England. However, a number of large natural lagoons are found in older geology, for instance on the Hebridean islands.

There are 36 species that are particularly associated with saline lagoons. Of these, 25 are confined to saline lagoon habitats: four plants, 20 invertebrates and one bird – the avocet (Table 4.25). Saline lagoon communities include some of the rarest plant and animals found in the UK (Plate

4.47) and some species are endemic to only one or two lagoons. There are about 360 saline lagoons covering 5,200 ha in the UK. Saline lagoons are listed as a priority Natura 2000 community.

Saline lagoons are relatively straightforward to create and are appropriate to most low-lying coastal morphology: they can quickly develop an outstanding value to wildlife. Examples of sites already created by mineral extraction include:

- Killingholme – clay extraction, Humberside
- Cliffe Pools – clay extraction, North Kent, see Box 4.7 (Plate 4.48)

Table 4.25 British lagoonal plant and animal species of conservation significance.
(from Bamber *et al*, in press)
Specialist species are defined as those that would have unsustainable populations in the UK without the presence of lagoons. There may be some populations or occurrences of these species in alternative habitats such as saltmarshes or brackish ditches. Species that are more likely to colonise newly created sites are emboldened.

Name	Scientific name
Plants	
Foxtail stonewort	*Lamprothamnium papulosum*
Bird's nest stonewort	*Tolypella nidifica*
Tasselweed	***Ruppia maritima***
Spiral tasselweed	***Ruppia cirrosa***
A filamentous algae	***Chaetomorpha linum***[1]
Cnidarians	
A sea-fir	*Clavopsella navis*
Ivell's sea anemone	*Edwardsia ivelli*
Starlet sea anemone	*Nematostella vectensis*
Bryozoans	
Lagoon sea-mat	***Conopeum seurati***
Trembling sea-mat	*Victorella pavida*
Worms	
Lagoon sandworm	*Armandia cirrhosa*
Molluscs	
Lagoon mud-snail	***Hydrobia ventrosa***
Southern lagoon mud-snail	***Hydrobia acuta***
A rissoid snail	*Onoba aculeus*
A sea slug	*Haminoea navicula*
Lagoon cockle	***Cerastoderma glaucum***
De Folin's snail	*Caecum armoricum*
Crustaceans	
An ostracod	***Cyprideis torosa***
Lagoon slater	***Idotea chelipes***
An isopod (slater)	***Lekanospheara hookeri***
Lagoon sand shrimp	***Gammarus insensibilis***
A sand shrimp	*Gammarus chevreuxi*
Lagoon corophium	***Corophium insidiosum***
Insects	
A cranefly	*Geranomyia bezzia*
A chironomid midge	*Glyptotendipes barbipes*
Birds	
Avocet	***Recurvirostra avocetta***

[1]Species not restricted to saline lagoons, but it has a distinct form found in saline lagoons.

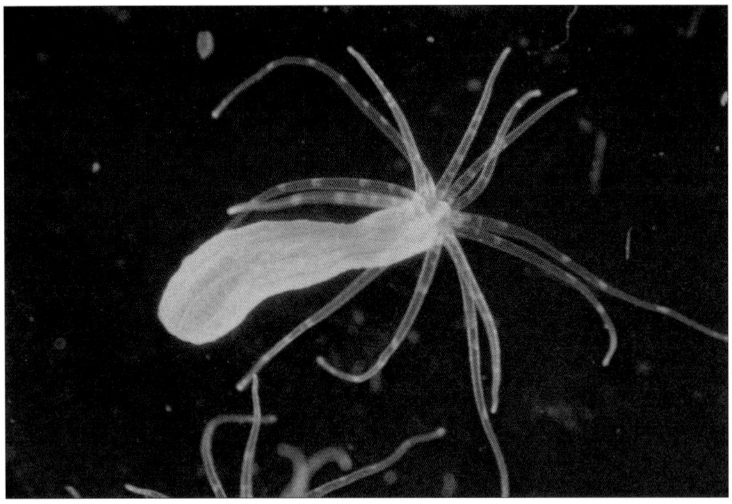

Plate 4.47
Starlet sea anemone – a specialist of saline lagoons.

Plate 4.48
The pools resulting from clay extraction at Cliffe, Kent are developing into an important saline lagoon habitat.

Plate 4.49
Snettisham pits – saline lagoons resulting from gravel extraction adjacent to The Wash, Norfolk.

- Snettisham Pits – gravel extraction, Norfolk (Plate 4.49).

However, there are few examples of deliberate creation of saline lagoons for wildlife. Lagoons created as a feature of a golf course in Hampshire attained important nature conservation interest within just five years and are likely to improve further. There is potential to create this habitat from sand and gravel extraction and other surface mining activities. Because of their extremely high conservation importance, saline lagoon creation should be a high priority when planning restoration of coastal mineral sites. With good design, new saline lagoons can be of outstanding value for breeding, passage and wintering birds, and for specialist flora and fauna. However, as with any habitat creation, location should be considered carefully, particularly if valuable habitats, such as shallow and/or seasonally dry brackish pools or ditches, are already present or is likely to develop: complement these rather than destroy them.

Areas of low-lying coast are likely to be affected by sea level rise in the foreseeable future. Many of the existing lagoons are vulnerable to the coastal erosion that may result. However, managed re-alignment of coastal defences to counter the effects of sea level rise can create opportunities for lagoon creation and coastal mineral extraction sites can be built into such plans.

4.4.6.1 Design

Saline lagoons can be created in low-lying coastal locations throughout the UK. Simple lagoons can benefit wildlife, although careful design can considerably enhance their value. Lagoons require regular, but not free, exchange of sea water, either by percolation through a porous barrier eg shingle, by over-topping during high tides, or through a channel. The most species-rich lagoons have a salinity between 20 and 35 parts per 1,000, are less than one metre deep and have a large edge to area ratio (Cadbury *et al*, 2001). However, certain species (Baltic stonewort, bearded stonewort and bird's-nest stonewort) prefer lower salinities. A

Box 4.7 Saline lagoon creation at Cliffe Pools

Cliffe Pools contains 111 ha of saline lagoons. These lagoons are nationally important for invertebrates and some are nationally important for feeding and roosting wildfowl. The RSPB has worked in partnership with Blue Circle Industries plc and Westminster Dredging Company to dispose sensitively of dredgings at the former clay workings. This involved changing the original planning consent, which allowed complete infilling of 12 pools. The dredging material will instead be used over a wider area to raise the bottom of the pools creating a variety of water depths with a mean depth of 1.5 m. A series of bunds will also be created to aid water retention and salinity control.

freshwater input, either from rainfall, surface or sub-surface movement or by managed input, is not required, but will increase species diversity (Table 4.26). Hyper-saline lagoons occur where freshwater input is less than the evaporation rate. These lagoons usually have a lower species diversity, but can support some specialist species.

A tidal exchange of up to 40% of the water volume will also produce conditions suitable for a high species diversity (Bamber *et al*, 1992; 1993). Constructed lagoons usually incorporate sluices or weirs to balance salinities and control lagoon water levels. The location and design of these structures is critical to the lagoon's success. In winter there is a need to remove high volumes of rainwater from the lagoon and to keep salinities within the tolerances of the specialist species. Water level control is critical to prevent lagoons from drying totally in summer and also for undertaking management, such as flooding to control vegetation on islands. Fine tuning of levels is important to provide suitable shallow feeding areas for nesting birds such as avocets.

Barriers preventing fish access may have to be included. Inlet structures should allow sea water ingress at a level a little below that of neap high tide. Landforming should aim to create a lagoon that has extensive areas less than one metre deep, though deeper sumps are beneficial where water level management cannot prevent levels from dropping. They also help buffer the effects of evaporation on salinity. Shallow margins provide areas for birds to feed and a number of low islands facilitate nesting by a range of important species. Avocets nest on bare mud close to the water; they benefit from smaller island size as this excludes black-headed gulls from nesting. Little terns nest on shingle-capped islands and Mediterranean gulls usually, among sparse grass.

Cadbury *et al* (2001) identified three types of saline lagoon that could be created deliberately:

- shallow and artificial – water exchange is usually partly natural and the lagoon may support both specialist lagoon species and important bird assemblages
- shallow scrapes or floods – tideless systems with artificially controlled input.

Table 4.26 Ecological requirements of saline lagoon species.
(after Bamber *et al*, 1993)

Group/species	General requirements
Specialist invertebrates*	Full strength sea water (35 ‰) required but tolerate some variation (± 10 ‰). Large lagoons are more secure from adverse impacts and tend to have higher diversity. Maximise edge:area ratio and provide varied depth conditions. Water should be retained during low phases of tidal cycle. Most species are adapted to living in fine sediment, but there is some value in a heterogeneous bed.
Birds	A sloping shoreline with abundant invertebrates. Bare shorelines must be managed to prevent invasion of emergent plants. Variable water levels required to expose bare mud.
Specialist plants	Similar conditions to those required by the specialist invertebrates, water must be retained in the lagoon at all times.

* eg lagoon cockle, lagoon sandworm, lagoon sand shrimp and starlet sea anemone.

They may support important assemblages of breeding waders, and wintering waders and wildfowl, but are unlikely to support specialist lagoon species
- deep and artificial – these may be separated from the sea by a permeable barrier, eg shingle, or by sluices and weirs. They may be colonised by specialist lagoon species, but are unlikely to support important bird assemblages.

4.4.6.2 Establishment techniques

Colonisation of new lagoons is by passive dispersal, ie eggs or larvae drifting on currents and tides. It may take some time for target species to colonise lagoons, although lagoons with direct exchange, rather than percolation, can be colonised by some species very quickly. It may be worth introducing material to assist with colonisation, particularly tasselweeds *Ruppia* spp, which can support a number of faunal species. Before making any introductions, very careful consideration should be given and the appropriate authorities consulted as a licence may be required to capture and transport biological material – many saline lagoon species have special protection. Channel inlets and sporadic inflows of large volumes of sea water may be important for colonisation.

D Tipling (rspb-images.com)

Plate 4.50
Cotton grass growing in raised bog.

4.4.6.3 Long-term management

It is necessary to:
- balance salinities
- maintain the exchange of sea water
- manage water level particularly during the bird nesting season
- ensure that emergent plants such as the common reed do not encroach the habitat.

A planned programme of management and monitoring is required. This need not be onerous, but is critical given that some of the specialist species have very precise requirements. Management for breeding birds, such as the avocet, and specialist lagoon species may not be compatible; salinities that benefit the avocet's prey are often lower than those for specialist species, for example higher salinity range has been shown to result in better spore production in the foxtail stonewort.

4.4.7 Fens and bogs

Fen and bog habitats are wetlands occurring on peat (Plate 4.50). Peat is an organic soil derived from the remains of plants that have accumulated *in situ*. This accumulation occurs because anoxic conditions prevent the decomposition of wetland plants. The vegetation communities of fens and bogs form a spectrum, with *Sphagnum* mosses more frequent in bogs, while reed and sedge species tend to dominate fens. Both habitat types occur on peat substrates with high and relatively stable water-tables. The high water-table in bogs is supplied purely by rainfall and leads to acidic conditions, whereas fens can be supported by seepage water as well as rainfall. The fens occurring in more rain-fed situations tend to be acidic and are referred to as poor fens. The fens supported by calcium-rich seepage water are usually neutral to alkaline and are referred to as rich (or alkaline) fens.

4.4.7.1 Establishment techniques

Fen and bog habitat may be restored in areas where peat has been left *in situ* following extraction at the site. Water control is a key issue. Natural colonisation is generally the most appropriate method of establishing the vegetation. *Sphagnum* mosses, cotton-grass, reed and other fen and bog species may colonise the peat substrate and the pools of open water within it. Plants such as *Sphagnum* mosses may form floating rafts on which non-raft forming species may colonise. The success of natural colonisation depends on the supply of propagules to the site. If there are remnants of fen or bog vegetation nearby, or topsoil from these habitats can be salvaged and spread on the habitat creation site, this will increase the chance of successful colonisation.

4.4.7.1.1 Fens

The water-table required to support fen vegetation should be high throughout the year, although seasonal fluctuation of around 0.5 m is typical. The water pH should be high. Creation of larger areas of fen habitat has not been trialled very widely, but smaller areas have been developed through natural regeneration where water quality and quantity, and the substrate, have been appropriate. Plug planting and spreading seeds from nearby propagule source may assist the process.

4.4.7.1.2 Bogs

The water-table should be stable and high. A fluctuating water-table would favour species from drier habitats such as birch, purple moor-grass, tufted hair-grass and soft rush. A widely fluctuating water-table also prevents the establishment of *Sphagnum* cover. Stable water-tables may be difficult to achieve in practice due to reduced water storage capacity in the peat remaining after extraction. This may be resolved by creating shallow lagoons thereby stabilising the water level relative to the vegetation surface. This increases water storage, reduces fluctuation in the water-table by retaining rainfall that would otherwise have drained away, and promotes the establishment of floating *Sphagna* rafts. The water pH and nutrient levels should be low.

Raft formation on open water is a valuable method of re-instating bog vegetation; it allows bog species to establish rapidly. Species initially forming rafts include bogbean, reed, reedmaces, common cotton-grass and aquatic *Sphagna* (especially *Sphagnum cuspidatum*). Water depths greater than 0.5 m tend to inhibit *Sphagnum* colonisation. Such an approach requires topography that can be flooded. Raft formation helps to create permanent wet conditions at the newly formed bog surface. This technique is probably the most successful at restoring functioning, bog surface vegetation over large areas. Where natural colonisation is unlikely to succeed, Wheeler and Shaw (1995) describe a technique to inoculate a site with locally collected *Sphagnum* moss.

Fen and bog vegetation is very sensitive to the pH and nutrient content of the water on which it depends. Care must be taken to ensure that the water used to re-wet the peat following extraction has the correct chemistry for the target vegetation (Wheeler and Shaw, 1995). Bogs should be fed by rainwater and not water that has been in contact with mineral soil, such as is often exposed by ditch-digging.

It is worth noting that bogs, particularly raised bogs, tend to form on sites that initially develop a fen habitat. Over time, succession and the build-up of peat can lead to the formation of more bog-like vegetation.

4.4.7.2 Long-term management

Fens and bogs are successional habitats and therefore require a degree of management to maintain their condition. Extensive grazing and mowing can be used where the peat is dry enough to support machinery and/or animals. If the site is to be grazed, then very low stocking rates should be used, eg 0.1 livestock units per hectare. If the site is to be managed by mowing, then low pressure machinery and careful timing is necessary. Mowing on a rotation of four to 10 years should be sufficient to prevent scrub invasion once fen or bog vegetation has established.

In areas where the water-table is too high to allow grazing or mowing, scrub invasion can be reduced by maintaining the water-table very close to the surface of the peat. Mechanical removal of the trees and scrub may be necessary if the hydrology cannot be managed as required.

4.4.8 Rivers and streams

Although only chalk streams are listed in the UK BAP, rivers and streams in general are the habitat of a number of BAP species, including invertebrates (such as the white-clawed crayfish), otters and water voles (see section 4.6.2). For more information consult Ward *et al* (1994), Strachan (1998) and RRC (1999). The habitat of dynamic gravel bed rivers is currently being added to the BAP list.

Many of our rivers have been modified in the past, either to protect land and property from flooding or for land drainage to increase agricultural production. However, these modifications can seriously damage the landscape, amenity, wildlife and natural functions of a river. In some limited circumstances short stretches of river may require restoration as part of a mineral working operation (see section 5.11 for work on the River Nith). In other cases, the opportunity may arise to enhance a river adjacent to a mineral site, for example, the creation of a braided channel in the River Tame adjacent to the Hanson quarry at Middleton Hall. Where such circumstances exist, opportunities to restore degraded river channels should be taken in consultation with the statutory authorities. Examples of work include:

- re-creating meanders
- re-shaping river channels, including the riverbed and banks
- re-opening culverts
- installing structures to concentrate or deflect the flow of water, where appropriate, so that a range of different water velocities and riverbed material develop along the course of the river
- replacing artificial beds or banks with natural materials
- creating new habitat for species such as the otter, water vole, kingfisher or white-clawed crayfish
- restoring free passage for fish by modifying or replacing weirs or re-opening culverts.

Some sand and gravel washings at mineral extraction sites develop a very similar fauna to the margins of dynamic gravel bed rivers (Plate 4.51), with extensive shoals of exposed sediment sand, silt, gravel and shingle. These habitats can be especially important for invertebrates (section 4.6.4.).

Plate 4.51 Eroding banks and sandy shoals along a Cumbrian river.

G J White

Further reading

Andrews, J and Kinsman, D (1990) *Gravel pit restoration for wildlife.* A practical manual. The RSPB, Sandy.

Bamber, R N, Batten, S D and Bridgwater, N D (1993) Design criteria for the creation of brackish lagoons. *Biodiversity and Conservation* 2: 127-137.

Biggs, J, Corfield, A, Walker, D, Whitfield, M and Williams, P (1994) New approaches to the management of ponds. *British Wildlife* 5: 273-287.

Bratton, J H (1990) Seasonal pools: an overlooked invertebrate habitat. *British Wildlife* 2(1): 22-29.

Brooks, A and Agate, E (1997) *Waterways and wetlands: a practical conservation handbook.* Third Edition. BTCV, Wallingford.

Collinson, N H, Biggs, J, Corfield, A, Hodson, M J, Walker, D, Whitfield, M and Williams, P J (1995) Temporary and permanent ponds: an assessment of the effects of drying out on the conservation value of aquatic macroinvertebrate communities. *Biological Conservation* 74: 125-133.

Giles, N (1992) *Wildlife after Gravel.* Game Conservancy Trust, Fordingbridge.

Hawke, C and José, P (1996) *Reedbed management for commercial and wildlife interests.* The RSPB, Sandy.

Merritt, A (1994) *Wetlands, Industry & Wildlife. A manual of principles and practices.* Wildfowl & Wetlands Trust, Slimbridge.

Nuttall, P M, Boon, A G and Rowell, M R (1997) *Review of the design and management of constructed wetlands.* CIRIA Report 180. CIRIA, London.

RRC (1999) *Manual of River Restoration Techniques.* RRC, Cranfield University, Bedfordshire.

RSPB, EN and ITE (1997) *The wet grassland guide: managing floodplain and coastal wet grasslands for wildlife.* The RSPB, Sandy.

Ward, D, Holmes, N and José, P (1994) *The new rivers and wildlife handbook.* The RSPB, Sandy.

Wheeler, B D and Shaw, S C (1995) *Restoration of damaged peatlands.* HMSO, London.

Williams, P, Biggs, J, Whitfield, M, Thorne, A, Bryant, S, Fox, G. and Nicolet, P (1999) *The pond book: A guide to the management and creation of ponds.* Ponds Conservation Trust, Oxford.

4.5 Field margins

J Day

Plate 4.52
Field margin.

G J White

Plate 4.53
Cornflowers and poppies in a cereal field.

4.5.1 General principles

Any land can be restored to agriculture, depending largely on the landowners requirements. Restoration managers designing agriculture restoration projects should not ignore the potential to include features that benefit wildlife (Table 4.27). All too often such schemes concentrate on returning land to agricultural productivity and ignore restoration of features such as species-rich hedgerows or the inclusion of cereal field margins (Plate 4.52), especially along watercourses (Andrews *et al*, 1992). This demonstrates the need to integrate biodiversity conservation into all aspects of the mineral extraction industry. Biodiversity conservation should not be 'pigeon-holed' and only considered during nature conservation restoration projects – the philosophy must pervade all spheres of work.

Restoration to agriculture has long been the favoured option for planners and government agricultural agencies. While agricultural restoration techniques have improved immensely over the last 50 years, there has been concern over the loss of wildlife habitats after restoration to very sterile, agricultural landscapes, eg in the South Wales coalfield (Andrews *et al*, 1992). This is still noticeable even in today's award-winning agricultural restoration projects. There is a need to ensure that wildlife features, such as species-rich hedgerows and cereal field margins, are incorporated into agricultural restoration schemes. Ponds can also form an integral feature of agricultural restoration schemes, providing care is taken to avoid over engineering.

4.5.2 Establishment techniques

4.5.2.1 Species-rich hedgerows

Design of new hedgerows should reflect the local type in both structure and species. Stock should be native and preferably local. Hedges should be functional and appropriate for the landscape. For functional stock-proof barriers, a 4:1 hawthorn to blackthorn mix should be used. If stock-proofing is not an issue, a much wider species selection can be used to create a

Table 4.27 Characteristic species of arable farmland.

Plants	Around 300 flowering plant species may occur in arable farmland. Many are widespread species, but many of the specialist cereal weeds are now severely restricted due to use of herbicides and changes in agricultural practice such as the shift to winter cropping. Typical plants include poppies, corn marigold, fumitories, speedwells and fluellens. Species such as pheasant's eye, narrow-fruited corn salad, corn gromwell, cornflower (Plate 4.53), broad-leaved spurge, corn parsley and corn buttercup are rare species.
Invertebrates	Many species of butterflies, grasshoppers and plant bugs are associated with farmland. Many polyphagous species (feed on a wide range of foods) breed in crops and overwinter in grassy banks, crop edges or hedges. Crop pollinators, such as bumblebees, depend on wild plants for nectar and pollen when the crop is not in bloom.
Birds	Most 'farmland' birds are open country generalists, but are now among our fastest declining species. Characteristic species are the skylark, lapwing, yellowhammer, corn bunting, grey partridge and turtle dove. Scarcer species with a more restricted distribution include the stone-curlew, cirl bunting and quail.
Mammals	Few mammals live entirely in arable farmland, even the most typical, such as the brown hare, favours a mosaic of arable, grass and hedgerow.

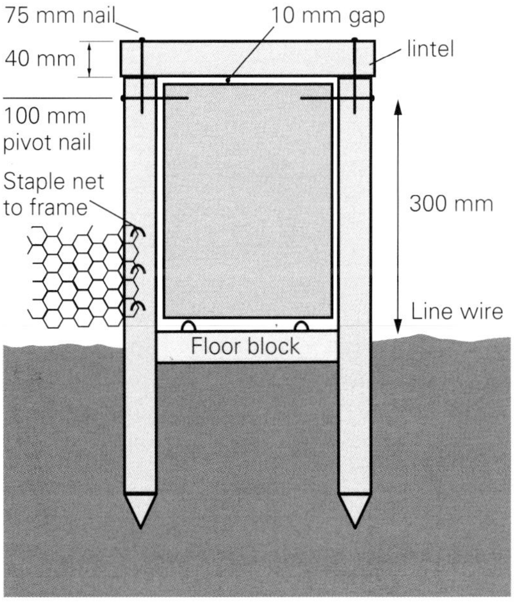

Lintel: 270 x 75 x 40 mm
Upright: 420 x 75 x 40 mm
Floor block: 190 x 75 x 40 mm
Door: 250 x 180 mm
(Either solid 40 mm thick or 30 mm wire mesh on 40 x 40 mm frame.)

Figure 4.22
Design of badger gates to incorporate into fence-lines built to protect tree plantings and hedgerows.

M Hamblin (rspb-images.com)

Plate 4.54
Newly planted hedgerow.

Table 4.28 Hedgerow planting mixture to maximise benefits to wildlife.
(Gilbert and Anderson, 1998)
Species should be chosen with full regard to soil type and geographical location.

Species	Percentage
Hawthorn	50
Field maple	20
Blackthorn	15
Dogwood, wayfaring tree, buckthorn, guelder-rose, hazel, spindle-tree, dog rose, privet and holly (where appropriate)	15

hedge of very high wildlife value. Gilbert and Anderson (1998) suggest the mixture presented in Table 4.28. Planting can be single row, ie plants 200–300 mm apart, or double row, ie plants staggered 300–450 mm apart with the two rows 500–1,000 mm apart (Plate 4.54). Where grazing animals are present, fencing is necessary to protect the hedge during establishment. Rabbit guards are also very important to protect young hedges. Weed control, using plastic or mulch matting, and rabbit guards are often necessary to protect saplings for the first few years. Fences should be one metre high and at least one metre from the hedge. Badger gates must be incorporated where this species is present (Figure 4.22). New hedgerows require annual pruning for the first two to three years to promote dense, bushy growth.

Where trees in hedges are commonplace, these should also be included in a planting scheme; maintaining them does, however, incur extra cost during hedge-cutting operations. Choose species appropriate to the area and plan to allow them to grow to old age. Oak and ash are frequent in hedges and both are valuable for a wide range of species.

Hedge translocation has been successfully undertaken by British Coal Opencast (BCO) with an 84% survival rate over the first two years. This method works for shrubs with a stem diameter of 20–200 mm:

- prior to translocation cut back shrubs to 750 mm to facilitate handling and transportation
- remove by excavating each side of the root zone to a depth of 400 mm and lifting shrub and associated root ball
- translocate immediately into a prepared trench, 500 mm wide and 400 mm deep, at the receptor site
- space shrubs at one metre intervals (or copy original density)
- backfill with topsoil/subsoil mix and finally top with hedgerow topsoil from the original site, ideally the top 75–100 mm, but can be up to 300 mm. However, note that topsoil should only be used if it supported a reasonable flora.

Ground flora should be re-introduced if necessary within 18 months of hedgerow establishment – after eliminating unwanted ground flora with routine herbicide application and before competition with

Figure 4.23 Repeatable hedgerow planting pattern for stock-proof hedge and showing the two methods for re-introducing hedgerow ground flora.

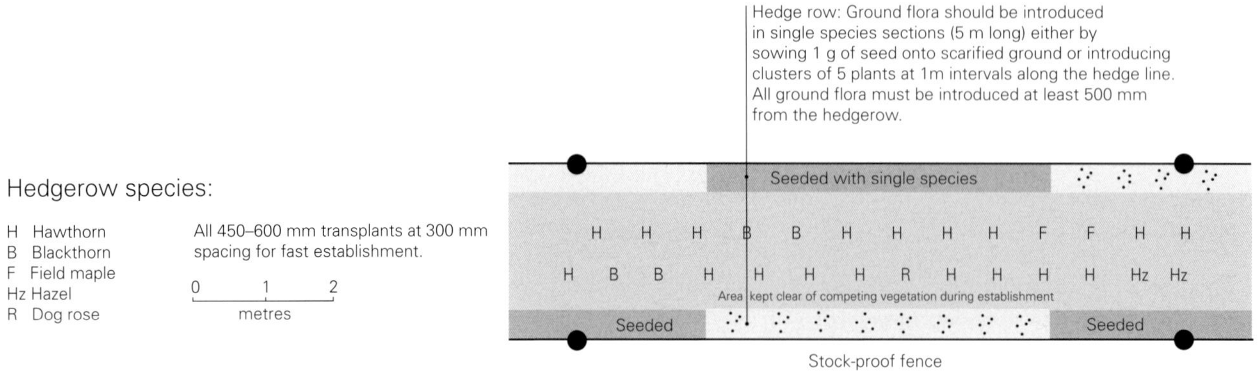

hedge species becomes severe. Species should be introduced in clusters (Figure 4.23). Some suitable species are included in Table 4.29. All material should be planted or sown at least 500 mm from the base of the hedge. Avoid re-seeding hedge-lines with agricultural mixes containing competitive species such as red fescue and white clover.

4.5.2.2 Cereal field margins

Cereal field margins provide a valuable habitat for invertebrates, small mammals and farmland birds. These areas may also be used as buffer strips to reduce the effects of spray drift and soil erosion, and to harbour predatory insects that attack crop pests. Unsprayed margins may also provide a valuable refuge area for scarcer arable weeds (Table 4.27). Strips, two to six metres wide, should be left uncultivated. Natural regeneration is most successful on light soils. Heavy soils with a history of intensive agriculture can become dominated by weeds and require intensive management. Selective herbicides may be used if invasive weed species establish in year one. An alternative is to use a perennial seed mix and ensure good establishment of the margin, thus excluding agricultural weeds. The seed mix should include a tussocky grass such as cocksfoot, Yorkshire fog or timothy to give good cover for nesting birds and wintering invertebrates. Some south facing margins could be sown with fine grasses and a wild flower mix for nectar-feeding insects. Regular cutting through the first spring will improve tillering and establishment. After that, cutting tussocky margins need only be carried out once every three years. Fertiliser or pesticides should be prevented from reaching the margins; this should maintain a stable margin and prevent weed ingress.

It should be noted that regularly ploughed, weedy, arable field margins without pesticide, especially on light soils are likely to be better for invertebrates (particularly early successional species) than tussocky grass margins, which tend to support only common species.

Table 4.29 Typical ground flora species suitable for introduction during hedgerow creation.
Species should be chosen with full regard to soil type and geographical location.

Species
Tufted vetch, dog's mercury, hogweed, cow parsley, hedge woundwort, bush vetch, foxglove, black bryony, woody nightshade, meadow vetchling, greater stitchwort, red campion, cowslip, primrose and perforate St John's-wort.

4.5.3 Long-term management

Both species-rich hedgerows and cereal field margins should be managed as part of the farming system after the initial establishment phase. The preferred method of hedgerow management for wildlife is regular trimming with hedge-laying on a rotation of 10–15 years. Annual trimming can be undertaken with limited harm to wildlife if it is undertaken in the winter. A two to three year rotation is better as it allows invertebrates overwintering in the hedge to survive somewhere on the farm each year. The best time to trim for birds is January/February after the berries have been taken and before nest building starts. Long-term management of cereal field margins is described above.

Further reading

Andrews, J and Rebane, M (1994) *Farming and wildlife: a practical handbook for the management, restoration and creation of wildlife habitats on farmland*. The RSPB, Sandy.

Brooks, A and Agate, E (1998) *Hedgelaying: A practical handbook*. BTCV, Wallingford.

Dodds, G W, Appleby, M J and Evans, A D (1995) *A management guide to birds of lowland farmland*. The RSPB, Sandy.

Dodds, G W, Appleby, M J and Campbell, L (1996) *A management guide to birds of upland farmland*. The RSPB, Sandy.

4.6 Additional habitat features

4.6.1 Bare rock and bare earth

Sparsely vegetated habitats are rarely considered valuable and management is often aimed at producing vegetation cover as fast as possible. However bare ground is an essential feature for a wide variety of specialist flora and fauna, but especially a suite of increasingly threatened invertebrates (Key, 2000). Mineral extraction sites often contain substrates unsuited to vegetation succession and have 'interesting', varied micro-topography (Plate 4.55). There may be spoil banks and areas of impeded drainage side by side and plenty of ruderal nectar- and pollen-bearing plants. Sand cliffs remaining after quarrying can be important for sand martins. Cliffs left in some hard rock quarries have become important nesting sites for choughs. These cliffs may also develop botanical value as crags and ledges are unavailable to grazing animals.

G J White

Plate 4.55
Retained cliffs and bare rock features in a restoration can be very valuable.

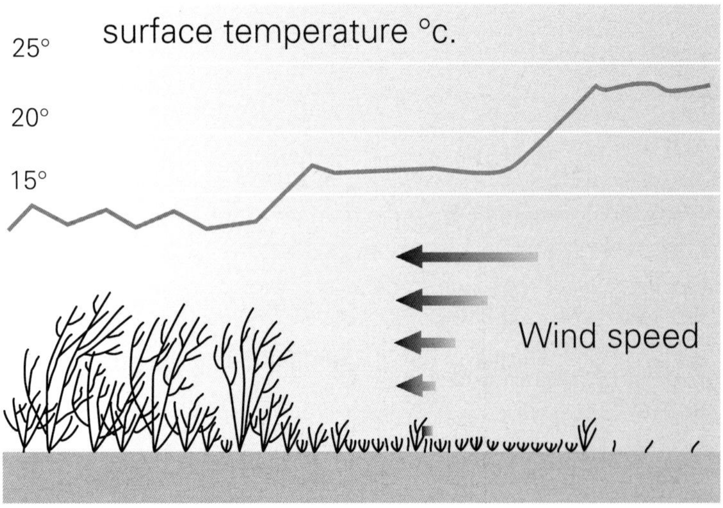

Figure 4.24
Surface temperature and wind speed difference between vegetated ground and bare ground.

4.6.1.1 Design

For specialist invertebrates and other groups, especially reptiles, bare ground offers (Key, 2000):

- warmth – wind speeds are drastically reduced at ground level and unshaded, bare ground warms up quickly in the sun by retaining heat (Figure 4.24). Bare ground can be 10–15 °C warmer than surrounding vegetation growth. This warmth is assimilated by basking or resting on warm surfaces to attain efficient operating temperatures and to incubate eggs laid in bare soil
- a substrate into which to burrow and/or lay eggs – the substrate must be friable enough to allow digging, but firm enough to prevent burrows collapsing. Sandy, peaty and calcareous soils are preferred. Different species have different requirements for particle size, slope aspect, patch size, degree of shelter and proximity to food sources
- ruderal plant colonists – these are important for plant-eating invertebrates that favour hot, dry conditions, and provide food for nectar- and pollen-feeding species.

Many species benefit from bare ground with nearby cover. Suitable cover includes small stones and plant debris. The margins of surrounding vegetated areas are often important, eg mats of overhanging heathland vegetation.

Native reptiles also require many of the features beneficial to invertebrates. Even small amounts of bare ground are valuable in any habitat, but it is especially important in habitats where it should be a regular feature, eg dry heathland (section 4.3), sandy or calcareous grassland (section 4.1.5) and woodland clearings (section 4.2). All these habitats have rich, bare ground invertebrate faunas (Key, 2000). Such bare areas may occur because physical or chemical factors that inhibit plant growth are present, or because of erosion or trampling. Bare ground, in the form of wet sand, mud or peat beside water, is also important in wetland habitats. Water fluctuation is essential in maintaining these areas.

There are a few general considerations to be noted.

- Natural regeneration is the favoured option to allow bare ground habitats to develop as part of a mosaic of other habitats.
- Avoid sowing seeds, planting trees and spreading soil on sites with the potential to support bare ground flora and fauna.
- Avoid re-surfacing paths with woodchips or other materials wherever possible.
- Where possible leave cliffs and slopes to erode naturally, allowing them to create bare areas continually through erosion and slippage.

Creating firebreaks by turf stripping or surface scraping in areas prone to fire, eg lowland heathland, can create important habitat. Try to create south-facing features during firebreak construction by angling the blade so that a spoil ridge accumulates along the northern edge of the break.

4.6.1.2 Long-term management

In many habitats, natural plant succession will ensure that bare areas are only temporary features, except in areas subjected to regular disturbance or grazing, for example by rabbits. Some native and non-native plant species, eg Canadian goldenrod, common fiddleneck, rosebay willowherb and birch, can be especially invasive on bare areas. It may be necessary to create new bare areas continually. In some circumstances, this can be achieved by allowing or encouraging small scale erosion.

It is possible to create and maintain bare ground on sites that have developed interesting communities, but are threatened by succession. This is possible using specially adapted, commercial, stone-picking/burying machines that either remove or bury turves to a depth where their nutrients become unavailable. At Fingringhoe Wick, rotational bulldozing of a former gravel pit continues to open up areas of bare ground and has greatly increased the site's biodiversity (Forsyth, 1999). If contemplating such action it is important to tell the general public what is happening – such management is sometimes alarming.

Further reading

Forsyth, L (1999) Creating bare ground habitats. *Enact* 7(1): 7-9.

Key, R (2000) Bare ground and the conservation of invertebrates. *British Wildlife* 11(3): 183-191.

Key, R and Gent, T (1993) Bare but not barren. *Enact* 1(2): 15-16.

4.6.2 Special features for mammals

4.6.2.1 Bats

The UK bat fauna constitutes a third of our mammal species (Plate 4.56). Species declines have resulted from a range of factors, but especially habitat loss and pesticide use. General requirements include the need for a range of roosting sites providing conditions suitable for resting, mating, raising young and hibernating, and

M Lane (rspb-images.com)

Plate 4.56 Daubenton's bat.

areas rich in invertebrates for feeding. Suitable roost sites are varied and include tree hollows and a range of artificial structures, such as bat boxes; these must be disturbance-free.

When feeding, bats depend on habitat mosaics and habitat corridors that connect up roosting and feeding areas. Mineral extraction sites and abandoned product treatment works can provide roosting sites (buildings, quarry faces and tunnels) and feeding sites (open water, wet grassland and other invertebrate-rich habitats). Caves, mines and structures such as lime kilns can provide the protected and stable conditions that many bats seek during hibernation. Within such sites, there is relatively little variation in humidity and temperature, although each site may provide a range of conditions.

Identified bat sites, especially hibernacula, may be enhanced or protected (Box 4.8). Old mine tunnels and natural caves exposed by quarrying should have bat-friendly barriers at the entrances to prevent access and disturbance by the general public; this is a requirement under the Mines and Quarries Act 1954 – see also MPG12. Access can be prevented by fitting grilles that permit bats in and out but restrict people. Suitable grilles should have openings at least 450 mm wide and 150 mm deep. If the site is already used by bats, the statutory nature conservation agencies must be contacted to obtain a licence before grilles are fitted.

When considering bats in general habitat creation schemes, ensure a wide variety of habitats and plant some trees which will attract abundant invertebrates and provide roost sites, eg oak, ash and beech. Where possible incorporate linking features such as hedgerows and tree-lines, which are favoured by bats for travelling and feeding.

Box 4.8 Creation of a bat hibernaculum in a disused lime kiln

The Herts and Middlesex Wildlife Trust successfully converted a disused and vandalised lime kiln in an old chalk quarry into bat hibernaculum. The site had previously been used by small numbers of bats in the winter months. However, the kiln's three open entrances caused problems: they allowed the internal temperature and humidity conditions to vary, and public access, which caused disturbance. The lime kiln's entrances were bricked up, leaving access holes for bats in each. A secure metal door was installed at one entrance to allow surveyors in for monitoring purposes. The roof vent was filled with chalk debris to allow in moisture and then covered with a grille. This work was undertaken to fulfil actions for Natterer's bat in the local BAP by safeguarding the integrity of roosting sites.

The kiln has been used by greater numbers of bats from the following winter; up to 20 Natterer's bats have been found. Up to three Daubenton's bats have also used the site. Specially constructed 'bat bricks' were installed to create more crevices, which the bats use as hibernation sites. These have been very successful, with the majority of bats found in the bat bricks, although a few continue to use the crevices in the original brickwork of the kiln.

Plate 4.57 Otters require cover in the form of rocks, cavities around tree roots or reedbeds etc.

WS Paton (rspb-images.com)

4.6.2.2 Otters

The otter population in England and Wales is recovering from a very low level, and all efforts should be made to encourage expansion. This can be achieved by increasing the availability of cover along watercourses (Plate 4.57). Where a watercourse is part of the mineral restoration area, otters can be encouraged by:

- planting trees and scrub – planting native trees, such as hawthorn and blackthorn, adjacent to the riverbank provides dense cover for lying up or breeding

- creating new wetland habitat – creation of backwaters in continuous connection with the main channel provides alternative feeding areas
- creating otter holts –these can be designed into most wetland creation projects (Figure 4.25). Ideally, they should be regarded as a short-term measure while the habitat develops. They should be sited as close as possible to the watercourse and be above frequently occurring flood levels. At Sevenoaks Nature Reserve, Kent, otter holts have been created by weaving live willows using hedge-laying techniques.

4.6.2.3 Water voles

Water voles have experienced a dramatic population decline across the UK. They are largely associated with slow-flowing rivers, ditches and canals, but also lakes, ponds and upland streams. Suitable habitat can be created where restoration sites are adjacent to such watercourses. Water voles prefer watercourses less than three metres wide and around one metre deep that do not show extreme water level fluctuations (Plate 4.58). They tend to use vegetated, earth river banks that are either stepped or steep so that they can burrow and create nest chambers above the water-table. The banks should be vegetated to the river's edge with species such as reed, rushes, bur-reed, reedmace and reed sweet-grass. Water voles may also use wetland areas such as wet grassland and fen where there are vegetation tussocks, particularly greater tussock sedge, which provides a dry nest site above the water-table (Strachan, 1998). Reedbeds are excellent refugia for water voles. Predation by American minks has a serious impact on water vole populations. Minks are now frequent in the countryside, having escaped from fur farms, and control is being promoted in key areas for Water Voles.

The following guidelines should be used to enhance habitat for water voles.

- Seek to create or enhance the habitat by carefully designing suitable banks to watercourses or create new water features following mineral extraction. These should be designed with a steep gradient on a proportion of the bank and be allowed to vegetate by natural colonisation.
- Maintain buffer strips of vegetation along watercourses. Where maintenance is required, minimise the impact on water voles by working in late summer/autumn, only cutting one bank in any one year, leaving a strip of vegetation at the toe of the bank, and keeping machinery as far back from the water's edge as possible.
- Where grasslands adjacent to watercourses are grazed, maintain low grazing densities, or fence, to minimise loss of vegetation and bank structure through over-grazing and poaching.
- Coppice or pollard waterside trees to prevent over-shading of marginal aquatic vegetation (except where unmanaged tree shade has a long history).

G J White

Plate 4.58 Water voles favour ditches with luxuriant marginal vegetation.

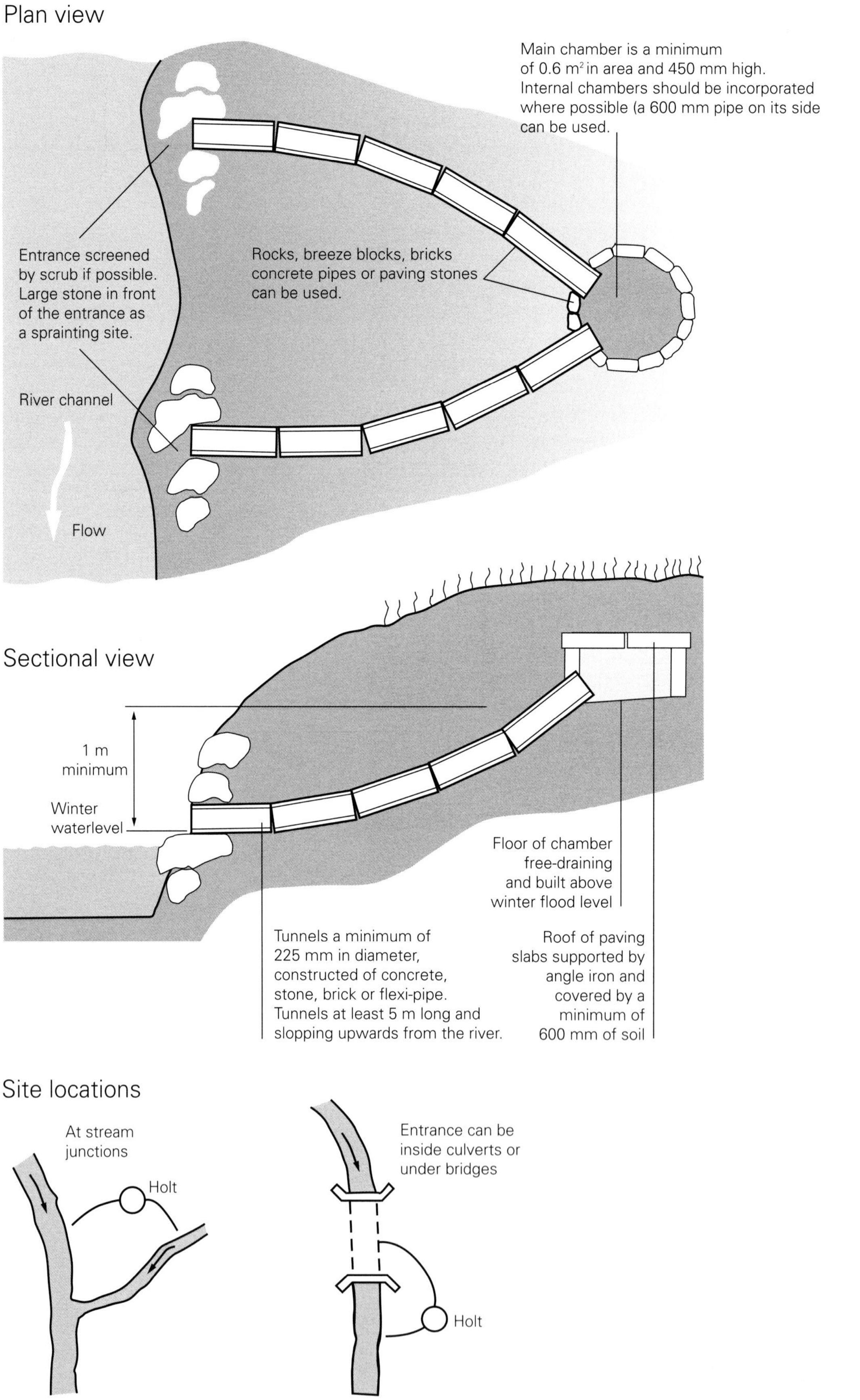

Figure 4.25 An example of a pipe and chamber otter holt.
(after NRA, 1993)

Table 4.30 Habitat requirements of British reptiles.
(Foster, 1997)

Species	Geographical range	Requirements
Grass snake	England and Wales	Found in grassland, heathland and wetland. Feeds mainly on amphibians and fish. Lays eggs in heaps of rotting vegetation, ideally 1 m^3.
Adder	Mainland Britain	Found on heathland, moorland, rough grassland and open woodland. Preys on small mammals, amphibians and lizards. Requires suitable, warm basking areas and shrubby cover.
Smooth snake	Very localised – dry southern heathlands	At the north-western edge of its range in the UK, probably limited to southern heathlands by climatic factors. Requires well-structured, dwarf shrub habitat for cover. Feeds on small mammals and lizards.
Common lizard	Widespread	Occurs in variety of habitats and feeds on insects and spiders. It has a higher tolerance of cooler conditions than the sand lizard, so depends less on unshaded habitat.
Sand lizard	Very localised – sand dunes in Merseyside and southern heathlands	Found in dry heathland and sand dunes. Feeds on insects and spiders, foraging among structurally diverse mature heath vegetation. Colonial. Requires unshaded, warm areas of soft, bare sand for egg-laying. Bare patches should exceed 2 m^2. Tolerates scrub and trees only at low density.
Slow worm	Widespread	Feeds on invertebrates. Found in a wide range of habitats. Likes warmth but instead of basking in the open prefers to hide under stones, logs or discarded debris exposed to the sun.

Further reading:

Hutson, A M, Mickleburgh, S and Mitchell-Jones, A J (1988) *Bats underground – a conservation code.* Flora and Fauna Preservation Society, Cambridge.

Stebbings, R E and Walsh, S T (1991) Bat boxes: *a guide to the history, function, construction and use in the conservation of bats.* Bat Conservation Trust, London.

Strachan, R. (1998) *Water Vole Conservation Handbook.* Wildlife Conservation Research Unit, Oxford.

4.6.3 Special features for reptiles and amphibians

4.6.3.1 Reptiles

There are six reptile species native to the UK. Two are endangered and are largely confined to heathland habitats and the remainder are in decline. All are protected under the Wildlife and Countryside Act 1981, with the sand lizard and smooth snake also receiving protection under the Conservation Regulations /99. For individual species requirements of reptiles see Table 4.30 and Foster (1997). General principles include:

- during design maximise southerly aspects with little or no vegetation to create basking areas
- vary micro-topography and consider introducing piles of rubble
- ensure egg-laying reptiles have suitable breeding sites
- create corridors between habitats within the site and to others off-site
- encourage a habitat mosaic, the structure of the vegetation is particularly important for reptiles
- protect from fire heathland sites with vulnerable species, especially during the summer months.

Amphibians

There are six native amphibians species and they may quickly colonise new waterbodies provided that there is an existing population nearby. Mineral extraction sites are potentially important for natterjack toads and great crested newts – both these species are protected under Schedule 5 of the Wildlife and Countryside Act 1981 and the Conservation Regulations /99. Heathland restoration on extraction sites may provide opportunities to create open, shallow, temporary pools suitable for natterjack toads.

Amphibians require breeding ponds adjacent to suitable habitat (Plate 4.59 and Plate 4.60); for the exact requirements of different species see Table 4.31 and Foster (1997). Suitable land habitats, generally a mosaic of grassland with scrub and trees, are vital. Log or rubble piles may be important for overwintering. If the

G J White

Plate 4.59
Ponds should ideally be set within grassland and scrub habitats.

R Brooks (rspb-images.com)

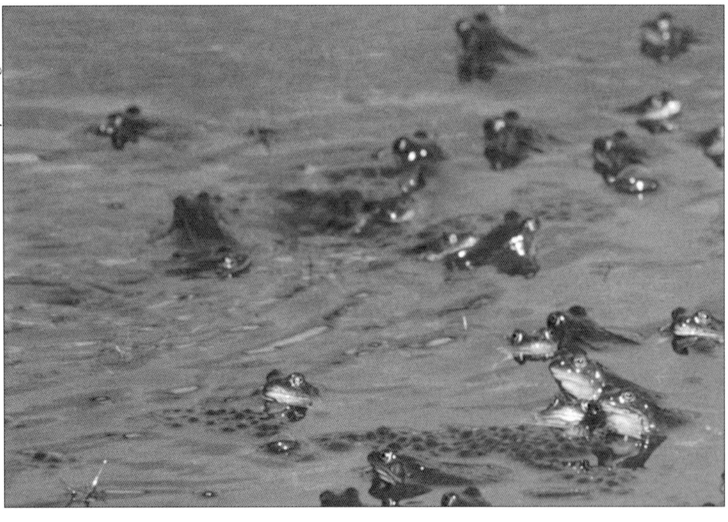

Plate 4.60
Spawning common frogs.

presence of protected species is suspected, a survey must be undertaken prior to restoration. When designing breeding ponds and ditches, consider the following (Bray, 1997):

- water quality must be high and water levels must usually be maintained during the breeding period – March to August
- pond areas should vary between 10 m^2 and 1,200 m^2 with depths generally ranging from 0.6 to 3.0 m. These may dry out in late summer
- pond and ditch profiles should vary, with sloping and shallow edges and deeper areas. Access to waterbodies should be facilitated by gently sloping banks
- ponds should be laid out in clusters of two to three within 50 m of each other and 250 m apart from other clusters
- pond design should vary within each cluster to increase diversity and provide security in abnormal wet or dry years
- occasionally ponds should be allowed to dry out, since this removes predators
- corridors linking ponds and clusters should be at least four metres wide.

Avoid shading by trees, open sumps, walls, fences and gates that impede movement at ground level, deep ponds with steep sides, and placing ponds near footpaths. Most pond and above ground management activities should take place in late autumn and early winter to avoid disturbing animals during the breeding season. Amphibian ponds are ideally fish-free and have no waterfowl. Management should be small scale, rotational, ensure that scrub and tree encroachment is kept in check, and ensure bare areas are created and maintained.

At Amwell Quarry in Hertfordshire, a huge colony of breeding common toads has developed necessitating the construction of a barrier on an adjacent road to minimise casualties during migration (Plate 4.61).

4.6.4 Special features for invertebrates

The enormous diversity in invertebrate requirements makes generalisation difficult. The complexity of the habitat tends to determine the diversity of invertebrates present. Some with specialised needs may have very small breeding colonies, for

Table 4.31 Habitat requirements of British amphibians.
(Foster, 1997)

Species	Geographical range	Requirements
Common frog	Widespread	Generally small (< $100m^2$), shallow, unshaded waterbodies with emergent and submerged vegetation.
Common toad	Widespread	A wide range of waterbodies (> 500 m^2) including lakes and slow-moving rivers.
Natterjack toad	Very localised	Highly specialised – temporary ponds with sparse vegetation surrounded by heathland and dune habitat including short turf interspersed with cover. Not tolerant of low pH (< 5). Cannot tolerate competition from common frogs or toads. Burrows in soft sand.
Common newt	Widespread, less common in the north and west	May occur in the full range of waterbodies, from garden ponds to shallow edges of lakes. On land, rough grassland habitats are important.
Palmate newt	Widespread	Particularly associated with heathland/moorland pools with low fertility and low pH. Less frequent than the smooth newt in lowland, agricultural landscapes.
Great crested newt	Widespread in England, uncommon in Scotland and Wales	Breeds in well-vegetated, lowland ponds but spends much of its life on land, associated with rough grassland, scrub and woodland, sometimes venturing several hundred metres from the pond. Populations often depend on several ponds close together, linked by suitable land habitats. Found in rural, suburban and urban locations.

example less than 1 m^2, whereas others may require much larger sites. Warmth, shelter and structural diversity are critical. These factors should be taken into account during site design and subsequent management. Useful information on invertebrate requirements can be found in Kirby (2001), Fry and Lonsdale (1991) and Key (2000).

Some features are particularly valuable:
- seepages and seasonal inundation
- ponds, which greatly enhance a site's importance for invertebrates (section 4.4.5)
- nectar sources, which are important to a wide range of invertebrate groups eg butterflies
- bare ground and piles of soil/sand/fine gravel, scattered rocks and brick, which can be important for many groups, eg wasps (section 4.6.1)
- dead wood retained on trees
- piles of dead wood, which provide habitat for specialist groups and fungi (Plate 4.62). Large piles are better than small, retain pieces as large as possible – partial burying can be beneficial.

G J White

Plate 4.61
Construction of an amphibian barrier, channelling animals to a safe road crossing.

G J White

Plate 4.62
Dead wood and tree stumps provide a habitat for the larvae of the stag beetle.

E A Janes (rspb-images.com)

Plate 4.63
Dragonfly larvae are often specific in their habitat requirements – empty larval case of the emperor dragonfly.

On bare ground surfaces in aggregate quarry restoration/creation projects care should be taken not to destroy any existing invertebrate interest. Specialist advice should be sought, as seemingly insignificant features may be very important. Wheelruts along seepage lines in chalk quarries may, for example, be important for pioneer invertebrates.

If a diversity of habitat cannot be maintained, for example due to natural succession, rotational management of a series of compartments may be employed. No one compartment should contain all of one particular habitat or the entire colony of a species. Such management could maintain a series of vegetation stages from bare substrate to mature vegetation if appropriate, maximising invertebrate diversity. Dragonflies and butterflies have enormous intrinsic appeal: their requirements are dealt with below.

It is essential to survey invertebrates before undertaking any restoration that may damage the existing interest. To minimise the cost, the survey should concentrate on those invertebrate groups likely to be favoured by existing conditions, eg ground beetles, bees and wasps in sand quarries, and water beetles in shallow gravel or brick pits.

4.6.4.1 Dragonflies

This group generally requires aquatic habitat with good water quality and abundant submerged and emergent vegetation for the larval stages (Plate 4.63). Waterbodies should be unshaded and fish-free. Adults emerge to feed on the wing on insects. Emergent plants are important allowing larvae to leave the water, as well as providing perches and egg-laying sites for adults. Ponds and ditches are favoured breeding sites.

Waterbody size is not important, but fish-free waters tend to be small (section 4.4.5). Shallow water is important and levels should not fluctuate extremely – although some species can survive in ponds subject to seasonal drying out. Ditches can support large dragonfly populations and have been specifically created at some sites eg Cow Lane, Cambridgeshire – see section 4.4.3 for ditch design specifications. It is important to include buffer strips of vegetated land, at least 15 m wide, around waterbodies if herbicides or fertilisers are used on adjacent land. For detail of individual species that may occur on mineral sites see Table 4.32.

4.6.4.2 Butterflies

A range of butterflies may be attracted to restored quarries, particularly those species that favour open grass swards with bare ground and a diverse range of associated herbs (Plate 4.64). It is advisable to consider attracting butterflies as part of a wider invertebrate assemblage by providing a range of general requirements. Warmth and shelter are important and south-facing aspects are favoured. The site should offer sufficient nectar plants throughout the season as well as a range of larval food plants (Table 4.33). Structural and topographic variety, and the presence of bare ground and patchy scrub are particularly important. As with most other invertebrates, butterflies benefit from stable conditions, preferring the same conditions each year.

G J White

Plate 4.64 Chalkhill blues have colonised many redundant chalk quarries.

Further reading

Dunbar, D (1994) *Saving butterflies: a practical guide to the conservation of butterflies*. British Butterfly Conservation.

Fry, R and Lonsdale, S D (1991) *Habitat conservation for insects – a neglected green issue*. Amateur Entomologists' Society, Middlesex.

Key, R (2000) Bare ground and the conservation of invertebrates. *British Wildlife* 11(3): 183-191.

Kirby (2001) *Habitat management for invertebrates*. The RSPB.

Table 4.32 Habitat requirements of selected British dragonflies and damselflies. (Merritt *et al*, 1996)

Name	Heathland habitat preference	Distribution and status
Beautiful demoiselle	Relatively fast-flowing streams with gravely bottoms. Tolerant of shade.	Locally abundant. Mostly west of a line between Liverpool and Folkestone.
Banded demoiselle	Slow-flowing streams with muddy substrate.	Common. Most of England and Wales.
Emerald damselfly	Shallow water with abundant emergent vegetation.	Locally common throughout Britain.
Scarce emerald damselfly	Densely vegetated shallow pools and drainage ditches.	Rare and local in south and east England.
White-legged damselfly	Breeds in clean, slow rivers.	Uncommon, though can be locally abundant in southern central England and in Devon.
Large red damselfly	Breeds in a range of still or slow-flowing waterbodies.	Widespread and common in Britain.
Red-eyed damselfly	Breeds on larger, less acidic ponds with abundant floating vegetation such as water lilies.	Locally common in southern England and the Welsh Borders.
Small red-eyed damselfly	Ponds and lakes with abundant submerged and floating vegetation.	Rare in south-east England but increasing.
Southern damselfly	Breeds in flowing, less acidic runnels and streams	Rare and protected by EU legislation. Hampshire, Pembrokeshire, Dorset and Devon, plus a few other isolated pockets.
Azure damselfly	Breeds in a wide range of still or slow-flowing waterbodies.	Very common throughout the British Isles except the northern half of Scotland.
Common blue damselfly	Breeds in a wide range of still or slow-flowing waterbodies, often abundant on well-vegetated, flooded mineral workings.	Abundant throughout the British Isles.
Scarce blue-tailed damselfly	Mineral-enriched, shallow water, especially flushes and springs, with sparse emergent vegetation.	Uncommon. Scattered populations in southern England and Wales.
Blue-tailed damselfly	Breeds in a wide range of still or slow-flowing waterbodies, commonly at flooded mineral workings.	Abundant throughout the British Isles. Common in western England, Wales and Scotland.
Common hawker	Favours acidic, nutrient-poor pools and pond margins.	Common and increasing its range: southern England, south coast of Wales.
Migrant hawker	Ponds and lakes with well developed, emergent vegetation, commonly at flooded mineral workings.	Very common in southern England and Wales, more local elsewhere.
Southern hawker	Ponds and lakes; avoids most nutrient-poor sites.	Common and widespread in southern and eastern England and the Welsh
Brown hawker	Breeds in slow rivers and lakes, commonly at flooded mineral workings.	Borders: absent from the South-west.
Emperor dragonfly	Larger pools and ponds with marginal vegetation, commonly at flooded mineral workings.	Widespread in southern England and southern Wales.
Hairy dragonfly	Well-vegetated ditches and ponds with tall, emergent vegetation.	Uncommon but increasing its range. Local populations in southern mainland Britain.
Downy emerald	Well-vegetated, mildly acidic ponds, avoids the most nutrient-poor.	Local: mainly south-east, but with scattered populations elsewhere in the British Isles.
Four-spotted chaser	Wide range of still or slow-flowing waterbodies, including acidic ponds	Wide distribution.
Scarce chaser	Slow-flowing, clean rivers, occasionally flooded mineral workings.	Scarce: colonies in southern and eastern England.
Broad-bodied chaser	Ponds with well-vegetated margins.	Widespread and common throughout southern England and Wales.
Black-tailed skimmer	Ponds or pools often with bare margins, which are used for basking, typically an early coloniser of newly flooded workings.	Fairly common: southern England, parts of Wales and Ireland.
Common darter	Wide range of still or slow-flowing, waterbodies, commonly at flooded mineral workings.	Abundant in England, Wales: less common in Scotland.
Ruddy darter	Ponds and ditches with plenty of emergent vegetation.	Resident in south-east England and increasing its range.
Black darter	Bog pools and boggy pond margins.	Widespread and can be abundant, especially in the north. Local in eastern and central England.

Table 4.33 Habitat preferences of selected butterflies.

Species	Habitat preference	Food plants of caterpillar	Status and distribution
Small skipper	Herb-rich, rough grassland.	Primarily Yorkshire fog, but other common grasses also used.	England and Wales, expanding: not threatened.
Essex skipper	Dry, herb-rich rough grassland.	Primarily cocksfoot, but other common grasses also used.	SE and central England, expanding: not threatened.
Large skipper	Herb-rich rough grassland, often in damp situations.	Primarily cocksfoot, occasionally other common grasses.	England and Wales, expanding: not threatened.
Dingy skipper	Open, herb-rich grassland where foodplants grow in a sparse sward with associated bare patches.	Bird's-foot trefoil, occasionally horseshoe vetch.	Patchy distribution in mainly England and Wales: declining.
Grizzled skipper	Herb-rich grassland where foodplants grow in a sparse sward with associated bare patches. Usually favours woodland rides, chalk grassland or disused industrial sites.	Plants of the Rosaceae family, mainly agrimony, creeping cinquefoil and wild strawberry.	Southern England, declining.
Brimstone	Scrubby grassland, woodland and hedgerows.	Buckthorn and alder buckthorn.	England and Wales, expanding.
Green-veined White	Woodland rides, hedgerows, meadows, especially with damp, lush vegetation.	Wild crucifers, notably garlic mustard, cuckoo flower and hedge mustard.	Throughout, stable.
Orange tip	Damp, grassy habitats.	Cuckoo flower and garlic mustard, occasionally other crucifers.	Throughout, expanding.
Green hairstreak	Scrubby grassland on chalk downland, heathland, woodland rides and old quarries.	Mainly common rock-rose, bird's-foot trefoil, gorse or broom, depending on habitat.	Throughout but patchy, stable.
Purple hairstreak	Woodlands and hedgerows.	Oak.	Mainly England and Wales, expanding.
Small copper	Dry grassland in a wide variety of habitat.	Common sorrel and sheep's sorrel, occasionally broad-leaved dock.	Throughout, stable.
Small blue	Calcareous grassland, on chalk, limestone or in quarries.	Kidney vetch	Mainly southern England, very patchy elsewhere, declining.
Silver-studded blue	Short or sparse vegetation on heathland, occasionally chalk grassland.	Heather, bell heather or cross-leaved heath, gorse, bird's-foot trefoil, common rock-rose, horseshoe vetch.	Patchy distribution in southern England and north Wales, declining.
Brown argus	Mainly chalk and limestone grassland but also disturbed soils with sparse vegetation, including quarries.	Common rock-rose, crane's-bill and stork's-bill.	Southern and central England and Wales, expanding.
Northern brown argus	As above.	Common rock-rose	Northern England and Scotland, declining in the south.
Common blue	Herb-rich grassland.	Mainly bird's-foot trefoil but also black medick, rest-harrow and lesser trefoil.	Throughout, stable.
Chalkhill blue	Chalk and limestone grassland, including old quarries.	Horseshoe vetch.	Southern England, declining.
Small tortoiseshell	Throughout.	Nettles.	Throughout, stable

Continued overleaf ▸▸▸

▸▸▸

Peacock	Throughout.	Nettles and hop.	Throughout, except northern Scotland, expanding.
Comma	Open woodland and wood edges.	Mainly nettles, also hop, elms and currants.	England and Wales, expanding.
Dark green fritillary	Flower-rich grasslands, often with scrub.	Violets.	Throughout, but very patchy in the east.
Speckled wood	Woodland, hedgerows and scrub.	Various grasses, mainly false brome, cocksfoot and Yorkshire fog.	England, Wales and northern Scotland, expanding.
Wall	Open, herb-rich grassland with associated bare patches.	Various grasses, including false brome, cocksfoot and Yorkshire fog.	England and Wales, declining in south-central England.
Marbled white	Rough grassland, mainly on chalk.	Various grasses, notably red fescue.	Southern and central England, expanding.
Grayling	Dry grassland with sparse vegetation and bare ground with fine grasses.	Sheep's fescue, red fescue, bristle bent and early hair-grass.	Throughout, but mainly coastal and patchy.
Gatekeeper	Rough, scrubby grassland.	Various grasses, mainly fine grasses such as bents.	England and Wales, expanding.
Small heath	Dry grassland with sparse open sward.	Fine grasses, especially fescues, meadow grasses and bents.	Throughout, some decline.

5 CASE STUDIES

5.1 Hanson-RSPB wetland project, Needingworth Quarry

Size: 700 hectares
Location: Cambridgeshire
Habitats created: wetland, predominantly reedbed with fen, open water and scrub
Operator: Hanson Aggregates

5.1.1 Background

Needingworth Quarry, situated near the town of St Ives in Cambridgeshire, covers 977 ha. It is one of the largest sand and gravel extraction sites in the UK to be covered by a single planning consent. The quarry will be operational for approximately 30 years, and almost 30 million tonnes of aggregates will be removed during this period. With a planned annual output of about one million tonnes per year, Needingworth Quarry is one of the largest and most modern sites in the UK. The scale of site restoration is equally ambitious; the phased creation of the Ouse Fen Nature Reserve will include the largest freshwater reedbed in the UK (460 ha), and will make a substantial contribution towards UK Biodiversity Action Plan wetland targets. Other habitats to be created include species-rich fen, open water meres and scrub.

5.1.2 Planning

The original application for planning permission was submitted in 1993. At this time, it was expected that the majority of the site would be graded as 3a agricultural land (ie the best and most versatile) (Plate 5.1). Government policy expects best and most versatile land to be restored to an equivalent quality. However, further surveys undertaken during the planning assessment demonstrated that most of the site was in fact grade 3b agricultural land, which therefore removed the policy presumption to restore the site to an agricultural after-use. At this stage, the RSPB and other conservation bodies indicated that the site would be ideally suited for restoration to wetland habitats in this unique location at the southern end of the Ouse Washes. In granting planning permission, Cambridgeshire County Council (the Minerals Planning Authority) included a proviso in the Section 106 agreement that required the company to produce a feasibility study investigating the site's potential for development of nature conservation after-uses. This resulted in further work being carried out by Hanson Aggregates, the RSPB and Cambridgeshire County Council, ultimately resulting in new restoration proposals whereby the majority of the area would be restored to wetland habitat, predominantly reedbed intersected by channels and meres. The 700 ha wetland will incorporate 32 km of new public rights of way, footpaths, bridleways and cycleways. These proposals formed the basis of a new Planning Application and Environmental Statement, which were prepared and submitted by Hanson Aggregates with input from the RSPB.

The Royal Town Planning Institute (RTPI) recognised the quality of the planning work in developing and facilitating this project and awarded it the RTPI National Planning Achievement Award (2000) for Planning and Biodiversity. The RTPI also nominated the project as one of four UK entrants for the 2002 European Urban and Regional Planning Awards.

Plate 5.1
Initial agricultural restoration plan.

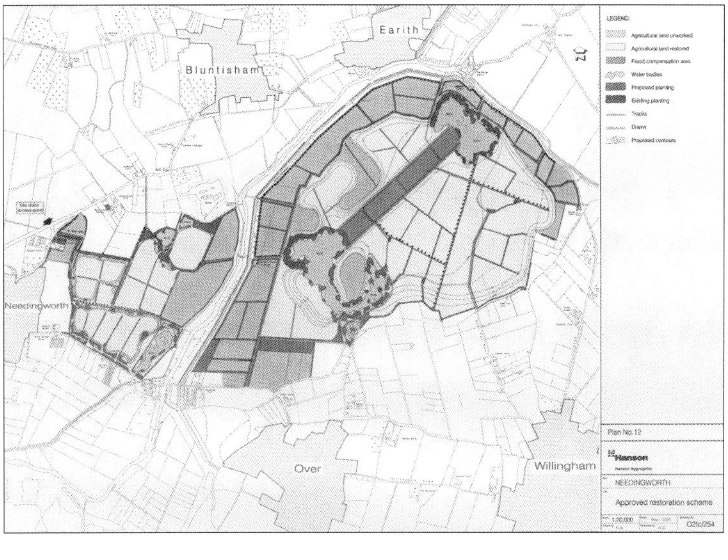

5.1.3 Consultation

The views of local people were important in developing the wetland restoration proposals. Public meetings were held to discuss the initial ideas and later as part of the planning application consultation. Artwork was produced to give an impression of how the area would look as a large wetland, with all its associated wildlife and accessibility to the public (Plate 5.2).

Bruce Pearson

Plate 5.2 Artist's impression of the final restoration.

A Hay (rspb-images.com)

Plate 5.3 Current excavation work.

5.1.4 Feasibility assessment

The feasibility of creating such an extensive wetland had to be investigated, and accurate estimates of the water supply and usage requirements in wet and dry years had to be made. Under the original plan for an agricultural after-use, an engineered, low-permeability, clay seal around the site had been proposed to isolate the area hydrologically from the surrounding water-table. The elevated level of the River Ouse in relation to the surrounding land will enable water to be abstracted under gravity to supply the site (under a winter abstraction licence issued by the Environment Agency). Owing to the low-lying nature of the site, an electric pump will be needed for drainage in exceptionally wet years. However, restoration at this low level provides additional benefits by enabling greater water management and hence the creation of a larger area of wetland habitat than would have been otherwise possible.

The original plan for agricultural restoration contained detailed requirements for careful re-instatement of the soil profile. Under the wetland creation proposal was a reduced constraint on substrate re-instatement; topsoil and subsoil will be replaced to produce a satisfactory medium for reed establishment, but to a shallower profile than would have been permitted for agricultural restoration.

5.1.5 Operational phase

Large-scale sand and gravel extraction began in 1996. The consented scheme includes requirements for detailed hydrological monitoring to ensure that there are no adverse impacts on adjacent sites of conservation importance: Berry Fen SSSI and the Ouse Washes SSSI, Ramsar Site and SPA. Operational sections are already attracting sand martins in areas prepared by the site staff each winter and prior to the spring migration. Additional measures have been implemented to trap oxidising iron to maintain water quality in adjacent ditches.

5.1.6 Restoration phase

The restoration has been planned using a modular system, with each module separated by clay-rich bunds. The modules are approximately 20–40 ha, the size of one or two years' worth of excavation. Landforming and reed planting will take place as the modules are completed. Accurate water level management will be possible within each module by constructing a peripheral ditch and sluice system. The restoration will be undertaken in close co-operation with the RSPB, who will take some responsibility for achieving successful reedbed establishment.

Reedbed creation will involve:

- covering the substrate with about 45 cm of subsoil and about 30 cm of topsoil
- assessing the soil seedbank and controlling weed growth by sowing a grass sward or cultivating the substrate if necessary
- planting reed seedlings at a density of 2 m^2 over 50% of the potential reedbed area in each module, and/or sowing reed seeds collected from local sources
- controlling competing ruderal plants by raising water levels or using appropriate herbicides
- managing water levels to provide optimum conditions for reed establishment, including spray irrigation if required
- monitoring reed establishment and deterring wildfowl grazing if necessary.

5.1.7 Long-term management and monitoring

Following the summer drawdown resulting from evapotranspiration, water levels will be maintained between 70 cm and 15 cm above ground surface to maximise the extent of established wet reedbed. Established reedbeds will be cut on a 10-year rotation to reduce litter build-up, maintain open structure and reed dominance, and remove nutrients. This will entail cutting 50 ha per year from two to four individual modules and the removal of cuttings from the site. Invading scrub will be controlled as appropriate, and stumps treated with herbicide if necessary. Some areas of isolated scrub will be permitted to develop on higher ground (excluding bunds) to a maximum limit of 8% of each module area. Cut reeds removed from site will be sold if possible, thereby generating some income to assist with the management and monitoring costs.

A programme of research, survey and monitoring will be introduced to enable the success of the habitat creation to be assessed. This will include:

- annual monitoring of breeding birds of conservation concern
- monthly WeBS counts of wintering waterfowl
- five-yearly surveys of mammals, fish, aquatic invertebrates and plants
- monitoring of BAP priority species
- monitoring of the water level and quality in each module
- a five-yearly aerial photograph survey to determine extent of major habitat types.

It is anticipated that this large and diverse wetland ecosystem will, when completed, make a substantial contribution to national BAP targets for reedbed and associated species including the bittern, and will support many species of conservation interest. The reserve will provide an important educational resource for raising awareness and support for biodiversity conservation. It will also be a substantial amenity resource for local people and visitors to the Fens.

5.2 Plenmeller

Size: 458 ha
Location: Northumberland
Habitats created: upland moorland – heather, cotton-grass, mat-grass and heath rush communities
Operator: RJB Mining (UK) Ltd (now UK Coal plc)

5.2.1 Background

Plenmeller is an opencast coal site situated at an altitude of about 300 m in the Pennines, within an area of important upland plant communities and including land designated as an AONB. Following a Public Inquiry in 1987, planning consent was issued to RJB Mining (UK) Ltd, with the condition that approximately 190 ha of the site had to be restored to cotton-grass, mat-grass, heath rush, heather and *Sphagnum* moorland plant communities. Planning conditions also required the construction of experimental trial plots to research and develop appropriate restoration techniques. Mineral extraction started in 1988. The site is still operational, producing about 5,000 tonnes of coal each week. A programme of restoration began in 1994.

5.2.2 Trials

Trial plots were established by the Liverpool University Environmental Advisory Unit (EAU) in 1990 to determine the basic principles for restoration. Each trial plot was divided into subplots with different management regimes, and some plots left to revegetate naturally. Plots were monitored for a five-year period. These trials provided the initial data for larger scale experimental plots established by ADAS in 1994.

Heather plots were established on both a peat and a mineral soil substrate. Mat-grass and cotton-grass plots were established on a peat substrate. In addition, trials were instigated to research methods for the control of soft rush and the effects of burning on controlling grasses and triggering germination of heather seeds.

5.2.3 Methods and results

5.2.3.1 Soil storage

All the existing peat was retained for future use in restoration. Where practical, the top 20 cm of soil was stored separately to maximise the opportunity for natural regeneration of moorland species from the seedbank. Initial results indicated that a reduction in the viability of grass and herb seeds occurs during soil storage, therefore limiting the contribution made by the seedbank to revegetation. Emphasis is now being placed on inoculation with seeds or fragments of desired species collected from local sources, to ensure that an adequate supply of plant material is available for restoration.

Plate 5.4 Overview of main restoration area at Plenmeller.

Simon Zisman

Simon Zisman

Plate 5.5 Heather seeded onto a peat substrate.

Soils replaced during the current trial period were taken from storage bunds and mounds, ie there has been little progressive restoration. Soils were replaced using excavators, trucks and bulldozers.

5.2.3.2 Habitat restoration

A variety of methods were trialled and monitored on site, to identify the most effective treatment. For heather restoration, a variety of seeding rates was used with different post-establishment management regimes and fertiliser applications. The development of vegetation communities was monitored and the relative success of the techniques used was assessed. This enabled the development of recommended guidelines for future restoration (see below). One problem with habitat creation at this site is the extremely short growing season due to the high altitude. NPK fertiliser was therefore used to hasten the establishment of nurse crops on some plots.

It was found that although heather initially established well on peat soils, strong competition from cotton-grass, mat-grass and soft rush led to a decline in the number of heather plants on many plots. This was attributed to various possible causes. The addition of NPK fertiliser on some plots probably shifted the competitive balance in favour of grass species. In addition, waterlogged conditions on re-laid peat substrates may have caused the heather roots to die back. In plots where fertiliser was not used, grazing was introduced after heather establishment. This grazing probably occurred too soon: the heather plants were overgrazed and therefore out-competed by less palatable species. Management techniques were developed to control soft rush on heather plots. A nurse crop was considered essential for sheltering immature heather seedlings if sown onto an otherwise bare substrate.

The results from the experimental plots were used to formulate recommended treatments to establish different plant communities at this altitude.

For establishing heather on a peat substrate (Plate 5.5):

- sow a nurse crop of 50:50 sheep's fescue and chewing's fescue at 10 kg/ha onto a prepared seedbed
- broadcast treated heather seed material at 20–25 kg/ha as soon as possible after sowing the nurse crop
- control soft rush by weed-wiper using a 50% glyphosate solution if necessary
- if other vegetation begins to out-compete the heather, introduce light grazing by sheep during May and June after the heather plants have flowered.

For establishing a cotton-grass community:

- prepare plant fragments taken from cotton-grass donor sites during late September – 20 m^2 donor site for one hectare of receptor site
- plant fragments at 1 m^2 during October either by hand or using a tractor-mounted planter
- control soft rush by weed-wiper using a 50% glyphosate solution if necessary.

For establishing a mat-grass community:

- sow a nurse crop of 50:50 sheep's fescue 67and chewing's fescue at 20 kg/ha onto a prepared seedbed with 350 kg/ha 17:17:17 NPK compound fertiliser
- cut and remove the vegetation twice each year until the sward will withstand light sheep grazing during the summer
- control soft rush by weed-wiper using a 50% glyphosate solution if necessary.

Restoration of cotton-grass and mat-grass communities was reasonably successful. Heather moorland restoration on peat soils also met with some success, with target populations consistently exceeding 15 plants/m^2. Heather restoration on mineral soils was less successful, and heather plants may not persist in the long-term on some of the experimental restoration plots. This may be due partly to unfavourable weather conditions during the establishment phase; heavy rainfall lead to waterlogging on mineral soil areas, which adversely effected the heathers' survival.

Best practice guidelines have been developed using the experience gained from these trials. These guidelines should ensure that future restoration at Plenmeller has a greater chance of success. They can also be usefully applied at similar sites elsewhere.

5.3 Inkerman

Size: 39.3 ha
Location: County Durham
Habitats created: moorland and heathland with small ponds
Operator: HJ Banks & Co Ltd

5.3.1 Background

The restored opencast coal site of Inkerman is situated on the outskirts of Tow Law in County Durham. A licence for extraction was granted in 1988; extraction commenced the same year and was completed by 1994. Conditions on the extraction licence required the restoration of a mixture of heathland and agricultural habitats with occasional small ponds. Restoration commenced in 1991, with a five-year aftercare period beginning in 1994.

5.3.2 Heathland restoration

Of the 39.3 ha at Inkerman, some 20 ha was heathland; the remainder comprised poor quality agricultural land. The heathland included areas of peat soils, in places up to five metres deep, with poor quality mineral soils covering the rest. A number of different experimental and conventional peat and soil stripping and storage techniques were used in the restoration. The restored site was split into areas of mineral soils and peat soils, each with a number of subdivisions based on the various stripping and replacement methods employed. This has created a mosaic of peat areas containing different peat depths restored with different techniques; six different replacement methods were used over 10 different zones.

5.3.3 Methods

5.3.3.1 Peat soils

Peat soil depth varied from one to five metres over the site. Stripping, storage and replacement methods varied depending on the depth of the soil and the time of working. The different methods used are outlined below.

1 Translocated heather strips

Peat was stripped from the site and stored in six-metre high piles. Heathland vegetation established on the stored peat. When restoration became possible, the top one metre of the storage mound was stripped with this re-established vegetation intact. This material was transplanted into previously prepared trenches of one metre depth, excavated into an area of previously restored overburden. This method was intended to preserve the heather in a relatively intact state, and therefore replicate the original conditions as closely as possible. Placing the turves into trenches prevented the peat from slipping away or otherwise eroding, thus increasing the heathers' chances of survival. The 1 m deep trenches dug on the receptor area were each between three to four metres wide. A Caterpillar 966 loading shovel with a modified bucket was used to translocate the heather. The modified bucket enabled the machine to excavate turves of 1 m x 3 m x 1 m depth. The turves were cut, transported and laid in the trenches in a single operation. Initially, the stability of the translocated peat turves was not known. Once the success of the first transplants became apparent, subsequent trenches were increased to six to seven metres wide, enabling two rows of turves to be laid side by side.

Following translocation, the ground between the trenches was spread with peat taken from the storage mounds. These areas were allowed to revegetate naturally.

Plate 5.6
Well established heather on translocated strips.

Simon Zisman

Simon Zisman

Plate 5.7
Area of restored moor gone to rough grazing.

2 Re-laid deep peat

The peat layer beneath the turves, stripped as described above, was excavated and block tipped onto overburden to a depth of two metres. The peat was stripped using a hydraulic excavator, and transported in articulated 25-tonne dump trucks. A hydraulic excavator and low ground pressure bulldozer were used to grade the re-laid peat.

5.3.3.2 Mineral soils

Areas of mineral soils were replaced with a soil profile comprising topsoil and subsoil of varying depths. During the soil stripping operation, careful note was made of the original location of the stripped soil, as soil depth and texture varied over the site. Soil was replaced as close as possible to its original location. Soils were stripped, stored and replaced according to standard techniques, using a combination of motor scrapers, tractors and boxes.

Plate 5.8
Red grouse breed at Inkerman.

L Campbell (rspb-images.com)

5.3.4 Results

The re-establishment of heather at Inkerman has been monitored yearly since 1991. The monitoring results have been used to identify where management was needed to maximise the success of restoration.

The heather on the translocated strips is now well-established and healthy (Plate 5.6). The peat between the heather strips has been colonised by a variety of moorland plants. Heather is establishing more slowly in these areas than on the translocated strips, but it is present throughout. Heather has failed to re-establish on re-laid mineral soil, mainly due to excessive competition from grasses and rushes (Plate 5.7).

The monitoring programme identified the need for soft rush control, and dense areas of this plant have been sprayed with glyphosate. The herbicide was applied using a weed-wiper mounted on an all-terrain vehicle. Dead stems and litter were strimmed and removed after the bird breeding season to prevent nutrient build-up. Encroaching scrub has been cut back also. Regular cutting is necessary to maintain the moorland in an open condition and discourage invasive grasses and shrubs. Currently the site is not grazed.

Overall, the restoration of heathland on peat soils has been very successful at Inkerman, and a number of bird species breed on the site, including red grouse (Plate 5.8), curlews, lapwings and snipe. Diverse invertebrate communities have been recorded from the translocated heather strips. In addition, the wet winter and spring of 1999 and 2000 have created conditions suitable for *Sphagnum* moss communities, and a diverse range of habitats have become established.

The experience at Inkerman suggests that heather restoration on peat soils can be highly successful if carefully planned and executed. However, competition from grasses and rushes seems to prevent the establishment of dense heather communities on mineral soils.

5.4 Nosterfield Reserve

Size: 46 ha
Location: North Yorkshire
Habitats created: open water and grazing marsh
Operator/Manager: Tarmac/Lower Ure Conservation Trust

5.4.1 Background

Nosterfield Reserve (Plate 5.9) was formerly a gravel extraction quarry operated by Tarmac. The portion of the site most recently worked is still owned by Tarmac, but the remainder was purchased by the Lower Ure Conservation Trust (LUCT) in 1997. Funding for the purchase and development of the majority of the site came from Yorventure Ltd, Tarmac and the local authorities. The site has been entered into a Countryside Stewardship agreement.

Site restoration was intended to benefit nature conservation by providing open water and grazing marsh habitats, with the emphasis on supporting populations of breeding and wintering birds. Restoration has been through natural regeneration of vegetation combined with grazing.

5.4.2 Restoration successes

The majority of the site was designed to attract breeding redshanks and shovelers. This has been successful, with eight pairs of shovelers, 11 broods of redshanks and 80 lapwing nests on or adjacent to the reserve recorded in 2001. Other bird species that have bred or probably bred include the ringed plover, curlew, turtle dove, yellow wagtail, linnet, tree sparrow and skylark. The site has also become important for migrating waders in autumn and spring, with black-tailed godwits, little stints, Temminck's stints, curlews sandpipers, ruffs and grey plovers being recorded. High numbers of wintering waders and wildfowl have also been recorded, including up to 4,000 lapwings, 1,000 golden plovers, 2,400 wigeons and 1,000 teals, as well as good numbers of shovelers, pintails and pochards. Nosterfield is now considered one of the prime inland sites for waders in north-east England.

Also over 200 plant species have been recorded at the site, including the nationally scarce mudwort. Red data book and nationally notable insect species have also been recorded. The site is excellent for brown hares.

5.4.3 Lessons learned from the site

Nosterfield is adjacent to an active landfill site, which attracts predators such as crows. Although the number of crows on the landfill site is low, they can still have serious impacts on breeding birds. To minimise the risk of damage to breeding bird populations, trees are prevented from developing, and the use of fence posts is avoided wherever practicable. This reduces the number of perching sites for crows overlooking the site.

Openness is very important for the waterfowl and wader species using the site, and landform design can considerably effect the number of birds attracted to a site. Birds will tolerate a steep bank along the edge of an extensive open area; however, a shallow bank can deter birds if it is associated with a more enclosed landform. Nosterfield has been designed to be very open, which helps to attract large numbers of birds.

Plate 5.9 Nosterfield Reserve, showing the newly constructed observation hide.

LUCT

While the creation of such an open site is beneficial, it does mean that visitors can disturb the birds. Public access paths need to be screened from open water and grazing marsh areas. But the amount of fencing and tree planting is restricted to minimise the perching and nesting sites for crows.

G J White

Plate 5.10 Water levels drop to reveal muddy pools and shallows in the area to the rear of this photograph.

Screening is probably best achieved by careful management of hedgerows (with attention to species and location) or by allowing a margin of uncut, tall, herbaceous vegetation to develop adjacent to paths.

Gravel islands were constructed in the lake to provide bird nesting sites free from predation. However, currently these islands only become exposed in the autumn, and are therefore not used by breeding birds. Water levels on the site fluctuate by two to three metres during the year, dropping by 100 mm per week in the summer months. As there is no control over the site's hydrology, water levels are 'adjusted' by optimising the landform, for example through the creation of a series of tiered scrapes (Plate 5.10). Rapid change in the conditions at a site can be a deterrent for breeding birds, as the suitability of a nesting location may change before the chicks have left the nest. Although Nosterfield has shown that large water level fluctuations can be managed successfully, in general, if water level control is possible, fluctuation should be minimised on wetland sites to allow more consistency during the breeding season.

Management of the site is primarily carried out by sheep grazing. Due to redshank nests being very susceptible to trampling by livestock, no grazing takes place until late June, when only a small number (c 0.3 livestock units per hectare) of animals are introduced. Later the numbers are increased significantly during mid-July to October. This grazing regime, combined with the large fluctuation in water level appears to create ideal conditions for redshanks to breed and rear young. Above the high water mark, tussocky grassland offers nesting sites; while the waterfowl-grazed, inundation grassland offers a short sward for feeding.

5.4.4 Strategic restoration planning

The LUCT has set up the Swale & Ure Washlands Project with the aim of co-ordinating a strategic approach to mineral working after-uses, particularly nature conservation, in the Swale and Ure catchments. The project was devised because although there are a substantial number of mineral workings in the area, each quarry was being restored as a separate unit. There was no consideration of the way the restored habitats could interact and complement each other. In consequence each quarry was often restored to a mixture of different after-uses, with small amounts of conservation, agriculture and amenity lands being created.

The Swale & Ure Washland Project aims to:
- maximise the nature conservation potential of mineral working sites
- link existing wildlife habitats by creating wildlife corridors and 'stepping stone' habitats
- contribute to national biodiversity targets through the creation of new habitats to encourage the spread of threatened species
- encourage the restoration of derelict and degraded land to a productive after-use
- create a network of managed nature reserves on former minerals sites
- involve local communities in the development of environmental projects.

5.5 Ham Wall

Size: 184 ha
Location: Somerset
Habitats created: mosaic of wetland habitats, predominantly reedbed
Operator/Manager: English Nature/The RSPB

5.5.1 Background

The RSPB Ham Wall nature reserve is located in the River Brue valley within the peat production zone (PPZ), at the eastern end of the Avalon Marshes (Plate 5.11). Drainage to enable peat extraction leaves groundwater levels in the PPZ lower than in the surrounding land. This lower level means that worked areas gradually fill with water once peat extraction and associated drainage cease – producing a major opportunity for wetland creation. Fisons (now The Scotts Company) gifted Ham Wall to English Nature in 1994, who in turn handed it over to the RSPB for habitat creation and management. The Ham Wall nature reserve initially comprised 77 ha; the remaining area has been acquired from English Nature and purchased from private landowners on a piecemeal basis in subsequent years.

5.5.1.1 Objectives of site restoration

The objective of wetland creation here is to develop the site as a nationally important wetland, which will form an integral part of the Avalon Marshes. The site design includes an extensive mosaic of reed-dominated swamp, open water and ditch systems to provide nesting habitat for reedbed species of high conservation priority, particularly the bittern, bearded tit and marsh harrier.

5.5.2 Reedbed creation

Areas of the former peat extraction site were re-profiled and bunded (Plate 5.12), and areas of deeper water and ditches were excavated. The design specified at least 20% of open water in each bunded phase and 250 m of reed/open water interface per hectare. Banks, sluices, pipes and pumps were installed to enable water levels to be manipulated.

5.5.3 Methods

Four different techniques were used to establish reedbeds in the phases, enabling comparisons to be made of effectiveness and costs. The methods used are outlined briefly below. Reedbed creation began in 1995 and is carried out in each phase after engineering work has been undertaken.

Sally Mills

Plate 5.11
Ham Wall, showing reed established in 1996.

Sally Mills

Plate 5.12
Bank building with borrow pit on the right-hand side.

Sally Mills

Plate 5.13 Reed seedlings in a polytunnel.

5.5.3.1 Seeds

Reed seeds were introduced as pre-germinated panicles or panicle fragments collected from the nearby Shapwick Heath NNR. Seeds were surface-spread at a density of about 80 seeds/m^2 in late May to early June. The original intention was to maintain the water level at or just below the surface after sowing, but a period of very dry weather prevented this. A rotary sprinkler was used to keep the soil surface damp.

5.5.3.2 Seedlings

For phase one, seedlings were grown in plugs by a commercial nursery from panicles collected in December 1994. In total, 100,000 seedlings were grown in plugs of sizes 200 cm^3 and 50 cm^3. Phase one received 18,000 seedlings, with the remainder being over-wintered and planted in phase two in the following year. Seedlings were only planted in areas where the soil water-table was no more than 14 cm below the surface. All future seedlings were grown on site in pots using a polytunnel (Plate 5.13), seeding in March and planting out in June/July (Plate 5.14). Weeds were controlled by raising water levels to cover the planting area, leaving a bare substrate for planting when water levels were lowered.

5.5.3.3 Transplanted rhizomes

Rhizome transplantation has been used extensively, mainly along the banks of the reedbed phases. An excavator was used to dig out clumps of reed approximately 2 m x 2 m x 0.5 m in size from a patch of nearby dry reedbed. These clumps were placed at 10 m intervals along the water's edge on the inside of the bunds. Individual rhizomes and spade-sized clumps have also been planted by hand, throughout the year, but making sure to leave erect dead stems above the surface to accommodate rising water levels and prevent drowning.

Sally Mills

Plate 5.14 Planting reed seedlings along a ditch edge.

5.5.3.4 Stem planting

Reed stems were cut and planted by volunteers; variations in volunteer availability meant planting was small scale in 1995 and 1996, but extensive in 1997. Stems were cut well before flowering during June and July. Vegetation in the planting area was cut and removed, and stems were planted in May, June and July. Stems were planted at about 16 stems/m^2 to a depth that ensured at least one, and preferably two nodes, were buried. Water levels were kept at or just below the soil surface during planting. Once the stems started to produce shoots, the water level was raised to discourage the growth of competitive vegetation.

Sally Mills

Plate 5.15 Creation of reedbed first planted June 1996.

5.5.4 Results

Two years after sowing seed, a mean density of 28.8 reed shoots/m^2 with mean percentage cover of 26.8 was achieved. This compares to a mean density of 80.3 shoots/m^2 with mean percentage cover of 28.0 achieved two years after planting of phase one seedlings. Phase two seedlings yielded a mean density of 146.5 shoots/m^2 and percentage cover 60.5 one year after planting. Hydrology appeared to have a greater effect than planting density on the amount of reed cover produced, with best results produced in areas with less than 20 drought-stressed days per year. However, in these wetter areas, after two years seedlings planted at 8 m^2 produced almost seven times the reed cover of seedlings planted at 4 m^2.

Rhizome transplantation was less successful than planting after one season, but after two seasons the mean density of stems had risen to 40.3 m^2. Approximately 50% of planted reed stems survived, producing 8 stems/m^2, each giving rise to a mean of three shoots. This provides an initial mean density of 24 shoots/m^2 one year after planting.

Sally Mills

Plate 5.16 The area shown in Plate 5.15 in January 1998.

5.5.5 Conclusions

- Planting seedlings grown on site is the most effective way to establish reed cover, and is one of the most cost-effective approaches. As long as the plants are part-flooded, a planting density as low as two plants/m^2 produces results over two years equal to higher planting densities.

- At sites where a damp, weed-free seedbed can be prepared and a good local seed source is available, sowing may be the most effective approach. It may not be suitable on sites with clay soils and abundant competitor rhizomes or in cooler areas such as northern England and Scotland.

- Rhizome transplantation is suitable for relatively small areas with a donor reedbed nearby. This technique is not appropriate for large scale reedbed creation but is a technique that can be used all year round.

- Reed establishes and achieves dominance more rapidly in areas with little or no competitive plant cover. Sites with marginal or emergent competitors such as soft rush and reedmace may require some weed control before reed is established.

- The rapid achievement of reed cover in the first season after planting is the most successful method of promoting long-term dominance. Such cover is best achieved by establishing seedlings at a high density, ie eight plants/m^2 or higher, particularly if there is no surface water.

Overall, the results at Ham Wall are highly encouraging. The wide range of the methods tried achieved stem densities and lengths comparable to those found in mature reedbeds after only one season. Planting of seedlings grown on site appears to be the most effective method of establishing reed. The control of water levels early in the establishment phase is critical and was probably the cause of some methods doing less well. Water level management in the early stages is important in all of the methods for controlling competing vegetation.

5.6 The Wetland Centre

Size: 42.5 ha
Location: London
Habitats created: wetlands, open water and grassland
Operator/Manager: Wildfowl & Wetlands Trust (WWT)

WWT

WWT

Plate 5.17 Aerial view of The Wetland Centre before and Plate 5.18 after construction.

5.6.1 Background

The Wetland Centre, on the site of a former Thames Water reservoir, consists of four concrete-lined waterbodies set in 53 ha of land. The reservoir became redundant following the construction of the London ring main in 1995. The Wetland Centre was created through a partnership between WWT, Thames Water and a property developer, Berkley Homes (Plate 5.17 and Plate 5.18). The developer was allowed to use 10 ha for housing in return for contributing substantial funds to the creation of wetland habitats and the construction of a visitors' centre and site offices. Thames Water provided the land on a 150 year lease for a peppercorn rent and also contributed funds towards the site's restoration. The creation of the Wetland Centre was a high budget operation with over £4 million spent on landforming and habitat creation and over £10 million spent on developing 'state of the art' visitor facilities.

Design constraints included planning conditions stipulating that no spoil could be taken off-site or left unlandscaped on site, and the requirement that eight hectares of open water be maintained at all times. A full soil analysis was carried out on all material extracted from the site, and a complex soil movement programme was devised to ensure that soils were stockpiled and laid according to type. The original site was a SSSI for its wintering wildfowl. The Wetland Centre has recently been re-notified as an SSSI on its wintering and breeding bird numbers.

5.6.2 Hydrological management

Water is taken from the River Thames at Hampton Court through an intake pipe, usually by gravity but is pumped when higher flows are required or there is a pressure drop in the supply pipe. The site has been designed so that if abstraction from the Thames is restricted due to a drought order, recirculation of water throughout the site is possible. This will prevent stagnation of the water and the attendant problems of de-oxygenation and algal growth. The water feeds into a storage reservoir, which is also managed as a habitat feature, and then into a reedbed filter system. The water level in the reservoir is one metre above the other waterbodies on the site, which allows the water management regime to be very flexible. A total of 27 separate waterbodies have been created. Full water control is possible via an array of tilting weir sluices (Plate 5.19). All the islands on the reserve can be flooded for weed control, and the wader scrape can be flooded and drained when necessary.

WWT

Plate 5.19 Tilting weir sluice.

deep, outer trench grading into a shallower centre, thus giving maximum protection from predators and also preventing encroachment of marginal and emergent plants. The complex of ponds was designed with cascading water supply systems to support a wide range of aquatic plant communities. Some ponds are isolated from all others. Instead they are supplied with water by run-off from peripheral bunds. All ponds were created using a clay blanket and vertical, clay, cut-off walls.

Marginal plants were protected from goose grazing by nine miles of orange plastic fencing. This fencing is easy to erect and was found to be the only effective barrier; green fencing and chicken wire were trialled at the site but did not work (Plate 5.20).

5.6.3 Habitat creation details

5.6.3.1 Open water

Some areas of open water were designed to provide good habitat for fish, with plenty of submerged reefs and shallow marginal habitat. The main lake was designed for breeding waterfowl; two types of island complex were provided. Islands are important for breeding waterfowl to prevent predators, such as foxes, from reaching nests. Some islands were surrounded by shallows for dabbling ducks, while others were surrounded by deeper water for diving ducks. The landforming operations created an ideal profile with a

5.6.3.2 Grazing marsh

Four hectares of grazing marsh with associated ditches were created (Plate 5.21). The intention was to create a grassland sward similar to the NVC MG13: chosen because it provides conditions suitable for wintering wildfowl and breeding waders. A variety of seed mixes were hand-sown in 1997. Sward development was monitored over a three-year period to ascertain the extent to which seed mixture and hydrological regime affected the establishment of the target plant community. Water levels were monitored using dip-wells, and a hydrological model used to interpret the hydrological regime across the marsh.

P Bensted

Plate 5.20 Reedbed one year after planting.

Plate 5.21 Open water and grazing marsh.

5.6.3.3 Limestone grassland

The overflow car park was selected for the establishment of limestone grassland as it was constructed from a thin layer of soil spread over crushed concrete (Plate 5.22). A seed mixture was sown that would provide a habitat for butterflies, but also remain relatively short to allow occasional car parking.

5.6.4 Wildlife successes and lessons learned

Results from the grazing marsh seeding experiments suggested that although significant differences between seed treatments were detected the first year after sowing, this difference had disappeared after three years; hydrological regime became the most important factor affecting sward composition. This suggests that the initial composition of seed mix is less important in the long-term than the establishment of appropriate soil conditions and water levels. Autumn sowing was more successful than spring sowing at suppressing weed growth, although weed control by cutting was necessary in all areas. An area left to colonise naturally also developed a community similar to MG13. This indicates that although it is necessary to introduce species on parts of a site, sowing an entire area is not required.

Using seeds collected from existing grassland is inexpensive, but the quantity of available seeds is limited by the size of the donor site. Commercial seeds are available in large amounts, but the number of species obtainable is limited. A good compromise would be to supplement commercial seed mixtures with seeds collected from existing grasslands.

A big weed problem developed on the grazing marsh due to an excess of nutrients in the soil provided for restoration. Intensive management by cutting and removal of plant material was required to combat the spread of weed species. Species diversity in all treatments gradually declined during the

Plate 5.22 Limestone grassland.

three-year monitoring period. This could be due to either the hydrological regime being inappropriate for some sown species, or to the high levels of available phosphorus in the soil. Successful establishment of an MG13 community requires appropriate hydrological conditions and soil fertility.

Limestone grassland creation was also successful. The Wetland Centre has become the only London site for a number of calcareous plant species including hare's-foot clover. Some non-native plant species are present in the aquatic plant communities. These species can be invasive and require management to prevent them becoming dominant.

One of the largest threats to the system is the high level of phosphorus within the water supplied direct from the River Thames. More work is being carried out to see how these levels can be reduced in at least some of the lakes and ponds within the Centre.

5.6.5 Interpretation

The Wetland Centre has extensive 'state of the art' visitor facilities, including a large interpretation centre. The Peter Scott Visitor Centre contains a discovery centre, an observatory, a theatre, an art gallery, a café and a shop. Facilities also include three outdoor exhibition areas. The site provides considerable educational opportunities for visitors and is a good example of the way in which habitat creation for wildlife can be integrated with extensive public access.

5.7 Langford Lowfields

Size: 167 ha
Location: Nottinghamshire
Habitats created: reedbed
Operator/Manager: Tarmac/The RSPB

5.7.1 Background

Langford Lowfields is an area of arable farmland within the River Trent floodplain. The site is being worked for sand and gravel extraction by Tarmac, and is being restored in phases (Plate 5.23). The entire site will eventually be restored to a reed-dominated wetland. Restoration work, commencing in 1996, will continue until 2025 and will create a 167 ha nature reserve. The reserve will comprise mostly reedbed and open water, capable of supporting a nationally important population of breeding bitterns and benefiting other specialist reedbed birds, mammals and invertebrates. The reserve will also contain other habitats including fen margins and dry grassland; these will support other bird species of conservation concern. At the time of writing, phase one of the restoration is under way, involving the creation of 12 ha of reedbed and 4.5 ha of open water.

5.7.2 Habitat creation methods

The phase one area was landformed using bulldozers and excavators (Plate 5.24). Soil was taken from storage piles and areas with excess soil to create a series of contoured beds and ditches with profiled edges. Surface grip drains were excavated through the beds. The beds were contoured to mimic a ridge and furrow landform, with about 20 m between each ridge. The reedbed was established by planting seedlings (Plate 5.25). Volunteers and site staff planted pot-grown seedlings by hand, using dibbers; the seedlings were bedded in so that at least one-third of the leaf remained above water.

5.7.3 Lessons learned from the site

The initial reed plantings at Langford Lowfields failed to establish. Of 10,000 seedlings planted in the first two years, only 1% survived. There are two theories why the plants did not survive. First is the theory of local provenance. There is very little information on the genetics of reed and the relative success of different ecotypes in

RSPB

Plate 5.23 Silt lagoons at Langford Lowfields.

RSPB

Plate 5.24 Landforming for reedbed restoration.

A Hay (rspb-images.com)

Plate 5.25 Planted reed seedling.

different conditions. Van der Toorn (1972) identified three consistent ecotypes adapted to brackish water, freshwater silt/clay and freshwater peat conditions respectively. It is possible that other variations exist influencing the ability of seedlings grown from one site to survive at another. The current recommendation is to source reed from nearby sites, but there is no guarantee that the seedlings will be adapted to the conditions on the new site. The first set of reeds planted at Langford Lowfields was grown from seeds from a Suffolk peat site and may explain why so many of the seedlings failed on the clay-based substrate at Langford. The second theory is that overgrazing by coots and geese penetrating the plastic fenced areas killed the plants.

Although it was not certain which of these factors was largely responsible, the reed seedlings for the third year of planting were taken from a more local, clay substrate source to increase the chances of the plants being adapted to the local conditions. In addition, rigid enclosures were erected around the newly planted seedlings to protect them from grazing. The enclosures were constructed from posts and plastic netting; the size of the enclosures varied, but was not large enough to permit grazing waterfowl to land inside.

The adoption of these measures has proved successful, and reed is now establishing on the site, with a 95% survival rate. Another technique employed has been to use stem transplants from self-sown reed on site. New planting of seedlings, translocation of rhizome material and stem planting, all from on-site material, will assist the natural expansion of the established reed. In addition, the edges of the enclosures will be moved out when the reed is sufficiently dense to continue to discourage grazing wildfowl.

5.7.4 Management and monitoring

A reedbed development monitoring programme has been set up: the development and spread of reed is assessed twice-yearly. Bird, fish and aquatic macrophyte communities will be monitored. The reedbed, once fully established, will be managed by rotational cutting on a four-year cycle. Initial management prescriptions include mowing shallow ditch margins on a two- or four-year rotation. This will maintain a dynamic reed edge suitable for feeding bitterns and spawning fish. Trees will be planted to screen open water and reedbed areas from access tracks. Planting will be the minimum necessary to reduce disturbance from human activity to waterfowl while minimising the availability of perching and nesting sites for corvids, eg crows. Areas of planted willow scrub will be controlled by selective coppicing on a seven- to ten-year rotation to maintain scrub height at a maximum of two metres – this will prevent corvids nesting. Further spread of scrub beyond planted areas will be controlled by hand-pulling or flooding if necessary.

When restoration is complete in 2025, the site will comprise approximately 22 ha of hay meadow, 52 ha of reedbed, 17 ha of open water, 56 ha of rough grassland and scrub, 3.5 ha of woodland and 23 ha of visitor facilities.

5.8 Fairburn Ings

Size: 276.5 ha
Location: West and North Yorkshire
Habitats created: grassland, wetland and woodland
Operator/Manager: RJB Mining (Now UK Coal plc)/The RSPB

C H Gomersall (rspb-images.com)

Plate 5.26 Fairburn Ings – view across the main lakes adjacent to the spoil heaps.

5.8.1 Background

Fairburn Ings is situated in the Lower Aire Valley near to Castleford (Plate 5.26). The site incorporates 105 ha of colliery spoil heaps, which were acquired and used for tipping by the Coal Board at the turn of the last century. RJB took over the tips from British Coal in 1994 intending to reclaim coal from the spoil using a washing process. Although some parts of the site contained up to 60% coal, the majority proved much less productive, making the operation economically unviable. The spoil processing was therefore halted in 1995, and site restoration commenced ahead of schedule (Plate 5.27).

The original restoration plan involved the creation of large woodland areas with small areas of open grassland and wetland features. The early cessation of spoil washing operations presented an opportunity to review the restoration plan, and it was subsequently re-designed by RJB ecologists with input from the RSPB and Leeds City Council. The reviewed plan maximised the areas of dry grassland and wetland habitats, restricting woodland planting to areas of high landscape value. The landscape design was modified to include existing contours and features.

5.8.2 Soil treatment and vegetation introduction

The colliery spoil at Fairburn is rich in iron pyrites. Acid leachate is produced when the pyrites comes into contact with air and water, and percolates through the site. This acidity can be neutralised by basic substances such as lime; most of the site was treated with lime prior to planting to buffer the soil against acidity. The lime also reduces the air contact with the pyrites and reduces the rate of breakdown, establishes sward quickly and prevents erosion. In areas where trees were to be planted, lime was ploughed into the spoil at a rate of 10 t ha^{-1}. A 10 cm layer of limestone subsoil was added as a top-dressing in the areas to be sown with a herb-rich grassland seed mix.

The lime treatment was insufficient to buffer the acidity over much of the tree planting areas, and the conductivity of the soil did not fall below 3,000 microsieverts, the upper threshold for tree plantings, for at least four years after landscaping. As ground conditions were unsuitable for trees, a salt-tolerant grassland mix was sown. This germinated well, quickly providing good ground cover and helping to prevent further erosion of the spoil, which in turn reduced the exposure of new pyrites.

Elsewhere, the liming treatments appear to have worked, at least in the short-term, but there are concerns about whether they will be sufficient in the long-term. A herb-rich mix of neutral grasses was sown in the top-dressed area (Plate 5.28). This has germinated well and has a low enough productivity to be suitable for species-rich grassland to develop.

Some areas were not treated with lime and not seeded (Plate 5.29). The intention was to produce bare areas and provide suitable

Plate 5.27 The restored spoil heap in 1996.

(rspb-images.com)

J Gilbert

Plate 5.28 In areas where buffering treatment was undertaken, species-rich mesotrophic pools developed.

habitat for the existing population of little ringed plovers and for early phase successional communities to develop. However, the acidic run-off from these areas appears to suppress plant growth within the adjacent seeded herb-rich areas. A similar situation is occurring in vegetated areas where small bare patches have developed, eg due to digging by rabbits. Run-off from these areas appears to be scorching vegetation lower down the slopes.

No fertiliser was used in areas where grassland species were sown, as herb-rich grassland requires a low soil nutrient status. However, sewage sludge was used as fertiliser in tree planting areas in the first phase of restoration, and trees have successfully established in this medium. Tree growth has been fast, but vigorous competition from weeds has been difficult to control. It appears that the soil will be too productive to support a diverse ground flora.

5.8.3 Wetland habitat creation

A variety of waterbodies has been created. Water chemistry varies according to the amount of acidity and buffering in the catchment of each waterbody. The presence of bare soil in the catchment tends to produce acidic pools, whereas well-vegetated, top-dressed catchments tend to produce mesotrophic pools. The old settlement lagoons have shallow margins, which are favoured by migrating and breeding waders, and reedbed is establishing in some areas. The black coal spoil beach provides an excellent habitat for invertebrates such as various species of small predatory ground beetles (*Bembidion*) and for burrowing dragonfly larvae.

J Gilbert

Plate 5.29 Where no buffering was undertaken the land remained bare and acidic, but was favoured by little ringed plovers and some invertebrates.

5.8.4 Lessons learned from the site

Bare substrate, although a necessary habitat for some species, should not have been located at or near the top of slopes, as it generates acid run-off adversely affecting downslope vegetation. Either bare soil areas should have been located at or near the lowest point in the catchment, or additional lime should have been applied. It is still not known whether the buffering treatment will work in the long-term, but it appears to be successful in areas that have remained fully vegetated.

Sewage sludge is too nutrient-rich to use in the restoration of diverse habitats such as herb-rich grassland, which requires low soil nutrient status. Although using sewage sludge fertiliser in tree planting areas helps the trees to establish and grow rapidly, it can create significant weed management problems. Weeds can reduce the diversity of woodland ground flora. The sewage sludge also provides no buffering of the pyrites acidity and run-off can be very acidic, leading to toxicity within parts of the drainage system and problems with disposal of sediment.

5.8.5 Wildlife interest in restored areas

The colliery spoil heaps support the majority of breeding little ringed plovers on the site – up to five pairs each year between 1991 and 1995. Wintering golden plovers also favour the spoil heaps, with a maximum of 7,000 recorded in 1995. The restoration of the spoil heap area is designed to retain habitat suitable for these species. Dragonfly species recorded from ponds include the emperor dragonfly, four- spotted chaser, common darter, ruddy darter, emerald damsel, common blue damsel and azure damsel. Extensive colonies of common blue butterflies have also been recorded.

5.9 Ballidon Quarry

Size: 51.5 ha
Location: Derbyshire
Habitats created: calcareous grassland, scree slopes and woodland
Operator: Tarmac

5.9.1 Background

Ballidon Quarry is in the Peak District National Park. Limestone has been extracted from the quarry since the 1950s, and 1.25 million tonnes of crushed limestone are currently produced each year. Efforts have been made to ensure that the quarry does not produce a visual impact on the National Park; a screening mound was created and contoured to blend in with the surrounding topography. A progressive restoration programme has also been adopted within the quarry itself.

5.9.2 Restoration details

The primary objective of restoration at Ballidon quarry is to heal the visual scar and promote the rapid establishment of vegetation cover in worked areas. The restoration scheme proposes the creation of a mosaic of habitats including 16 ha of calcareous grassland, 12 ha of deciduous woodland, 12 ha of open water, 7.5 ha of Daleside landscape and bare rock face, and four hectares of alder woodland.

Experimental work at Ballidon has proved very instructive in the restoration of such sites. The limestone was blasted and cut into large benches during quarrying operations, producing a series of obviously artificial steps. Once limestone extraction finished, the benches were re-profiled, using a combination of blasting and leaving buttresses of unquarried rock, to create a more natural-looking sloping landform. Trials of this technique demonstrated that a large quantity of blasting is needed to break up the benches. Site constraints mean it has not been possible to create scree slopes, which continue for more than one bench height. Leaving unquarried areas of limestone, as in some areas, significantly improves the final appearance of the rock face, but carries a cost in reduced production.

To provide a suitable growing medium for vegetation, an additional layer of waste material (scalpings) was placed onto the restored landform. An experiment was carried out using different proportions of topsoil mixed with the scalpings. Using 100% scalpings produced a weedy community, with very low vegetation cover after one year. A 1:4 soil:scalping mix produced a thin vegetation cover with an interesting flora, presumably from the seedbank, including salad burnet, sweet vernal grass and sheep's fescue. A soil:scalping mix of 1:2 and 3:4 produced faster-growing vegetation, but plant species characteristic of calcareous grassland were out-competed by more aggressive ruderal species. The ideal mixture can now be used extensively across the site.

Large areas of the re-profiled bench surfaces were planted with trees. Breaking up the linear appearance of the benches by tree planting helps to reduce the visual impact of quarry's worked areas.

5.9.3 Lessons learned from the site

Requests from planners to establish vegetation rapidly on the restored landform has lead to habitats with less conservation

Plate 5.30 Ballidon Quarry.

Tarmac

interest than if more time had been allowed to 'green' the site. Of course, it is recognised that ameliorating visual impacts is an important part of site restoration, and may be the primary factor governing restoration after-use in especially sensitive areas. However, in areas where visual amenity is not the primary concern, ie in those parts of the site not visible from the surrounding countryside, a bare limestone quarry face provides a good opportunity to create a range of early successional habitats. Such habitats are likely to be more diverse and of greater ecological interest than the habitat produced by planting trees into a fertile substrate.

Allowing vegetation to develop by natural re-colonisation promotes the development of a range of habitats from bare rock to grassland. Grassland management can be introduced if necessary as the habitats develop. Tree planting is appropriate on a small scale and in areas of particular landscape sensitivity, especially if shrubs favoured by butterflies are planted; extensive tree planting should be avoided.

Future management of Ballidon Quarry provides the potential for the site to contribute towards local BAP targets. The habitat considered to make the most valuable contribution is calcareous grassland. Other habitats of value include ash woodland, hay meadow and rock faces.

An interesting comparison with the restoration carried out at Ballidon Quarry is nearby Hopton Wood Quarry. This latter site has been designated an SSSI for its habitats and plant species, and is managed by Derbyshire Wildlife Trust. Hopton Quarry was worked several decades ago; no landscape restoration was undertaken, and the site has developed entirely through natural colonisation. It now supports a very diverse calcareous flora including several notable species such as the frog orchid and dark red helleborine. A short grassland turf appears to be maintained by rabbit grazing, although scrub invasion is becoming a problem in some areas. This shows that over time natural colonisation can produce habitats with considerable conservation value. It is not suggested that large sites such as Ballidon should be left entirely to natural colonisation. However, it is certainly possible to include natural colonisation within a restoration plan to maximise the conservation benefits of restoration.

5.10 Aymestrey Quarry

Size: 46 ha
Location: Herefordshire
Habitats created: agricultural land and woodland
Operator: Hanson Aggregates

5.10.1 Background

Aymestrey Quarry lies in a designated Area of Great Landscape Value within the Lugg Valley in north-west Herefordshire. The surrounding landscape contains broadleaved woodland, commercial forestry plantations on the steeper hills and predominantly livestock pasture on shallower slopes and the valley floor. Sand and gravel was quarried from Aymestrey between 1952 and 1990. Restoration progressed in phases, with the final phase completed in 1996.

5.10.2 Habitat creation details

The restoration at Aymestrey aimed to create an agricultural landscape with woodland compatible with the surrounding rural land. Topsoil and subsoil were stripped and stored separately prior to mineral extraction, and were replaced at an average depth of 30 cm (subsoil) and 20 cm (topsoil) on top of a layer of overburden. A total of 24 ha of pasture were restored. Under-drainage ditches were installed in the fields after restoration.

Soil was not replaced over the silt lagoons in the centre of the site. In places, the lagoons had dried to the point where the lagoon bed soil could be ripped before tree planting. These lagoons (7 ha) were planted with native broadleaved species appropriate to the local area, including ash, oak, hazel and beech. In addition, numerous birch and alder trees had naturally colonised parts of the lagoons, giving rise to a diverse age structure within the woodland block. A central woodland ride was created to increase woodland habitat diversity. A 1.6 m high deer exclusion fencing, to protect the trees from grazing damage, surrounded this area of woodland. Trees and shrubs were planted as whips into pits, with compost incorporated into the backfill.

Over 700 m of native hedgerow species, predominantly hawthorn and blackthorn with oak and ash standards, were planted at the site and protected by rabbit fencing. The hedgerows were planted on both sides of a bridleway, which runs through the site and along field boundaries. One large pond, formed during the quarry's operational phase, was left in *situ*.

5.10.2.1 Restoration successes

In general, restoration has been very successful, and the restored landform blends well with the surrounding landscape. The phased restoration,

Plate 5.32 Woodland planting at Aymestrey Quarry

Hanson

Hanson

Plate 5.33 A large pond was retained from the extraction phase

combined with natural woodland colonisation, has produced a more natural-looking and more diverse woodland block than would have been created if all trees had been planted at the same time. The retention of some landscape features has further enhanced habitat diversity. A small, steep-sided sinkhole has developed naturally into woodland with seasonal pools at the bottom; the slopes provide good habitat for badgers – at least one active sett was observed in 2002.

A shortfall of available soils for restoration led to the creation of an area of hard standing adjacent to the bridleway. This was surfaced with stone chippings, and has developed a ruderal vegetation community not found elsewhere on site. It also provides additional habitat for a range of plant and invertebrate species that may not have occurred had the entire area been restored to pasture.

5.10.3 Lessons learned from the site

There is evidence that stocking density is too high on some of the restored pasture. Also some of the hedgerows have been over-managed, with standard trees cut to the same height as the hedge species, and the entire hedge cut too low. Weed control in some of the younger hedges also appears to have stopped, resulting in competition from tall ruderals potentially affecting the growth of the planted species. Even when restoration and the initial five-year aftercare period are carried out to a high standard, as at Aymestrey, inappropriate long-term management, after the operator's involvement ceases, can compromise the success of the restoration.

Some of the planted trees on the silt lagoon areas have been relatively slow-growing compared with the naturally colonised trees in the same area. This may be due to compaction caused by machinery used to rip the soil prior to planting. Although ripping soil is standard tree-planting practice, it may have been inappropriate to use heavy machinery on the unstructured, damp, silty soil remaining in the lagoon beds. Unstructured, immature soils are more prone to compaction. However, tree mortality has not been higher than expected, so the eventual development of diverse woodland will not be affected.

In general, planning requirements dictate that agricultural land used for mineral extraction must be restored to agricultural land of similar quality. Aymestrey Quarry demonstrates that restoration to agriculture with associated features of conservation interest, such as woodland, ponds and hedgerows, can produce a landscape with higher conservation value than originally occurred on site.

5.11 House of Water, River Nith

Size: 3 km
Location: Ayrshire
Habitats created: river channel
Operator: Scottish Coal

5.11.1 Background

The River Nith supports a good population of Atlantic salmon *Salmo salar*, and is therefore an important local recreational and economic resource. The Atlantic salmon is listed on Annex II of the 1992 EU Habitats & Species Directive, and the River Nith has conservation interest due to its salmon population. Trout and several coarse fish species are also found in the river.

At the House of Water site, the River Nith flowed past an opencast coal mine (Plate 5.34) owned by Scottish Coal. Surveys revealed that the land surrounding the river at this point was underlain by a substantial amount of coal. Following extensive consultation with the West Galloways Fisheries Trust and the River Nith District Salmon Fishery Board, a plan was submitted to move a 1.5 km river section to the opposite side of the floodplain, thus enabling the expansion of the existing coal mine. The river was diverted into the new channel in late summer 2000. Once the opencast coal mining is complete, the whole floodplain will be restored. Scottish Coal intends to create about 100 ha of wet grassland with some open water features on the reconstructed floodplain. The aim is to manage the grassland for breeding waders: high water-tables in spring without extensive flooding. The RSPB is advising on the creation of appropriate hydrological and soil conditions.

5.11.2 Habitat creation details

To minimise the detrimental impacts of moving the watercourse on the river ecosystem, the new watercourse was designed to be as similar as possible to a natural watercourse (plate 5.35). A fish rescue operation was conducted, which transported approximately 50,000 fish from the obsolete river channel to the newly created watercourse. A 10-year monitoring programme of the fish population commenced in 2000, along with short-term monitoring of aquatic invertebrates, aquatic plants and channel stability.

5.11.2.1 Habitat creation successes

Biological monitoring has established that the river diversion is being recolonised by riverine flora and fauna. Aquatic plants on gravel exposures and depositional zones are developing well, and the marginal species toad rush and sharp-flowered rush are becoming well-established. Results suggest that species richness is rapidly reaching levels comparable with undisturbed reaches upstream of the new channel, although

Plate 5.34 The opencast coal mine at House of Water.

J Gilbert

abundance and cover are still comparatively low. The constructed backwaters have been rapidly colonised, and support some species that have not been found in the main flow channel.

Aquatic invertebrate monitoring suggests that gravel conditions are well suited to surface dwellers, with abundant cased caddis-fly, stonefly and mayfly larvae being recorded. Healthy densities of salmon fry have been found, showing that adult salmon have migrated to the new channel and that spawning was successful. Juvenile salmon and trout were also observed, indicating successful trout spawning and the survival of a number of fish from the rescue operation. Some coarse fish species, such as stone loach and eel, also survive in the new channel. Fish populations both within the new channel and downstream are at sustainable levels, and re-stocking is not required.

Bird surveys showed that the majority of species expected in such an upland channel, such as the oystercatcher, grey wagtail and reed bunting, appear to be using the new watercourse.

5.11.3 Lessons learned from the site

Caseless caddis-fly larvae, riffle beetles and sessile species such as the pea mussel, which are present in the natural channel, have yet to be observed in any abundance in the new channel. In part, this reflects the comparatively low mobility of these species and the absence of a fully developed aquatic and marginal plant community. It is possible that these species will colonise in greater numbers in the future. However, the introduction of plants and sediment containing invertebrates, either from the old watercourse or from upstream sites, would speed up the development of a diverse aquatic invertebrate community.

Plate 5.35 The restored river channel.

J Gilbert

Some of the marginal plants that were introduced have not survived. It is apparent that these were exotic species not adapted to the physical environment, and would in any case be out-competed by naturally colonising flora. It is preferable, wherever possible, to plant local provenance, native species in any habitat restoration scheme, particularly when there is a suitable source: in this case, the original river channel. There is a higher chance that the plants will be adapted to the local conditions, and should therefore hasten the development of a natural aquatic plant community.

Riparian vegetation, especially on bank faces, has also been slow to establish. The sown grass mix was washed out by floods, which occurred in late autumn and winter 2000. Establishment problems were compounded further by drought the following summer. It is likely that river-borne seeds from upstream will remedy this situation. However, repeated inoculations of seeds and/or plants would ensure that riparian vegetation develops rapidly and would help to minimise bank erosion.

Remedial works within the river channel would increase habitat diversity for fish, particularly for coarse species. In-stream habitat diversity is currently low; although trout and salmon parr were present, the establishment of this age group has been hindered by the absence of suitable habitat. Although in-stream cover is currently a good standard for juvenile salmonids, cover suitable for older fish is lacking. As a potential remedial measure, a number of boulders could be placed in selected locations along the river channel. Planting occasional deciduous trees along the banks would create bankside cover and provide a source of woody debris in the river and increase habitat diversity. Tree planting would also increase bank stability.

5.12 Sandy Heath Quarry

Size: 28 ha
Location: Bedfordshire
Habitats created: acid grassland/heathland
Operator: Lafarge Aggregates

5.12.1 Background

Sandy Heath Quarry is situated on the Greensand Ridge, an elevated area of land in Bedfordshire. Between the late medieval period and the mid-19th century, the area around Sandy and the nearby Everton Heath formed an extensive area of open heathland, comprising a mixture of heather, grassland and bare ground. This area survived almost intact until around 1825. Since then, much of the heath has been lost to agricultural encroachment and tree planting, and little heathland vegetation now remains. Sand has been extracted in the Sandy area for around 40 years. Extraction permission was first given in 1965 and a further permission was awarded in 1985. Early plans for restoration included tree planting, but since 1990 the emphasis has shifted towards the re-establishment of heathland and grassland. The restoration of current areas of extraction will increase the area considerably.

5.12.2 Habitat creation details

Sandy Heath Quarry presents an opportunity to create a large heathland block that will contribute to both national and local BAP targets. Sand extraction sites provide good conditions for heathland creation, as there is no problem with excessive soil fertility: one of the main obstacles to successful heathland creation on more nutrient-rich sites.

Existing nature conservation interest at Sandy Heath Quarry centres on early successional bare ground and acid grassland habitats and their associated invertebrate and plant communities. The aim of restoration is to create a mosaic of heathland habitats characteristic of the local area, maintaining early successional habitats in some areas while encouraging the colonisation of mature heathland communities in others.

Shallow, seasonal pools will also be created. Site restoration on recently quarried areas aimed to create a landform similar to that found in local valleys. Sand extraction lowered the site surface by up to 30 m, and the final landform was designed to accommodate this change. Three valley forms were created which flow between and

G J White

Plate 5.36
The restoration at Sandy Heath aimed to create a landform similar to that found in local valleys.

around retained areas of woodland. Heather establishment was achieved by transplanting year-old heather plants grown from local provenance seed. An additional method, spreading heather litter containing seeds, was also employed. Areas of heather were fenced to exclude rabbits.

5.12.3 Lessons learned from the site

The restoration challenge at Sandy Heath Quarry is striking a balance between the establishment of mature heather communities and the maintenance of bare ground and the naturally colonising, early successional habitat important for the existing invertebrate assemblage. Maintaining early successional habitats requires reasonably heavy grazing, by rabbits in this case, over quite substantial areas of the site. Early management is essential; coarse grassland and scrub can develop within a few years on ungrazed areas, and once developed it can be hard to return to its previous condition.

Rabbit grazing generally maintains an open-structured vegetation community, although sheep grazing has been suggested as an appropriate long-term management technique. However, heavy grazing is detrimental to the successful establishment of heather. Fenced exclusion plots were therefore constructed to allow heather seedlings to develop. This has led to an issue with broom colonisation. The majority of the dry scrub on site is broom, and although the plant supports a significant invertebrate fauna, including at least one nationally scarce species, it is capable of rapidly colonising new areas. Broom is a nitrogen-fixing legume, so can raise soil nutrient levels to the point where communities requiring low nutrient status are unable to establish due to competition from coarse grasses and other undesirable species.

Excluding rabbits from heather plots has allowed colonisation by broom. To prevent broom from dominating areas of heather, gaps have been made in the rabbit fencing to allow the rabbits to control the broom. Accurately judging the appropriate time to allow rabbits access to the enclosures is not straightforward. It needs to be early enough to allow the young broom plants to be grazed and controlled, but late enough to allow the heather seedlings to be established sufficiently to withstand rabbit grazing. There is also a risk that rabbits will establish warrens inside the enclosures. Using a greater number of smaller enclosures to cover the same area as the original large enclosures can reduce this risk.

Sandy Heath Quarry is an interesting example of the need to balance potentially conflicting management requirements that enable the co-existence of early successional bare ground and grassland communities together with more mature heathland communities. This case study demonstrates that with careful management planning it is possible to achieve a balance between different habitats on the same site.

Appendix 1 Glossary of scientific and technical terms

aftercare
the period defined in the planning permission where the operating company has an obligation to care for the site (may have a formal definition).

after-use
the use to which a mineral extraction site is put after extraction has ceased.

available nutrients
the nutrients in the soil available to plants ie the sum of those absorbed in the exchange complex plus the soluble nutrients.

available water capacity
the amount of water in the soil available to plants, assessed as the difference in water contents of a soil at field capacity and permanent wilting point.

bioassay
methods of assessment using plants as an indicator, for example to determine a soil's potential for sustaining plant growth.

biomass
a quantitative estimate of animal and/or plant matter.

brash
the finer branches or twigs that result from woody growth being cut down.

bulk density
the dry weight of a unit volume of soil in its field state.

decomposition
break down of organic matter by microbial action.

dibber
device for creating a hole in the soil of suitable size to receive a plant plug.

drawdown
the removal of water from a wetland habitat.

ecotone
a narrow and fairly sharply defined transition zone between two communities. Such edge communities are typically species-rich.

eutrophic
nutrient-enriched.

evapotranspiration
total loss of water from the soil surface by combination of evaporation and transpiration from plants. Potential evapotranspiration is calculated using measured rainfall, wind and sunshine data.

field capacity
the moisture condition of a wet soil when all excess water has been drained away, the remaining water being held by capillary action.

fixation capacity
the ability of the soil to precipitate nutrients in a form unavailable to plants, usually by chemical reaction with other soil constituents.

grip
a small ditch or foot-drain designed to enable a flow of water to be maintained in a reedbed.

growing season
period of the year when climatic conditions are suitable for plant growth.

heeling in
the process of making a slot in the soil, inserting a tree or shrub root and the using one's heel to firm the ground around the root.

hydraulic conductivity
a measure of the potential water flow through a soil.

hydroseeding
method of applying seeds, soil amendments and fertiliser to areas inaccessible to agricultural machinery, eg steep slopes.

hypertrophic
with an abnormally high nutrient loading.

infiltration
movement of water from the surface into the soil by percolation.

inoculation
addition to soil of dormant spores of bacteria or fungi, usually nitrogen-fixing species associated with species being planted, or soil invertebrates, eg worms.

landfill
disposal of relatively inert domestic and industrial wastes by burial.

leaching
removal of soluble chemicals from the surface soil layers by percolating water.

legume
plants from family *Legumininosae*, which are able to fix atmospheric nitrogen through their association with *Rhizobium* bacteria in their roots.

mesotrophic
containing moderate amounts of plant nutrients

microclimate
localised climatic and atmospheric conditions affected by factors such as topography, soil texture, aspect, slope etc.

micro-topography
small scale variations (<1.0 m) in topography.

mulch
protective covering applied to bare soil or substrate, over planted seedbeds or around newly planted trees.

mycorrhiza
fungi associated symbiotically with the roots of most species of trees and shrubs.

nutrient
mineral element essential for plant growth obtained from the soil.

NVC
National Vegetation Classification. A comprehensive description of all types of British vegetation using a standardised system.

oligotrophic
containing low levels of plant nutrients.

ombrotrophic
derived solely from rainwater.

overburden
non-processible material overlying mineral deposits that must be stripped before extraction can proceed.

perimeter tipping
method of constructing large spoil tips whereby the outer faces are built first, so that vegetation establishment can commence while the remaining void is infilled.

permanent wilting point
the moisture condition of a dry soil when all the free water is lost, the remaining water being chemically bound or absorbed onto the soil particles and thus unavailable to plants.

porosity
the amount of air space in soil and the distribution of the pore sizes.

progressive working
method of extracting shallow mineral deposits by placing overburden, spoil and fill in worked out sections, allowing progressive restoration of soils and vegetation.

pyrite
metallic sulphides, usually iron pyrites FeS_2, present in some spoils.

reclamation
process of bringing back a derelict or disused site to some form of productive or useful purpose.

restoration
process of bringing back a derelict or disused site to a properly functioning state – often the original state prior to development.

ripping
deep cultivation of compacted soil using a shanked ripping tool attached to a crawler tractor.

scarification
i) light cultivation of soil surface to prepare seedbed or prevent lamination between successive soil layers as they are replaced
ii) mechanical treatment to hard-coated seeds to provoke germination.

soil
any mineral or organic material used as a plant growth medium, whether fertile or sterile.

spoil
bulk waste material produced alongside marketable mineral.

stratification
seed treatment to overcome dormancy involving exposure to cold and moisture.

subsoil
subsurface soil material, within the plant root zone, made up of decomposed rocks, but containing little organic matter.

substrate
plant growth medium.

topsoil
surface soil material enriched with organic matter.

toxicity
presence of chemicals in a concentration antagonistic to growth or survival of plants and animals.

vernalisation
is the requirement of repeated chilling of moist seeds before they can successfully germinate. Seeds may be artificially vernalised by mixing with wet sand and subjecting to freeze/thaw conditions for about one month.

weathering
breakdown of rock minerals under the combined action of water, heat, cold, wind and time.

whips
tree transplants less than about one metre tall.

Appendix 2 Acronyms used in the text

ADAS Agricultural Development and Advisory Service
AONB Area of Outstanding Natural Beauty
ASLF Aggregates Levy Sustainability Fund
ASSI Area of Special Scientific Interest (Northern Ireland only)
BAP Biodiversity Action Plan
BBOWT Berkshire, Buckinghamshire and Oxfordshire Wildlife Trust
BCO British Coal Opencast
BTO British Trust for Ornithology
CAA Civil Aviation Authority
CCW Countryside Council for Wales
CRoW Countryside and Rights of Way Act 2000
CPRE Council for the Protection of Rural England
CPRW Council for the Protection of Rural Wales
DARD Department of Agriculture (Northern Ireland)
DCAN Development Control Advice Note (Northern Ireland only)
DEFRA Department for Environment, Food and Rural Affairs
DETR Department of Environment, Transport and the Regions
DoE Department of Environment
DoENI Department of Environment Northern Ireland
DWT Durham Wildlife Trust
EU European Union
EN English Nature
ET evapotranspiration
FC Forestry Commission
GIS Geographical Information System
IDB Internal Drainage Board
IDO Interim Development Order
HLF Heritage Lottery Fund
HSE Health and Safety Executive
JNCC Joint Nature Conservation Council
LUCT Lower Ure Conservation Trust
MAFF Ministry of Agriculture, Fisheries and Food
MKPT Milton Keynes Park Trust
MLP Mineral Local Plan (England and Wales only)
MOD Ministry of Defence
MPA Mineral Planning Authority
MPG Mineral Planning Guidance (England and Wales only)
NCC Nature Conservancy Council
NGO Non-governmental organisation
NNR National Nature Reserve
NPPG National Planning Policy Guidelines (Scotland only)
NVC National Vegetation Classification
OCCS Opencast coal site
OS Ordnance Survey
PAN Planning Advice Notes (Scotland only)
PPG Planning Policy Guidance (England and Wales only)
PPS Planning Policy Statement (Northern Ireland only)
PPZ peat production zone
QPA Quarry Products Association
ROMP Review of Old Mineral Permissions
RPG Regional Planning Guidance
RSPB The Royal Society for the Protection of Birds
RTPI Royal Town Planning Institute
SAC Special Area of Conservation
SAM Scheduled Ancient Monument
SEERAD Scottish Executive Environment and Rural Affairs Department
SEPA Scottish Environmental Protection Agency
SNH Scottish Natural Heritage
SAP Species Action Plan
SPA Special Protection Area
SSSI Site of Special Scientific Interest
WeBS Wetland Bird Survey
WGS Woodland Grant Scheme
WFD Water Framework Directive
WWT Wildfowl & Wetlands Trust

Appendix 3 Scientific names of species mentioned in the text

Plants

Adder's-tongue spearwort	*Ranunculus ophioglossifolius*
Agrimony	*Agrimonia eupatoria*
Alder (common)	*Alnus glutinosa*
Alder buckthorn	*Frangula alnus*
Ash	*Fraxinus excelsior*
Autumn hawk	*Leontodon autumnalis*
Baltic stonewort	*Chara baltica*
Bearded stonewort	*Chara canescens*
Beech	*Fagus sylvatica*
Bee orchid	*Ophrys apifera*
Bell heather	*Erica cinerea*
Betony	*Stachys officinalis*
Bilberry	*Vaccinium myrtillus*
Birch	*Betula spp*
Bird's-eye primrose	*Primula farinosa*
Bird's-foot trefoil	*Lotus corniculatus*
Bird's-nest stonewort	*Tolypella nidifica*
Black bryony	*Tamus communis*
Black medick	*Medicago lupulina*
Black poplar	*Populus nigra*
Blackthorn	*Prunus spinosa*
Bluebell	*Hyacinthoides non-scripta*
Blue sesleria (blue moor-grass)	*Sesleria caerulea*
Bogbean	*Menyanthes trifoliata*
Bog rosemary	*Andromeda polifolia*
Bracken	*Pteridium aquilinum*
Bramble spp	*Rubus spp*
Bristol rockcress	*Arabis scabra*
Bristle-leaved bent	*Agrostis setacea*
Broad-leaved cudweed	*Filago pyramidata*
Broad-leaved dock	*Rumex obtusifolius*
Broad-leaved pondweed	*Potamogeton natans*
Broad-leaved spurge	*Euphorbia platyphyllos*
Broom spp	*Cytisus spp*
Buckthorn	*Rhamnus catharticus*
Bugle	*Ajuga reptans*
Bulbous buttercup	*Ranunculus bulbosus*
Burnet saxifrage	*Pimpinella saxifraga*
Burnt-tip orchid	*Orchis ustulata*
Bur-reed (branched)	*Sparganium erectum*
Bush vetch	*Vicia sepium*
Canadian goldenrod	*Solidago canadensis*
Carline thistle	*Carlina vulgaris*
Cat's-ear	*Hypochoeris radicata*
Chewings fescue	*Festuca rubra ssp commutata*
Cocksfoot	*Dactylis glomerata*
Common bent	*Agrostis capillaris*
Common dog-violet	*Viola riviniana*
Common fiddleneck	*Amsinkia micrantha*
Common knapweed	*Centaurea nigra*
Common mouse-ear	*Cerastium alpinum*
Common sorrel	*Rumex acetosa*
Common reed	*Phragmites australis*
Common rock-rose	*Helianthemum nummularium*
Corn buttercup (corn crowfoot)	*Ranunculus arvensis*
Cornflower	*Centaurea cyanus*
Corn gromwell	*Buglossoides arvensis*
Corn marigold	*Chrysanthemum segetum*
Corn parsley	*Petroselinum segetum*
Cotton-grass	*Eriophorum angustifolium*
Cowbane	*Cicuta virosa*
Cow parsley	*Anthriscus sylvestris*
Cowslip	*Primula veris*
Crane's-bill	*Geranium spp*
Creeping bent	*Agrostis stolonifera*
Creeping buttercup	*Ranunculus repens*
Creeping cinquefoil	*Potentilla reptans*
Crested dog's-tail	*Cynosurus cristatus*
Crested hair-grass	*Koeleria macrantha*
Cross-leaved heath	*Erica tetralix*
Cuckoo flower (lady's smock)	*Cardamine pratensis*
Cut-leaved germander	*Teucrium botrys*
Dark red helleborine	*Epipactis atrorubens*
Deptford pink	*Dianthus armeria*
Devil's-bit scabious	*Succisa pratensis*
Dog's mercury	*Mercurialis perennis*
Dog rose	*Rosa canina*
Dogwood	*Cornus sanguinea*
Dwarf sedge	*Carex humilis*
Early gentian	*Gentianella anglica*
Early hair-grass	*Aira praecox*
Early spider orchid	*Ophrys sphegodes*
Elder (common)	*Sambucus nigra*
Enchanter's nightshade	*Circaea lutetiana*
English sandwort	*Arenaria norvegica anglica*
Erect brome (upright brome)	*Bromus erectus*
False brome	*Brachypodium sylvaticum*
False oat-grass	*Arrhenatherum elatius*
Field maple	*Acer campestre*
Field scabious	*Knautia arvensis*
Flattened meadow-grass	*Poa compressa*
Fluellen	*Kickxia spp*
Fly orchid	*Ophrys muscifera*
Floating water-plantain	*Luronium natans*

Foxglove	*Digitalis purpurea*
Foxtail stonewort	*Lamprothamnium papulosum*
Frogbit	*Hydrocharis morsus-ranae*
Frog orchid	*Coeloglossum viride*
Garlic mustard	*Alliaria petiolata*
Gentians	*Gentianella spp*
Glabrous rupturewort	*Herniaria glabra*
Goat's-beard	*Tragopogon pratensis*
Gorse	*Ulex spp*
Grass-poly	*Lythrum hyssopifolia*
Grasswrack pondweed	*Potamogeton compressus*
Great burnet	*Sanguisorba officinalis*
Greater bird's-foot trefoil	*Lotus uliginosus*
Greater bladderwort	*Utricularia vulgaris*
Greater stitchwort	*Stellaria holostea*
Greater tussock sedge	*Carex paniculata*
Greater water-parsnip	*Sium latifolium*
Great spearwort	*Ranunculus lingua*
Great sundew	*Drosera anglica*
Ground-pine	*Ajuga chamaepitys*
Guelder-rose	*Viburnum opulus*
Hairy oat-grass	*Helictotrichon pubescens*
Hairy St John's-wort	*Hypericum hirsutum*
Hoary willow-herb	*Epilobium parviflorum*
Hard fescue	*Festuca longifolia*
Hare's-foot clover	*Trifolium arvense*
Hawthorn	*Crataegus monogyna*
Hazel	*Corylus avellana*
Heath bedstraw	*Galium saxatile*
Heath rush	*Juncus squarrosus*
Heather	*Calluna vulgaris*
Hedge bedstraw	*Galium mollugo*
Hedge mustard	*Sisymbrium officinale*
Hedge woundwort	*Stachys sylvatica*
Hemp-agrimony	*Eupatorium cannabinum*
Hoary plantain	*Plantago media*
Hogweed	*Heracleum sphondylium*
Holly	*Ilex aquifolium*
Hop	*Humulus lupulus*
Hornbeam	*Carpinus betulas*
Hornwort spp	*Ceratophyllum spp*
Horseshoe vetch	*Hippocrepis comosa*
Ivy-leaved duckweed	*Lemna trisulca*
Jacob's ladder	*Polemonium caeruleum*
Juniper	*Juniperus communis*
Kidney vetch	*Anthyllis vulneraria*
Lady's bedstraw	*Galium verum*
Lesser reedmace	*Typha angustifolia*
Lesser spearwort	*Ranunculus flammula*
Lesser trefoil	*Trifolium dubium*
Lesser water-plantain	*Baldellia ranunculoides*
Lords and ladies	*Arum maculatum*
Man orchid	*Aceras anthropophorum*
Marsh foxtail	*Alopecurus geniculatus*
Marsh marigold	*Caltha palustris*
Mat-grass	*Nardus stricta*
Meadow oat-grass	*Helictotrichon pratense*
Meadowsweet	*Filipendula ulmaria*
Meadow barley	*Hordeum secalinum*
Meadow buttercup	*Ranunculus acris*
Meadow crane's-bill	*Geranium pratense*
Meadow fescue	*Festuca pratensis*
Meadow foxtail	*Alopecurus pratensis*
Meadow saxifrage	*Saxifraga granulata*
Meadow thistle	*Cirsium dissectum*
Meadow vetchling	*Lathyrus pratensis*
Military orchid	*Orchis militaris*
Mouse-ear hawkweed	*Hieracium pilosella*
Mudwort	*Limosella aquatica*
Musk-mallow	*Malva moschata*
Narrow-leaved cudweed	*Filago gallica*
Narrow-fruited corn salad	*Valerianella dentata*
New Zealand pigmy-weed	*Crassula helmsii*
Oak spp	*Quercus spp*
Oxeye daisy	*Leucanthemum vulgare*
Pasque flower	*Pulsatilla vulgaris*
Pennyroyal	*Mentha pulegium*
Pepper saxifrage	*Silaum silaus*
Perfoliate pennycress	*Thlaspi perfoliatum*
Perforate St John's-wort	*Hypericum perforatum*
Pheasant's eye	*Adonis annua*
Pignut	*Conopodium majus*
Pillwort	*Pilularia globulifera*
Pond sedge	*Carex spp*
Poplar spp	*Populus spp*
Poppy (common)	*Papaver rhoeas*
Prickly sedge	*Carex muricata ssp muricata*
Primrose	*Primula vulgaris*
Privet	*Ligustrum vulgare*
Purple moor-grass	*Molinia caerulea*
Purple ramping fumitory	*Fumaria purpurea*
Quaking-grass (common)	*Briza media*
Ragged robin	*Lychnis flos-cuculi*
Ramsons (wild garlic)	*Allium ursinum*
Red campion	*Silene dioica*
Red fescue	*Festuca rubra*
Red-tipped cudweed	*Filago lutescens*
Reedmace (bulrush)	*Typha latifolia*
Reed sweet-grass	*Glyceria maxima*
Rest-harrow (common)	*Ononis repens*
Ribbon-leaved water-plantain	*Alisma graminea*
Ribwort plantain	*Plantago lanceolata*
Rosebay willowherb	*Chamerion angustifolium*
Rough hawkbit	*Leontodon hispidus*
Rough meadow-grass	*Poa trivialis*
Rushes	*Juncus spp*
Rye grass (perennial)	*Lolium perenne*
Salad burnet	*Sanguisorba officinalis*
Scots pine	*Pinus sylvestris*
Sedges	*Carex spp*

Self-heal	*Prunella vulgaris*
Sharp-flowered rush	*Juncus acutiflorus*
Sheep's fescue	*Festuca ovina*
Sheep's sorrel	*Rumex acetosella*
Silverweed	*Potentilla anserina*
Small-flowered catchfly	*Silene gallica*
Small scabious	*Scabiosa columbaria*
Smooth brome	*Bromus racemosus*
Smooth cat's-ear	*Hypochoeris glabra*
Smooth meadow-grass	*Poa pratensis*
Snake's-head fritillary	*Fritillaria meleagris*
Sphagnum	*Sphagnum spp*
Soft brome	*Bromus mollis*
Soft rush	*Juncus effusus*
Spiked speedwell	*Veronica spicata (ssp hybrida)*
Spindle-tree	*Euonymus europaeus*
Spiny rest-harrow	*Ononis spinosa (campestris)*
Spring gentian	*Gentiana verna*
Starfruit	*Damasonium alisma*
Stinging nettle	*Urtica dioica*
Strapwort	*Corrigiola litoralis*
Stoneworts	*Charophyte spp*
Stork's-bill (common)	*Erodium cicutarium*
Sweet vernal grass	*Anthoxanthum odoratum*
Sweet violet	*Viola odorata*
Tasselweeds	*Ruppia spp*
Thistles	*Carduus and Cirsium spp*
Thyme	*Thymus spp*
Timothy	*Phleum pratense*
Toad rush	*Juncus bufonius*
Tor grass	*Brachypodium pinnatum*
Tormentil	*Potentilla erecta*
Tower mustard	*Arabis glabra*
Tufted hair-grass	*Deschampsia caespitosa*
Tufted vetch	*Vicia cracca*
Upright hedge-parsley	*Torilis japonica*
Violet spp	*Viola spp*
Water crowfoot	*Ranunculus spp*
Water fern	*Azolla filiculoides*
Water lilies	*Nyphaea spp and Nuphar spp*
Water milfoil	*Myriopyllum spp*
Wayfaring tree	*Viburnum lantana*
Wavy hair-grass	*Deschampsia flexuosa*
Wavy St John's-wort	*Hypericum undulatum*
White clover	*Trifolium repens*
White willow	*Salix alba*
Whorled caraway	*Carum verticillatum*
Wild carrot	*Daucus carota*
Wild chamomile	*Chamaemelum nobile*
Wild cherry	*Prunus avium*
Wild strawberry	*Fragaria vesca*
Willow spp	*Salix spp*
Wood anemone	*Anemone nemorosa*
Wood avens (Herb Bennet)	*Geum urbanum*
Wood millet	*Milium effusum*
Woodruff	*Galium odoratum*
Wood sage	*Teucrium scorodonia*
Wood sorrel	*Oxalis acetosella*
Woody nightshade (bittersweet)	*Solanum dulcamara*
Woolly willow	*Salix lanata*
Yarrow	*Achillea millefolium*
Yellow archangel	*Lamiastrum galeobdolon*
Yellow iris	*Iris pseudacorus*
Yellow oat-grass	*Trisetum flavescens*
Yellow rattle	*Rhinanthus minor*
Yorkshire fog	*Holcus lanatus*

Invertebrates

Insects

Damselflies and dragonflies	***Odonata***
Azure damselfly	*Coenagrion puella*
Black-tailed skimmer	*Orthetrum cancellatum*
Common blue damselfly	*Enallagma cyathigerum*
Common darter	*Sympetrum striolatum*
Emerald damselfly	*Lestes sponsa*
Emperor dragonfly	*Anax imperator*
Four-spotted chaser	*Libellula quadrimaculata*
Hairy dragonfly	*Brachytron pratense*
Keeled skimmer	*Orthetrum coerulescens*
Norfolk hawker	*Aeshna isosceles*
Red-eyed damselfly	*Erythromma najas*
Ruddy darter	*Sympetrum sanguineum*
Scarce blue-tailed damselfly	*Ischnura pumilio*
Scarce chaser	*Libellula fulva*
Scarce emerald damselfly	*Lestes dryas*
Variable damselfly	*Coenagrion pulchellum*
White-faced darter	*Leucorrhinia dubia*

Stoneflies	***Plecoptera***
Water boatmen	*Hempitera (Corixidae)*

Beetles	***Coleoptera***
(a) beetle	*Helophorus longitarsus*
(a) ground beetle	*Bembidion humerale*
Predatory ground beetles	*Bembidion spp*
Riffle beetles	*Elmidae*
Tiger beetles	*Cicindelidae*
Water beetles	*Dytiscidae*
Great silver water beetle	*Hydrophilus piceus*

True flies	***Diptera***
(a) hoverfly	*Lejops vittata*
(a) soldierfly	*Odontomyia argentata*
(a) soldierfly	*Odontomyia ornata*

Butterflies	***Lepidoptera***
Adonis blue	*Lysandra bellargus*

Brimstone	*Gonepteryx rhamni*
Common blue	*Polyommatus icarus*
Durham brown argus	*Aricia artaxerxes salmacis*
Grayling	*Hipparchia semele*
Grizzled skipper	*Pyrgus malvae*
Large blue	*Maculinea arion*
Large heath	*Coenonympha tullia*
Marsh fritillary	*Euphydryas aurinia*
Northern brown argus	*Aricia artaxerxes*
Orange tip	*Anthocharis cardamines*
Pearl-bordered fritillary	*Boloria euphrosyne*
Silver-studded blue	*Plebejus argus*
Small blue	*Cupido minimus*

Moths ***Lepidoptera***

Fenn's wainscot moth	*Photedes brevilinea*
Narrow-bordered bee hawk moth	*Hemaris tityus*
Small eggar moth	*Eriogaster lanestris*
Reed leopard moth	*Phragmataeica castanea*
Caddis-flies	*Trichoptera*
Wasps	*Hymenoptera*

Other invertebrates

Fairy shrimp	*Chirocephalus diaphanus*
Ivell's sea anemone	*Edwardsia ivelli*
Lagoon cockle	*Cerastoderma glaucum*
Lagoon sand-shrimp	*Gammarus insensibilis*
Lagoon sandworm	*Armandia cirrhosa*
Lagoon sea slug	*Tenellia adspersa*
Lagoon winkle	*Littorina tenebrosa*
Medicinal leech	*Hirudo medicinalis*
Mire pill beetle	*Curimopsis nigrita*
Shining ramshorn snail (a) mollusc	*Segmentina nitida*
Pea mussel	*Pisidium tenuilineatum*
Starlet sea anemone	*Nematosella vectensis*
Tadpole shrimp	*Triops cancriformis*
Tentacled lagoon-worm	*Alkmaria romijni*
Trembling sea-mat	*Victorella pavida*
White-clawed crayfish	*Austropotamobius pallipes*
Wolf spiders	*Lycosidae*

Amphibians and reptiles

Adder	*Vipera berus*
Common frog	*Rana temporaria*
Common lizard	*Lacerta vivipara*
Common toad	*Bufo bufo*
Grass snake	*Natrix natrix*
Great crested newt	*Triturus cristatus*
Marsh frog	*Rana ridibunda*
Natterjack toad	*Bufo calamita*
Palmate newt	*Triturus helveticus*
Slow worm	*Anguis fragilis*
Smooth snake	*Coronella austriaca*
Smooth newt	*Triturus vulgaris*
Sand lizard	*Lacerta agilis*

Fish

Atlantic salmon	*Salmo salar*
Bream	*Abramis brama*
Eel	*Anguilla anguilla*
Perch	*Perca fluviatilis*
Pike	*Esox lucius*
Roach	*Rutilus rutilus*
Rudd	*Scardinius erythrophthalmus*
Spined loach	*Cobitis taenea*
Stone loach	*Nemacheilus barbatula*
Tench	*Tinca tinca*
Trout	*Salmo trutta*

Mammals

American mink	*Mustela vison*
Barbastelle	*Barbastella barbastellus*
Brown hare	*Lepus europaeus*
Brown long-eared bat	*Plecotus auritus*
Shrew (common)	*Sorex araneus*
Daubenton's bat	*Myotis daubentonii*
Field vole	*Microtus agrestis*
Hazel dormouse	*Muscardinus avellanarius*
Harverst mouse	*Micromys minutus*
Greater horseshoe bat	*Rhinolophus ferrumequinum*
Grey long-eared bat	*Plecotus austriacus*
Harvest mouse	*Micromys minutus*
Lesser horseshoe bat	*Rhinolophus hipposideros*
Natterer's bat	*Myotis nattereri*
Otter	*Lutra lutra*
Pine marten	*Martes martes*
Pipistrelle	*Pipistrellus pipistrellus*
Red squirrel	*Sciurus vulgaris*
Water shrew	*Neomys fodiens*
Water vole	*Arvicola terrestris*
Wild cat	*Felis sylvestris*

Birds

Aquatic warbler	*Acrocephalus paludicola*
Avocet	*Recurvirostra avocetta*
Barn owl	*Tyto alba*
Bearded tit	*Panurus biarmicus*
Bewick's swan	*Cygnus columbianus*
Bittern	*Botaurus stellaris*
Blackcap	*Sylvia atricapilla*
Black grouse	*Tetrao tetrix*
Black-headed gull	*Larus ridibundus*
Black-tailed godwit	*Limosa limosa*
Cetti's warbler	*Cettia cetti*
Chough	*Pyrrhocorax pyrrhocorax*

Cirl bunting	*Emberiza cirlus*
Common tern	*Sterna hirundo*
Coot	*Fulica atra*
Curlew	*Numenius arquata*
Dartford warbler	*Sylvia undata*
Fulmar	*Fulmarus glacialis*
Gadwall	*Anas strepera*
Garden warbler	*Sylvia borin*
Garganey	*Anas querquedula*
Goldeneye	*Bucephala clangula*
Golden plover	*Pluvialis apricaria*
Grasshopper warbler	*Locustella naevia*
Great crested grebe	*Podiceps cristatus*
Great spotted woodpecker	*Dendrocopos major*
Greenland white-fronted goose	*Anser albifrons flavirostris*
Greenshank	*Tringa nebularia*
Grey partridge	*Perdix perdix*
Grey plover	*Pluvialis squatarola*
Hawfinch	*Coccothraustes coccothraustes*
Hen harrier	*Circus cyaneus*
Jack snipe	*Lymnocryptes minimus*
Kingfisher	*Alcedo atthis*
Lapwing	*Vanellus vanellus*
Lesser spotted woodpecker	*Dendrocopos minor*
Linnet	*Acanthis cannabina*
Little ringed plover	*Charadrius dubius*
Little tern	*Sterna albifrons*
Mallard	*Anas platyrhynchos*
Marsh harrier	*Circus aeruginosus*
Marsh tit	*Parus palustris*
Mediterranean gull	*Larus melanocephalus*
Merlin	*Falco columbarius*
Montagu's harrier	*Circus pygargus*
Nightingale	*Luscinia megarhynchos*
Nightjar	*Caprimulgus europaeus*
Nuthatch	*Sitta europaea*
Oystercatcher	*Haematopus ostralegus*
Peregrine	*Falco peregrinus*
Pintail	*Anas acuta*
Pochard	*Aythya ferina*
Raven	*Corvus corax*
Red grouse	*Lagopus lagopus*
Redshank	*Tringa totanus*
Reed bunting	*Emberiza schoeniclus*
Ringed plover	*Charadrius hiaticula*
Ruff	*Philomachus pugnax*
Sand martin	*Riparia riparia*
Savi's warbler	*Locustella luscinoides*
Sedge warbler	*Acrocephalus schoenobaerius*
Short-eared owl	*Asio flammeus*
Shoveler	*Anas clypeata*
Skylark	*Alauda arvensis*
Snipe	*Gallinago gallinago*
Sparrowhawk	*Accipiter nisus*
Spotted flycatcher	*Muscicapa striata*
Stone-curlew	*Burhinus oedicnemus*
Tawny owl	*Strix aluco*
Teal	*Anas crecca*
Treecreeper	*Certhia familiaris*
Tree pipit	*Anthus trivialis*
Tree sparrow	*Passer montanus*
Tufted duck	*Aythya fuligula*
Turtle dove	*Steptopelia turtur*
Water rail	*Rallus aquaticus*
Whinchat	*Saxicola rubetra*
Whitethroat	*Sylvia communis*
Whooper swan	*Cygnus cygnus*
Wigeon	*Anas penelope*
Woodlark	*Lullula arborea*
Yellowhammer	*Emberiza citrinella*
Yellow wagtail	*Motacilla flava*

Appendix 4 Biodiversity Action Plan species which could potentially benefit from mineral workings in England

(after Bate *et al*, 1998)

Species	BAP list	Habitat requirements and distribution
Mammals		
Water vole	Short	Vertical banks associated with open water, lakes, ponds, rivers, streams and drainage channels, with plenty of emergent vegetation.
Otter	Short	Wetlands with good water quality and high fish biomass.
Brown hare	Short	Open farmland. Widespread.
Red squirrel	Short	Broadleaved and coniferous woodland (now restricted to the north of England and Northern Ireland).
Greater horseshoe bat	Short	Roosts in caves, mines and buildings. Restricted to SW England and S Wales.
Pipistrelle	Short	Widespread.
Daubenton's bat	Long	Hibernates in caves and mines, often feeds over open water.
Brown long-eared bat	Long	Roosts in houses, hibernates in underground sites.
Grey long-eared bat	Long	Similar to brown long-eared bat. Restricted to SW England.
Lesser horseshoe bat	Long	Associated predominately with large old buildings. Restricted to Wales and SW England.
Birds		
Aquatic warbler	Short	Autumn migrant to wetland sites along the south coast from Kent to Cornwall.
Skylark	Short	Associated with open farmland (resident).
Bittern	Short	Reedbeds. Breeding birds confined to few known sites in East Anglia and Lancashire (resident).
Grey partridge	Short	Lowland farmland, associated with grassy hedge banks and cereal field margins (resident).
Woodlark	Middle	Heathland and Breckland. Restricted southerly distribution to a number of discrete heathland areas (resident/summer visitor).
Turtle dove	Middle	Lowland bird, feeding on open farmland. Associated with S and SE England (summer visitor).
Sparrowhawk	Long	Breeds in woodland and scrub – distributed throughout England (resident).
Peregrine	Long	Breeds on cliffs, buildings and in quarries.
Chough	Long	Breeds on cliffs in the west of the British Isles in close proximity to grasslands and heaths.
Kingfisher	Long	Feeds in shallow and slow-moving freshwater. Nests in burrows in sandy/muddy steep banks (resident).
Great spotted woodpecker	Long	Prefers mature broadleaved woodland, but also found in plantation woodland. Distributed throughout country (resident).
Lesser spotted woodpecker	Long	Almost exclusively associated with broadleaved woodland. Restricted to Wales, S and W England and Midlands (resident).

Continued overleaf ▸▸▸

▸▸▸

Sand martin	Long	Nests communally in sandy banks and gravel pits (summer visitor).
Tawny owl	Long	Woodland bird, also nesting in trees in farmland and gardens (resident).
Pintail, shoveler, teal, wigeon, mallard, garganey, gadwall, tufted duck and goldeneye	Long	Open waters with good marginal habitat. Breeding species.
jack snipe, greenshank and redshank	Long	Wetland, waterbody margins. Breeding species.
Amphibians and reptiles		
Great crested newt	Short	Aquatic habitats for breeding preferring still, slow-flowing with good weed growth. Terrestrial outside breeding season.
Palmate newt	Long	Variety of still, shallow waterbodies including ponds, heath and woodland pools. Prefers clear, acid water.
Smooth newt	Long	Variety of damp habitats. Breeds in still, shallow water (ponds, ditches etc).
Sand lizard	Short	Restricted to coastal sand dunes and sandy heaths.
Common toad	Long	Variety of often fairly dry habitats.
Common frog	Long	Wide range, largely terrestrial occurring in damp areas. Found in waterbodies during breeding.
Slow worm	Long	Pastures, heather and hedge banks.
Grass snake	Long	Found in damp places, swims well and may hunt in waterbodies.
Invertebrates		
Pearl-bordered fritillary	Short	Woodland clearings in England and Wales, more common in south.
Northern brown argus (Durham brown argus)	Long	Rough, grassy banks and hillsides. (Southern race occurs from Derbyshire to Scottish Border.)
Silver-studded blue	Middle	Heathland, also occurs on chalk/limestone grassland.
Adonis blue	Middle	Restricted to S England chalk and limestone hills and lowlands.
Small blue	Long	Chalk/limestone grassland.
Large blue	Short	Reintroduced species – rough southern grassland, with wild thyme and Myrmica ants.
Medicinal leech	Short	Muddy ponds, poached edges.
Starlet sea anemone	Short	Saline lagoons
Ivell's sea anemone	Short	Saline lagoons, extinct
Scarse chaser	Long	River floodplains, water meadows and occasionally gravel pits. Preference for nutrient-rich backwaters with prolific emergent vegetation.
Vascular plants		
Ground-pine	Long	Known from small scale abandoned chalk quarry workings in N Kent.
Ribbon-leaved water-plantain	Short	Shallow water/eutrophic. Main site is an artificial lake. Very rare.
Tower mustard	Middle	Dry, grassy, rocky and waste places. Decreasing in England only.

Continued overleaf ▸▸▸

▸▸▸

Bristol rockcress	Long	Limestone rocks near Bristol. Very rare.
English sandwort	Long	Bare limestone, Yorkshire. Very rare.
Dwarf sedge Very common.	Long	Short turf in species-rich limestone/chalk grassland.
Prickly sedge	Middle	Very rare on steel dry limestone slopes.
Wild chamomile England.	Long	Short grassy places on sandy soils. Central/southern
Deptford pink disturbed places.	Middle	Rare on gravel pits and banks and other open and Southern.
Narrow-leaved cudweed	Long	Sandy and gravelly ground. Introduced. Now extinct except Sark (formerly England).
Red-tipped cudweed England.	Middle	Bare sandy places. Very local and decreasing in S and E
Broad-leaved cudweed	Middle	Rare on sandy soils in S England. Present in bottoms of worked out chalk pits.
Purple ramping fumitory	Middle	Rare in waste places and other artificial habitats. Scattered but western endemic.
Early gentian	Short	Successfully colonised some small scale chalk and limestone quarries in Lincs and Glos.
Spring gentian	Long	Stony, grassy places on limestone. N England – very local.
Glabrous rupturewort	Long	Dry, sandy places, very localised and decreasing, East Anglia.
Smooth cat's-ear	Long	Grassy/open ground on sandy soils. Decreasing.
Floating water-plantain	Short	Acidic, oligotrophic lakes, (2 m of mud), sometimes mesotrophic. NW distribution.
Early spider orchid	Long	Grassland or spoil heaps on chalk or limestone – including quarry debris. Local, southern.
Military orchid	Long	Chalk grassland/old chalk pit with invading trees and shrubs. Very rare (four sites in Bucks and Suffolk).
Burnt-tip orchid	Long	Short grassland on chalk and limestone. Rare and local.
Pillwort	Long	Silty or gravelly mud by lakes, ponds, reservoirs. Submerged for at least part of year. On acid soil, including clay/gravel pits (especially new).
Jacob's ladder	Long	Very localised (Peak District, Yorkshire Dales) on limestone grassland, scree and rock ledges.
Grasswrack pondweed	Middle	Calcareous/mesotrophic water. Recorded from a few flooded clay and gravel pits. Rare.
Small-flowered catchfly	Middle	Waste, open, cultivated places on sandy and gravelly soil. Local and often casual.
Cut-leaved germander	Short	Chalky fields/open habitats in chalk grassland. Very rare. Southern.
Perfoliate pennycress (Cotswold pennycress)	Middle	Limestone spoil/bare, stony limestone in Wilts, Oxon, Glos, casual elsewhere. Known from quarry sites.
Spiked speedwell	Long	Limestone rocks in few scattered localities.

Appendix 5 Useful addresses

The Charity Commission
London Office: Harmsworth House, 13–15 Bouverie Street, London EC4Y 8DP Tel: 0870 333 0123 www.charity-commision.gov.uk

National Council for Voluntary Organisations
Regent's Wharf, 8 All Saints Street, London N1 9RL Tel: 020 7713 6161 www.ncvo-vol.org.uk

Countryside Agency
John Dower House, Crescent Place, Cheltenham, Gloucestershire GL50 3RA Tel: 01242 521381 www.countryside.gov.uk

Groundwork UK
85–87 Cornwall Street, Birmingham B3 3BY Tel: 0121 236 8565 www.groundwork.org.uk

The Bat Conservation Trust
15 Cloisters House, 8 Battersea Park Road, London SW8 4BG Tel: 020 7627 2629 www.bats.org.uk

The Community Forest Unit
c/o Countryside Agency, John Dower House, Crescent Place, Cheltenham, Gloucestershire GL50 3RA Tel: 01242 521381

Forestry Commission
www.forestry.gov.uk
National Office for England: Great Eastern House, Tenison Road, Cambridge CB1 2DU Tel: 01223 314546
National Office for Scotland:
231 Corstophine Road, Edinburgh EH12 7AT
Tel: 0131 334 0303
National Office for Wales: Victoria Terrace, Aberystwyth, Ceredigion SY23 2DQ Tel: 01970 625866

The Woodland Trust
Autumn Park, Grantham, Lincolnshire NG31 6LL Tel: 01476 581111 www.woodland-trust.org.uk

The RSPB
UK Headquarters, The Lodge, Sandy, Bedfordshire SG19 2DL Tel: 01767 680551 www.rspb.org.uk

The Wildlife Trusts
The Kiln, Waterside, Mather Road, Newark, Nottinghamshire NG24 1WT Tel: 0870 036 7711 www.wildlifetrusts.org

Wildfowl and Wetland Trust
Slimbridge, Gloucestershire GL2 7BT
Tel: 01453 891900 www.wwt.org.uk

The Game Conservancy Trust Fordingbridge, Hampshire SP6 1EF
Tel: 01425 652381 www.gtc.org.uk

Environment Agency
Rio House, Waterside Drive, Aztec West, Almondsbury, Bristol BS32 4UD
Tel: 0845 933 3111 www.environment-agency.gov.uk

British Trust for Conservation Volunteers
36 St Mary's Street, Wallingford, Oxfordshire OX1 0EU
Tel: 01491 821600 www.btcv.org

The Amateur Entomologists' Society
PO Box 8774, London SW7 5ZG www.theaes.org

British Entomological and Natural History Society
The Pelham-Clinton Building, Dinton Pastures country Park, Davis Street, Hurst, Reading, Berkshire RG10 0TH www.benhs.org.uk

British Dragonfly Society
The Secretary, The Ahywain, Hollywater Road, Borden, Hants GU35 0AD www.dragonflysoc.org.uk

Butterfly Conservation
Manor Year, East Lolworth Road, Nr Wareham, Dorset BH20 5QP Tel: 01929 400209 www.butterfly-conservation.org

The British Herpetological Society
c/o The Zoological Society of London, Regents Park, London NW1 4RY www.thebhs.org

English Nature
Northminster House, Peterborough PE1 1UA
Tel: 01733 455000 www.english-nature.org.uk

Scottish Natural Heritage
12 Hope Terrace, Edinburgh EH9 2AS
Tel: 0131 447 4784 www.snh.org.uk

Countryside Council for Wales
Maes-y-Ffynnon, Penrhosgarnedd, Bangor, Gwynedd LL57 2DN Tel: 0845 130 6229 www.ccw.gov.uk

Bibliography and references

Agate, E (1986) *Fencing: a practical conservation handbook.* BTCV, Wallingford.

Allen, R B and Wilson, J B (1991) A method for determining indigenous vegetation from simple environmental factors, and its use for vegetation restoration. *Biological Conservation* 56: 265-280.

Allen, S E (1989) *Chemical analysis of ecological materials.* Second Edition. Blackwell Scientific, Oxford.

Allen, S E, Grimshaw, H M, Parkinson, J A B and Quarmby, C (1974) *Chemical analysis of ecological materials.* Blackwell Scientific Publications, Oxford.

Anderson, P (1994) *Flower-rich grassland creation.* Enact 2(3): 21-22.

Anderson, P (1995) Can we see the woodland through the trees? *Journal of Practical Ecology and Conservation* 1(1): 3-6.

Andrews, J (1990) Principles of restoration of gravel pits for wildlife. *British Wildlife* 2(2): 80-88.

Andrews, J (1991) *The creation of wildlife habitats on restored opencast sites.* The RSPB, Sandy.

Andrews, J (1992) The creation of wetlands in opencast restorations. *Opencast Mining* 1992: 45-47.

Andrews, J (1993) The reality and management of wildlife corridors. *British Wildlife* 5(1): 1-7.

Andrews, J and Etherington, J R (1989) *Wildlife restoration on opencast sites in South Wales. Some practical constraints and proposals for management and experiment.* The RSPB, Sandy.

Andrews, J and Kinsman, D (1990) *Gravel pit restoration for wildlife. A practical manual.* The RSPB, Sandy.

Andrews, J, Kinsman, D and Tyler, S (1992) Opencast operations in the South Wales Coalfield. *RSPB Conservation Review* 6: 74-78.

Andrews, J and Rebane, M (1994) *Farming and wildlife: a practical handbook for the management, restoration and creation of wildlife habitats on farmland.* The RSPB, Sandy.

Andrews, J and Ward, D (1991) The management and creation of reedbeds – especially for rare birds. *British Wildlife* 3(1): 81-91.

Ash, H J, Bennett, R and Scott, R (1990) *Flowers in the grass: creating and managing grassland with wildflower.* English Nature, Peterborough.

Atkinson, M D, Trueman, I C, Millett, P, Jones, G H and Besenyei, L (1995) The use of hay strewing to create species-rich grasslands. (ii) Monitoring the vegetation and the seed bank. *Land Contamination and Reclamation* 3(2): 108-110.

Auld, M, Davies, S and Pickess, B (1992) Restoration of lowland heathland in Dorset. *RSPB Conservation Review* 6: 68-73.

Backshall J, Manley J and Rebane M (eds) (1998) *The upland management handbook.* English Nature, Peterborough.

Bamber, R N, Batten, S D and Bridgwater, N D (1993) Design criteria for the creation of brackish lagoons. *Biodiversity and Conservation* 2: 127-137.

Bamber, R N, Batten, S D, Sheader, M and Bridgwater, N D (1992) On the ecology of brackish lagoons in Great Britain. *Aquatic Conservation: marine and freshwater ecosystems* 2: 65-94.

Bamber, R N, Gilliland, P M and Shardlow, M E (2001) *Saline lagoons: a guide to their management and creation.* English Nature, Peterborough.

Banks (1993) *Restoration techniques employed on heathland at Inkerman OCCS.* Report Number BP/SJT CM/N/113. Banks Ltd, Ferryhill.

Bate, R, Bate, J, Bradley, C, Peel, H and Wilkinson, J (1998) *The potential contribution of the mineral extraction industries to the UK Biodiversity Action Plan.* English Nature Research Report No 279. English Nature, Peterborough.

BCC (1993) *Extraction and Restoration. An environmental code for the heavy clay industry.* British Ceramic Confederation, Stoke-on-Trent.

Beaumont, D, O'Brian, M and Flemming, J (2001) *Management of open grazed grassland for birds – RSS prescription.* Information and Advice Note 4. The RSPB, Edinburgh.

Beebee, T and Denton, J (1996) *The natterjack toad conservation handbook.* English Nature, Peterborough.

Bell, M C, Delany, S N, Millett, M C and Pollitt, M S (1997) Wintering waterfowl community structure and the characteristics of gravel pit lakes. *Wildlife Biology* 3(2): 65-78.

Bending, N A D and McRae, S G (1999) *Soil-forming materials: their use in land reclamation.* HMSO, London.

Bennett, A, Watson, D and Hill, D (2001) Water Voles and development – a case study of mitigation techniques. *British Wildlife* 12: 167-172.

Bentham, H, Harris, J A, Birch, P and Short, K C (1992) Habitat classification and soil restoration assessment using analysis of soil microbiological and physico-chemical characteristics. *Journal of Applied Ecology* 29: 711-718.

BGS (1997) *United Kingdom Minerals Yearbook 1996. Statistical data to 1995.* British Geological Survey, Nottingham.

Biggs, J, Corfield, A, Walker, D, Whitfield, M and Williams, P (1994) New approaches to the management of ponds. *British Wildlife* 5: 273-287.

Bisgrove, R and Dixie, G (1994) Wildflowers: plugging the gap. *Enact* 2(1): 18-20.

Boyce, D V M (1995) The creation of damp grassland and wetland on a site restored without topsoil following opencast coal mining. *The Journal of Practical Ecology and Conservation* 1(2): 31-37.

Box, J (1993) Conservation or greening? The challenges of post-industrial landscapes. *British Wildlife* 4(4): 273-279.

Box, J (1995) Improving the quality of the habitat creation process by defining outputs. *Journal of Practical Ecology and Conservation* 1(1): 20-23.

Box, J (1999) Habitat translocation and mineral workings. Mineral Planning 79: 11-14.

Box, J and Hill, A (1999) Mineral extraction and

heathland restoration. *Mineral Planning* 80: 5-8.
Box, J, Mills, J and Coppin, N (1996) Natural legacies: Mineral workings and nature conservation. *Mineral Planning* 68: 24-27.
Bradshaw, A D (1983) The reconstruction of ecosystems. *Journal of Applied Ecology* 20: 1-17.
Bradshaw, A D (1989) Wasteland management and restoration in Western Europe. *Journal of Applied Ecology* 26: 775-786.
Bradshaw, A D and Chadwick, M J (1980) *The restoration of land. The ecology and reclamation of derelict and degraded land*. Studies in Ecology Volume 6. Blackwell Scientific Publications, Oxford.
Bradshaw, A D, Marrs, R H and Roberts, R D (1982) Succession. In B N K Davis (ed) *The ecology of quarries. The importance of natural vegetation*, pp 47-52. Institute for Terrestrial Ecology, Cambridge.
Bratton, J H (1990) Seasonal pools: an overlooked invertebrate habitat. *British Wildlife* 2(1): 22-29.
Bray, R (1997) Design opportunities: amphibians. In R Bray and T Gent (eds) *Opportunities for amphibians and reptiles in the designed landscape*, pp 31-40. English Nature Science Series 30. English Nature, Peterborough.
Brooks, A (1980) *Woodlands: a practical handbook.* BTCV, Wallingford.
Brooks, A (1988) *Hedging: a practical conservation handbook.* BTCV, Wallingford.
Brooks, A and Agate, E (1997) *Waterways and wetlands: a practical conservation handbook.* Third Edition. BTCV, Wallingford.
Brooks, A and Agate, E (1998) *Hedgelaying: A practical handbook.* BTCV, Wallingford.
Brooks, S and Stoneman, R (1997) *Conserving bogs: the management handbook.* HMSO, Edinburgh.
Buckley, G P (1989) *Biological habitat reconstruction.* Bellhaven Press.
Buckley, G P and Knight, D J (1989) The feasibility of woodland reconstruction. In G P Buckley (ed) *Biological Habitat Reconstruction*, pp 171-88. Bellhaven Press.
Bullock, J M (1998) Community translocation in Britain: setting objectives and measuring consequences. *Biological Conservation* 84(3): 199-214.
Burgess, N D and Becker, D (1989) *The creation and management of islands and rafts on RSPB reserves.* Unpublished report. The RSPB, Sandy.
Butt, K R and Frederickson, J (1995) Earthworm cultivation and soil inoculation: a practical technique for land restoration. *Journal of Practical Ecology and Conservation* 1(1): 14-19.
Cadbury, J, Shardlow, M and Buisson, R (2001) Saline lagoons: A scarce habitat of biodiversity importance. *RSPB Conservation Review* 13: 75-84.
CEC (1985) 85/337/EEC. Directive on the assessment of effects of certain public and private projects on the environment. *Official Journal of the European Communities* L175: 40-48.
Chapman, R and Younger, A (1995) The establishment of a species rich hay meadow community in lowland SE Northumberland, England. In L t'Maneetje and J Frame (eds) *Grassland and Society*. Proceedings of the 15th General Meeting of the European Grassland Federation, June 6-9, 1994, Wageningen, Netherlands.
Clarke, C T (1997) Role of soils in determining sites for lowland heathland reconstruction in England. *Restoration Ecology* 5: 256-264.
Cohn, E V J and Millett, P (1995) Problems of the implementation and management of urban woodland habitat creation schemes. *Land Contamination and Reclamation* 3(2): 89-92.
Cohn, E V J and Packham, J R (1993) The introduction and manipulation of woodland field layers: seeds, plants, timing and economics. *Arboricultural Journal* 17(1): 69-83.
Collins, D J (1993) *Heather restoration on opencast coal sites.* 7th ADAS National Land Restoration Seminar, October 1993. ADAS, Wolverhampton.
Collins, D J (1996) Lowland heathland restoration on opencast coal sites in Co Durham. *Aspects of Applied Biology* 44: 345-50.
Collinson, N H, Biggs, J, Corfield, A, Hodson, M J, Walker, D, Whitfield, M and Williams, P J (1995) Temporary and permanent ponds: an assessment of the effects of drying out on the conservation value of aquatic macroinvertebrate communities. *Biological Conservation* 74: 125-133.
Cooper, B (1993) *The purpose and management of grass on mineral extraction sites.* 7th ADAS National Land Restoration Seminar, October 1993. ADAS, Wolverhampton.
Coppin, N J and Bradshaw, A D (1982) *Quarry reclamation. The establishment of vegetation in quarries and open pit non-metal mines.* Mining Journal Books.
Coppin, N J and Box, J D (1998) After-use options for reclaimed land – a land suitability approach. In H R Fox, H M Moore and A D McIntosh *Land reclamation: Achieving sustainable benefits*, pp 351-360. AA Balkema, Rotterdam.
Cordrey, L (1997) *Action plan for biodiversity in the south-west, a series of habitat and species plans to guide delivery*. The RSPB, Exeter.
Countryside Commission (1993) *Opencast coal mining. Advice on landscape and countryside issues.* Countryside Commission, Cheltenham.
Cranfield University (2002) *The water regime requirements and the response to hydrological changeof grassland plant communities.* DEFRA-commissioned project BD1310.
Crofts, A (1991) *Pastures new: how to create and care for wild flower meadows.* RSNC, Lincoln.
Crofts, A and Jefferson, R G (eds) (1999) *The Lowland Grassland Management Handbook.* 2nd Edition. English Nature/The Wildlife Trusts, Peterborough.
Cullen, W C, Wheater, C P and Dunleavy, P J (1998) Establishment of species-rich vegetation on reclaimed limestone quarry faces in Derbyshire, UK. *Biological Conservation* 84: 25-33.
Danell, K and Sjöberg, K (1982) Successional patterns of plants, invertebrates and ducks in a man-made lake. *Journal of Applied Ecology* 19: 395-409.
Davis, B N K (ed) (1982a) *The ecology of quarries. The importance of natural vegetation.* Institute for Terrestrial Ecology, Cambridge.
Davis, B N K (1982b) Regional variation in

quarries. In B N K Davis (ed) *The ecology of quarries. The importance of natural vegetation*, pp 12-19. Institute for Terrestrial Ecology, Cambridge.

Davis, B N K, Lakhani, K H, and Brown, M C (1993) Experiments on the effects of fertilizer and rabbit grazing treatments upon the vegetation of a limestone quarry floor. *Journal of Applied Ecology* 30: 615-628.

DETR (2000) *Effectiveness of provisions for the aftercare of mineral workings*. Department of the Environment, Transport and the Regions, London.

Dixon, J M and Hambler, D J (1994) An experimental approach to the reclamation of a limestone quarry floor. The first three years. *Environmental Conservation* 2(1): 19-28.

Dobson, M C and Moffat, A J (1993) *The potential for woodland establishment on landfill sites*. HMSO, London.

Dodds, G W, Appleby, M J and Campbell, L (1996) *A management guide to birds of upland farmland*. The RSPB, Sandy.

Dodds, G W, Appleby, M J and Evans, A D (1995) *A management guide to birds of lowland farmland*. The RSPB, Sandy.

DoE (1990) *Planning Policy Guidance (PPG) 16: Archaeology and Planning*. HMSO, London.

DoE (1991) *Survey of land used for mineral workings in England*. HMSO, London.

DoE (1992a) *Digest of Environmental Protection and Water Statistics No 15*. HMSO, London.

DoE (1992b) *The UK Environment*. HMSO, London.

DoE (1994) *Digest of Environmental Protection and Water Statistics No 16*. HMSO, London.

DoE/Welsh Office (1989) *Mineral Planning Guidance (MPG) 7: The reclamation of mineral workings*. HMSO, London.

Down, C G (1982) *The re-creation of conservation value in mineral workings. In B N K Davis (ed) The ecology of quarries. The importance of natural vegetation*, pp 62-66. Institute for Terrestrial Ecology, Cambridge.

Drake, C M and Sheppard, D A (1998) *Changes in the fortunes of invertebrates of floodplain habitats. In R G Bailey, P V José and B R Sherwood (eds) United Kingdom Floodplains*, pp 229 - 236. Westbury Academic and Scientific Publishing, Otley.

Dryden, R (1997) *Habitat restoration project: fact sheets and bibliographies*. English Nature Research Report No 260. English Nature, Peterborough.

Duffey, E, Morris, M G, Sheail, J, Ward, L K, Wells, D A and Wells, T C E (1974) *Grassland ecology and wildlife management*. Chapman and Hall, London.

Dunbar, D (1994) *Saving butterflies: a practical guide to the conservation of butterflies*. Butterfly Conservation.

EAU (1988) *Heathland restoration: a handbook of techniques*. British Gas, Southampton.

Elliot, T and Port, C (undated) *Moorland restoration on opencast coal sites*. Unpublished conference/seminar speech. ADAS, Newcastle upon Tyne.

Emery, M (1986) *Promoting nature in towns and cities*. Croom Helm, London.

English Nature (1994) *Facts about great crested newts*. English Nature, Peterborough.

English Nature, Quarry Products Association and Silica and Moulding Sands Association (1999) *Biodiversity and minerals – extracting the benefits for wildlife*. Entec UK Ltd, Leamington Spa.

English Nature, Quarry Products Association and the Silica and Moulding Sands Association (2002) *'Geodiversity and Minerals, a guide to planning, operating, restoring and managing sites for geological constuction'* English Nature, Peterborough.

Etherington, J R (1989) *The restoration of opencast coal mining sites in South Wales: future implications for wildlife*. University of Wales, Cardiff.

Eurosite (1999) *Toolkit: management planning*. Eurosite, Tilburg.

Farmer, R E, Cunningham, M and Barnhill, M A (1982) First-year development of plant communities originating from forest topsoils placed on southern Appalachian minesoils. *Journal of Applied Ecology* 19: 283-294.

Forestry Commission (1991) *Community woodland design guidelines*. HMSO, London.

Forestry Commission (1994a) *Reclaiming disturbed land for forestry*. FC Bulletin 110. HMSO, London.

Forestry Commission (1994b) *Management guides for semi-natural woodlands*. Forestry Commission, Edinburgh.

Forestry Commission (1997) *Recycling land for forestry*. FC Technical paper 22. HMSO, London.

Forsyth, L (1999) *Creating bare ground habitats*. Enact 7(1): 7-9.

Foster, J (1997) Amphibians and reptiles – the species and their ecology. In R Bray and T Gent (eds) *Opportunities for amphibians and reptiles in the designed landscape*, pp 4-17. English Nature Science Series 30. English Nature, Peterborough.

Francis, J L, Morton, A J and Boorman, L A (1992) The establishment of ground flora species in recently planted woodland. *Aspects of Applied Biology* 29: 171-78.

Francis, J L and Street, M (1993) The establishment of woodland herbs in new plantations. *Urban Nature* 1: 107-110.

Free, A and Kitson, M T (1992) *Heathland habitat creation*. Nuclear Electric/Suffolk Wildlife Trust.

Fry, R and Lonsdale, S D (1991) *Habitat conservation for insects – a neglected green issue*. Amateur Entomologists' Society, Middlesex.

Fuller, R M (1987) The changing extent and conservation interest of lowland grasslands in England and Wales: a review of grassland surveys 1930-84. *Biological Conservation* 40: 241-300.

Galán, P (1997) Colonization of spoil benches of an opencast lignite mine in northwest Spain by amphibians and reptiles. *Biological Conservation* 79: 187-195.

Gault, C (1997) *A moving story. Species and community translocation in the UK: a review of policy, principle, planning and practice*. WWF-UK, Godalming.

Gault, C (ed) (1998) *Cornwall's Biodiversity Volume*

2; *Action Plans.* Cornwall Biodiversity Inititative, Cornwall Wildlife Trust.

Gibson, C W D, Watt, T A and Brown, V K (1987) The use of sheep grazing to recreate species-rich grassland from abandoned arable land. *Biological Conservation* 42: 165-183.

Gilbert, J C (2000) *High soil phosphorus availability and the restoration of species-rich grassland.* PhD thesis, Cranfield University, Bedfordshire.

Gilbert, J C, Gowing, D J G, Higginbottom, P R G and Godwin, R J (2000) The habitat creation model: A decision support system to assess the viability of converting arable land into semi-natural habitat. *Computers and Electronics in Agriculture* 28: 67-85.

Gilbert, J C, Higginbottom, P R G, Gowing, D J G, Bradley, R I, Kerr, D M, Leeds-Harrison, P B, Spoor, G and Godwin, R J (1996) *The habitat creation model: A model to assess the viability of converting arable land into semi-natural habitat.* MAFF commissioned project CSA 2373. Cranfield University, Bedfordshire.

Gilbert, O L and Anderson, P (1998) *Habitat Creation and Repair.* Oxford University Press, Oxford.

Gilbert, O L and Wathern, P (1976) Towards the production of extensive Calluna swards. *Landscape Design* 117: 35.

Gilbert, O L and Wathern, P (1980) The creation of flower-rich swards on mineral workings. *Reclamation Review* 3: 217-221.

Giles, N (1992) *Wildlife after Gravel.* Game Conservancy Trust, Fordingbridge.

Gillham, D A (1980) *The conservation and restoration of heathland vegetation disturbed by industrial operations.* PhD thesis, University of Liverpool, Liverpool.

Gillham, D A and Putwain, P D (1977) *Restoring moorland disturbed by pipeline installation.* Landscape Design 119: 34-36.

Gilmour, W N G (1983) The making of the Rother Valley Country Park. *ILAM Journal* October 1983: 14-18.

Gimingham, C H (1992) *The Lowland Heath Management Handbook.* English Nature, Peterborough.

Gough, M W and Marrs, R H (1990) A comparison of soil fertility between semi-natural and agricultural plant communities: implications for the creation of species-rich grassland on abandoned agricultural land. *Biological Conservation* 51: 83-96.

Graveland, J (1998) Reed die-back, water level management and the decline of the Great Reed Warbler *Acrocephalus arundinaceus* in The Netherlands. Ardea 86(2): 187-201.

Green Balance and AERC Ltd (1998) *The potential contribution of the mineral extraction industries to the UK Biodiversity Action Plan.* English Nature Research Report No 279.

Grime, J P, Hodgson, J G and Hunt, R (1988) *Comparative plant ecology.* Unwin Hyman, London.

Guthrie, I (1996) *Heather regeneration on disturbed sites.* The Heather Trust 12th Annual Report, pp 28-32. The Heather Trust.

Harper, P, Glenn-Lewis, and Werger, M J A (1983) Early revegetation of Calluna heathland under various fertilisation treatments. *Oecologia* 58: 208-214.

Hawke, C and José, P (1996) *Reedbed management for commercial and wildlife interests.* The RSPB, Sandy.

Hill, A and Box, J (1999) Experimental translocation of wet heathland in Dorset, England: implications for restoration of mineral workings. In P E K Fuchs, M R Smith and M J Arthur (eds) *Mineral Planning in Europe*, pp 342-351. The Institute of Quarrying, Nottingham.

HMSO (1994) Biodiversity: *The UK Action Plan.* HMSO, London.

HMSO (1995) *Biodiversity* (2 vols). HMSO, London.

HMSO (1996) *Survey of land for Mineral Workings in England 1994.* HMSO, London.

Hodge, S J (1995) *Creating and managing woodlands around towns.* Forestry Commission Handbook 11. HMSO, London.

Hodgson, J M (ed) (1976) *Soil survey handbook: Describing and sampling soil profiles.* Soil Survey Technical Monograph No 5, Harpenden.

Hodgson, J G (1982) State and Status. In B N K Davis (ed) *The ecology of quarries. The importance of natural vegetation*, pp 3-11. Institute for Terrestrial Ecology, Cambridge.

Holl, K D (1996) The effect of coal surface mine reclamation on diurnal Lepidopteran conservation. *Journal of Applied Ecology* 33: 225-236.

Holmes, N T H (1998) Floodplain restoration. In R G Bailey, P V José and B R Sherwood (eds) *United Kingdom Floodplains*, pp 331-348. Westbury Academic and Scientific Publishing, Otley.

Hopkins, J J (1989) Prospects for habitat creation. *Landscape Design* 179: 19-23.

Hopkins, J J (1996) Scrub ecology and conservation. *British Wildlife* 8(1): 28-36.

Horne, R and Frost, S (1991) *Opencast coal mining in England and Wales: a review of legislation and policy.* Landuse Policy 8(1): 29-35.

Hutson, A M, Mickleburgh, S and Mitchell-Jones, A J (1988) *Bats underground – a conservation code.* Flora and Fauna Preservation Society, Cambridge.

Hutson, B R (1980) The influence on soil development of the invertebrate fauna colonising industrial reclamation sites. *Journal of Applied Ecology* 17: 277-286.

Jefferson, R G (1984) Quarries and wildlife conservation in the Yorkshire Wolds, England. *Biological Conservation* 29: 363-380.

Jefferson, R G, Gibson, C W D, Leach, S J, Pulteney, C M, Wolton, R and Robertson, H J (1999) *Grassland habitat translocation: The case of Brocks Farm, Devon.* English Nature Research Report No 304.

Jefferson, R G and Usher, M B (1987) The seedbanks of disused chalk quarries in the Yorkshire Wolds, England: implications for conservation management. *Biological Conservation* 42: 287-302.

Jefferson, R G and Usher, M B (1989) Seed rain

dynamics in disused chalk quarries in the Yorkshire Wolds, England, with special reference to nature conservation. *Biological Conservation* 47: 123-136.

Jones, G (1990) Learning from experience. *Landscape Design* 193: 40-44.

Jones, G H (1993) *Factors controlling the establishment of species-rich grasslands in urban landscaping schemes.* PhD thesis, University of Wolverhampton, Wolverhampton.

Jones, G H, Trueman, I C and Millett, P (1990) The ecological significance of grasslands created using hay from ancient English meadows. In H G Hughes and T M Bonnicksen (eds) *Restoration 89: The new management challenge*, pp 520-531. First Annual meeting of the Society for Ecological Restoration, Oakland, California January 1989.

Jones, G H , Trueman, I C and Millett, P (1995) The use of hay strewing to create species-rich grasslands. (i) General principles and hay strewing versus seed mixes. *Land Contamination and Reclamation* 3(2): 104-107.

Key, R (2000) Bare ground and the conservation of invertebrates. *British Wildlife* 11(3): 183-191.

Key, R and Gent, T (1993) Bare but not barren. *Enact* 1(2): 15-16.

Kirby, K (1994) Where should you put your new woods? *Enact* 2(3): 12-14.

Kirby, P (1992) *Habitat management for invertebrates: a practical handbook.* The RSPB, Sandy. Reprinted 2001.

Land Use Consultants (1992a) *Amenity reclamation of mineral workings.* Main report. Report to DoE. HMSO, London.

Land Use Consultants (1992b) *The use of land for amenity purposes. A summary of requirements.* Report to DoE. HMSO, London.

Land Use Consultants (1996) *Reclamation of Damaged Land for Nature Conservation.* HMSO, London.

Lane, A (1992) *Practical Conservation. Grasslands, Heaths and Moors.* Hodder and Stoughton, London.

Larson, P (1999) Mineral development. A net contributor to heathland in the South-West. *Quarry Management* March: 39-44.

Luscombe, G and Scott, R (1994) *Wildflowers work: a technical guide to creating and maintaining wildflower landscapes.* Landlife, Liverpool.

Lyle, E S (1987) *Surface mine reclamation manual.* Elsevier, Amsterdam.

MAFF (1996) *Water storage reservoirs – getting control over your water resource.* Booklet PB2512. MAFF, London.

Manchester, S, Treweek, J, Mountford, O, Pywell, R and Sparks, T (1998) Restoration of a target wet grassland community on ex-arable land. In C B Joyce and P M Wade (eds) *European wet grasslands: biodiversity, management and restoration*, pp 277-294. John Wiley and Sons, Chichester.

Marrs, R H (1993) Soil fertility and nature conservation in Europe: theoretical considerations and practical management solutions. *Advances in Ecological Research* 24: 241-300.

Marrs, R H and Bradshaw, A D (1980) Ecosystem development on reclaimed china clay wastes. III. Leaching of nutrients. *Journal of Applied Ecology* 17: 727-736.

Marrs, R H, Roberts, R D and Bradshaw, A D (1980) Ecosystem development on reclaimed China clay wastes. I. Assessment of vegetation and the capture of nutrients. *Journal of Applied Ecology* 17: 709-717.

McDonald, A W, Bakker, J P and Vegelin, K (1996) Seed bank classification and its importance for the restoration of species-rich flood-meadows. *Journal of Vegetation Science* 7: 157-164.

McDougall, D (1997) Agriculture or alternative uses? *Mineral Planning* 7(3): 27-30.

McLean, M (1992) *New hedges for the countryside.* Farming Press Books, Ipswich.

McRae, S (1979) The agricultural restoration of sand and gravel quarries in Great Britain. *Reclamation Review* 2: 133-42.

Meadon, D P (1983) *The restoration and creation of heather moorland vegatation.* PhD thesis, University of Liverpool, Liverpool.

Merrilees, D W, Tiley, G E D and Gwynne D C (1995) Restoration of wet heathland after opencast mining. In B D Wheeler, S C Shaw, W J Fojt and R A Robertson (eds) *Restoration of Temperate Wetlands,* pp 523-532. John Wiley and Sons, Chichester.

Merritt, A (1994) *Wetlands, Industry & Wildlife. A manual of principles and practices.* Wildfowl & Wetlands Trust, Slimbridge.

Merritt, R, Moore, N W and Eversham, B C (1996) *Atlas of dragonflies of Britain and Ireland.* ITE Research Publication 9. HMSO, London.

Milne-Redhead, E (1990) The BSBI black poplar survey, 1973-1988. *Watsonia* 8: 1-5.

Milsom, T P, Ennis, D C, Haskell, D J, Langton, S D and McKay, H V (1998) Design of grassland feeding areas for waders during winter: the relative importance of sward, landscape factors and human disturbance. *Biological Conservation* 84: 119-129.

Moffat, A and McNeill, J (1994) Reclaiming disturbed land for forestry. Forestry Commission Bulletin 110. HMSO, London.

Mortimer, S R, Tomer A J, Brown, V K, Fuller, R J, Good, JEG, Bell, S G, Stevens, P A, Norris, D, Bayfield, N and Ward, L K (2000) *The Nature Conservation Value of Scrub in Britain.* JNCC Report 308. JNCC, Peterborough.

NCC (1988) *Site management plans for nature conservation – a working guide.* Nature Conservancy Council, Peterborough.

NCC (1990) *Handbook for Phase 1 Habitat Survey. A technique for environmental audit.* Nature Conservancy Council, Peterborough.

NRA (1993) *Otters and river habitat management.* Conservation Technical Handbook 3. National Rivers Authority, Bristol.

Nuttall, P M, Boon, A G and Rowell, M R (1997) *Review of the design and management of constructed wetlands.* CIRIA Report 180. CIRIA, London.

Office of the Deputy Prime Minister (2002) *Survey of land for mineral workings in England 2000.*

Orford, R (1996) Reservoir design – for wildlife and landscape. *Farming & Conservation* July 1996: 20-24.

Parker, D M (1995) *Habitat creation, a critical guide.* English Nature Science Series No 21. English Nature, Peterborough.
Parkyn, Stoneman, and Ingram, (1997) *Conserving peatlands.* CAB, Wallingford.
Parr, T W (1987) *Experimental studies on the propagation and establishment of reeds* (Phragmites australis) *for root zone treatment of sewage.* Institute for Terrestrial Ecology, Monks Wood.
Peterken, G F (1993) *Woodland conservation and management.* Second Edition. Chapman and Hall, London.
Peterken, G F and Hughes, F M R (1998) Limitations and opportunities for restoring floodplain forest in Britain. In R G Bailey, P V José and B R Sherwood (eds) *United Kingdom Floodplains,* pp 423-436. Westbury Academic and Scientific Publishing, Otley.
Petts, G E and Amoros, C (eds) (1996) *Fluvial hydrosystems.* Chapman and Hall, London.
Porter, K (1994) Seed harvesting – a hay meadow dilemma. *Enact* 2: 4-5.
Putwain, P D (1992) The creation of heathland vegetation: theory and practice. *Aspects of Applied Biology* 29: 33-40.
Putwain, P D and Gillham, D A (1988) Restoration of heather moorland. *Landscape Design* 172: 51-56.
Putwain, P D and Gillham, D A (1990) The significance of dormant viable seed bank in the restoration of heathlands. *Biological Conservation* 52: 1-16.
Pywell, R F (1991) Heathland translocation and restoration. In M H D Auld, B P Pickess and N D Burgess (eds) *History and management of Southern lowland heaths,* pp 18-26. Proceedings of Heathlands Conference II. Harrow House, Dorset, 4-6 June 1990. The RSPB, Sandy.
Pywell, R F, Putwain, P D and Webb, N R (1996) Establishment of heathland vegetation on mineral workings. *Aspects of Applied Biology* 44: 285-292.
Pywell, R F, Veitch, N and Webb, N R (1991) *Locating and reconstructing former heathlands.* ITE Annual Report 1991-1992, pp 66-69. Institute for Terrestrial Ecology, Monks Wood.
Pywell, R F, Webb, N R and Putwain, P D (1994) Soil fertility and its implications for the restoration of heathland on farmland in southern Britain. *Biological Conservation* 70: 169-181.
Pywell, R F, Webb, N R and Putwain, P D (1996) Harvested heather shoots as a resource for heathland restoration. *Biological Conservation* 75: 247-254.
Ranson, C E and Doody, J P (1982) Quarries and nature conservation: objectives and management. In B N K Davis (ed) *The ecology of quarries. The importance of natural vegetation,* pp 20-26. Institute for Terrestrial Ecology, Cambridge.
RRC (1999) *Manual of River Restoration Techniques.* RRC, Cranfield University, Bedfordshire.
Reed, S M and Singh, R N (1986) Groundwater recovery problems associated with opencast mine backfills in the United Kingdom. *International Journal of Mine Water* 5(3): 47-74.
Rehfisch, M M (1994) Man-made lagoons and how their attractiveness to waders might be increased by manipulating the biomass of an insect benthos. *Journal of Applied Ecology* 31: 383-401.
Richardson, J A and Evans, M E (1986) Restoration of grassland after Magnesian limestone quarrying. *Journal of Applied Ecology* 23: 317-332.
RMC (1986) *A practical guide to restoration.* RMC Group plc, Feltham.
Roberts, R D, Marrs, R H and Bradshaw, A D (1980) Ecosystem development on reclaimed china clay wastes. II. Nutrient compartmentation and nitrogen mineralisation. *Journal of Applied Ecology* 17: 719-725.
Robinson, G R and Handel, S N (1993) Forest restoration on a closed landfill: rapid addition of new species by bird dispersal. *Conservation Biology* 7(2): 271-78.
Rodwell, J (1991a) *British Plant Communities. Volume 1. Woodland and scrub.* Cambridge University Press, Cambridge.
Rodwell, J (1991b) *British Plant Communities. Volume 2. Mires and heaths.* Cambridge University Press, Cambridge.
Rodwell, J (1992) *British Plant Communities. Volume 3. Grasslands and montane communities.* Cambridge University Press, Cambridge.
Rodwell, J (1995) *British Plant Communities. Volume 4. Aquatic communities, swamp and tall herb fen.* Cambridge University Press, Cambridge.
Rodwell, J S and Patterson, G S (1994) *Creating new native woodland.* Forestry Commission Bulletin 112. HMSO, London.
RPS Clouston and Wye College (1992) *The reclamation of mineral workings to agriculture.* HMSO, London.
The RSPB (1999) *Good practice guide to mineral restoration.*
RSPB, EN and ITE (1997) *The wet grassland guide: managing floodplain and coastal wet grasslands for wildlife.* The RSPB, Sandy.
Rust Consulting Ltd (1994a) *Hydrology and mineral workings: effects on nature conservation (Technical Annexe).* English Nature Research Report No 106. English Nature, Peterborough.
Rust Consulting Ltd (1994b) *Hydrology and mineral workings: effects on nature conservation (Guidelines).* English Nature Research Report No 107. English Nature, Peterborough.
Sansen, U, and Koedam, N (1996) Use of sod cutting for restoration of wet heathlands: revegetation and establishment of typical species in relation to soil conditions. *Journal of Vegetation Science* 7: 483-486.
Scottish Office (1994a) *Planning Advice Note (PAN) 42. Archaeology – the planning process and scheduled monument procedures.* Scottish Office.
Scottish Office (1994b) *National Planning Policy Guidelines (NPPG) 4: Land for mineral working.* Scottish Office.
Scottish Office (1994c) *National Planning Policy Guidelines (NPPG) 5: Archaeology and Planning.*

Scottish Office.

Scullion, J (1994) *Restoring farmland after coal: the Bryngwyn project.* Report to British Coal Opencast. University of Wales, Aberystwyth.

Scullion, J, Mohammed, A R A and Richardson, H (1988) Effect of storage and reinstatement procedures on earthworm populations in soils affected by opencast coal mining. *Journal of Applied Ecology* 25: 233-240.

Self, M (1999) *Creating new reedbeds: a practical guide.* Unpublished report. The RSPB, Sandy.

Self, M, Hawke, C and José, P (1996) Reedbed enhancement and creation at RSPB nature reserves. *RSPB Conservation Review* 10: 45-53.

Sheldon, J C and Bradshaw, A D (1977) The development of a hydraulic seeding techniques for unstable sand slopes. I. Effects of fertilizers, mulches and stabilisers. *Journal of Applied Ecology* 14: 905-918.

Skeffington, R A and Bradshaw, A D (1980) Nitrogen fixation by plants grown on reclaimed China clay waste. *Journal of Applied Ecology* 17: 469-477.

Smith, R E N, Webb, N R and Clarke, R T (1991) The establishment of heathland on old fields in Dorset, England. *Biological Conservation* 57: 221-34.

Souch, C A, Gilbert, J C, Gowing, D J G and Hess T M (2000) *Anglian region joint study on water resource availability for wetland creation.* Unpublished. Cranfield University, Bedfordshire.

Soutar, R G and Peterken, G F (1989) Regional lists of native trees and shrubs for use in afforestation schemes. *Arboricultural Journal* 13: 33-43.

Standen, V (1995a) The effect of transplantation of a blanket bog. I Impact on vegetation and selected invertebrate groups. *The Journal of Practical Ecology and Conservation* 1(2): 7-17.

Standen, V (1995b) The effect of transplantation of a blanket bog. II Impact on spiders. *The Journal of Practical Ecology and Conservation* 1(2): 18-21.

Standen, V (1997) Invertebrate community succession on heath and bog created by translocation and recolonisation. In A Cooper and J Power (1997) *Species dispersal and land use processes.* Proceedings of the sixth annual IALE (UK) conference, University of Ulster, Coleraine 9th-11th September 1997. The UK Region of the International Association for Landscape Ecology.

Stebbings, R E and Walsh, S T (1991) *Bat boxes: a guide to the history, function, construction and use in the conservation of bats.* Bat Conservation Trust, London.

Strachan, R (1998) *Water vole conservation handbook.* Wildlife Conservation Research Unit, Oxford.

Street, M (1989) *The restoration of gravel pits for wildfowl.* ARC.

Stubbs, A E and Chandler, P (1978) *A dipterist's handbook.* Amateur Entomologist Volume 15. AES, Hanworth.

Stubbs, A E and Falk, S J (1983) *British hoverflies.* The British Entomological and Natural History Society, London.

Sutherland (1996) *Ecological Census Techniques: A Handbook.* Cambridge University Press.

Swan, M J S and Oldham, R S (1993) *Herptile sites. Volume 1: national amphibian survey.* English Nature Research Report 38. English Nature, Peterborough.

Tacey, W H and Glossop, B L (1980) Assessment of the topsoil handling techniques for rehabilitation of site mined for bauxite within the jarrah forest of Western Australia. *Journal of Applied Ecology* 17: 195-201.

UK Biodiversity Group (1998) *Tranche 2 action plans. Vol. II – terrestrial and freshwater habitats.* English Nature, Peterborough.

Usher, M B, Brown, A C and Bedford, S E (1992) Plant species richness in farm woodlands. *Forestry* 65: 1-13.

Van der Toorn, J (1972) *Variability of Phragmites australis in relation to the environment.* Van Zee tot Land 48: 1-122.

Walker, K J, Manchester, S J, Mountford, J O, Stevens, P A and Pywell, R F (2001) *Methodology for restoring and re-creating semi-natural lowland grassland. A review and quantitative model.* CCW Contract Science Report No 437.

Wallace, I D (1991) *A review of the Trichoptera of Great Britain. Research and survey in nature conservation 32.* Nature Conservancy Council, Peterborough.

Walsh, A L and Harris, S (1996) Foraging habitat preferences of vespertilionid bats in Britain. *Journal of Applied Ecology* 33: 508-518.

Ward, D and Andrews, J (1993) Waterfowl and recreational disturbance on inland waters. *British Wildlife* 4(3): 221-229.

Ward, D, Holmes, N and José, P (1994) *The new rivers and wildlife handbook.* The RSPB, Sandy.

Wells, T, Bell, S and Frost, A (1981) *Creating attractive grasslands using native species.* Nature Conservancy Council, Peterborough.

Wheeler, B D (1995) Introduction: wetlands and restoration. In BD Wheeler, S C Shaw, W J Fojt and R A Robertson (eds) *Restoration of temperate wetlands*, pp 1-18. John Wiley and Sons, Chichester.

Wheeler, B D and Shaw, S C (1995) *Restoration of damaged peatlands.* HMSO, London.

Williams, L M S (1989) Soil-less restoration to agriculture/amenity afteruse of worked out mineral sites. *Mineral Planning* 41: 8-10.

Williams, P, Biggs, J, Corfield, A, Fox, G, Walker, D and Whitfield, M (1997) Designing new ponds for wildlife. *British Wildlife* 8: 137-150.

Williams, P, Biggs, J, Whitfield, M, Thorne, A, Bryant, S, Fox, G and Nicolet, P (1999) *The pond book: A guide to the management and creation of ponds.* Ponds Conservation Trust, Oxford.

Wilson, G (1998) Habitat translocation. In *Minerals, Land and the Natural Environment. The foundations of wealth*, pp 253-256. Papers presented at the 'Minerals, Land and the Environment' conference organised by the Institution of Mining and Metallurgy, London, 24 June 1998.

Woodrow, W, Symes, N and Auld, M (1996) RSPB Dorset Heathland Project 1989-1995: *a*

management case study. The RSPB, Sandy.
Worthington, T R and Helliwell, D R (1987) Transference of semi-natural grassland and marshland onto newly created landfill. *Biological Conservation* 41: 301-311.

Planning Guidance mentioned in the text

MPG3 *Coal mining and colliery disposal*
MPG7 *The reclamation of mineral workings*
MPG13 *Peat guidance*
MPG14 *Review of mineral planning permissions*
MPG15 *Provision of silica sand in England*
NPPG16 *Opencast coal and related m inerals*
PPG9 *Nature conservation*

Other RSPB habitat management handbooks

European wet grassland. Guidelines for management and restoration by P J Benstead, P V José, C B Joyce and P M Wade. The RSPB, Sandy. 1999. ISBN 1 901930 01 7. £15.95.
The wet grassland guide: managing floodplain and coastal wet grasslands for wildlife by P Benstead, M Drake, P José, O Mountford, C Newbold and J Treweek. The RSPB, Sandy. 1997. ISBN 0 903138 86 7. £17.95.
Reedbed management for commercial and wildlife interests by C J Hawke and P V José. The RSPB, Sandy. 1996. ISBN 0 903138 81 6. £14.95.
The new rivers and wildlife handbook edited by D Ward, N Holmes and P José. The RSPB, Sandy. 1994. ISBN 0 903138 79 9. £19.95.
Farming and wildlife – a practical management handbook by J Andrews and M Rebane. The RSPB, Sandy. 1994. ISBN 0 903138 67 0. £21.95.
Habitat management for invertebrates: a practical handbook by P Kirby. The RSPB, Sandy. 1992. ISBN 0 903138 55 7. £9.95. (Reprinted with modifications 2001.)
Gravel pit restoration for wildlife by J Andrews and D Kinsman. The RSPB, Sandy. 1990. ISBN 0 903138 60 3. £12.00.

These books are available at good booksellers or directly from the RSPB.

Index

Notes: *Italic* page numbers refer to photographs and **bold** numbers indicate cases, figures and tables.

RSPB

Habitat creation handbook for the minerals industry questionnaire

Dear handbook user

We're keen to keep improving the quality of advice in our handbooks, so we'd appreciate it if you would fill out this short feedback questionnaire and return it to us, together with any other comments you would like to make. The instructions for returning this questionnaire are printed overleaf.

With many thanks
Peter Robertson, Head of RSPB Conservation Management Advice

1 Which ONE of these statements best describes how you have used the handbook to date?

I have read most/all of it ☐1 (11)
I have read some of it ☐2
I have flicked through it but not read any of it thoroughly ☐3

2 Overall, how do you rate the handbook?

Very good ☐1 Good ☐2 Fair ☐3 Poor ☐4 Very poor ☐5 (12)

3 How much do you feel you learned from the handbook about managing land for conservation?

A lot ☐1 A little ☐2 Nothing at all ☐3 (13)

4 How strongly do you agree or disagree with the following statements?
The advice in the handbook is...

	Agree strongly	Agree slightly	Disagree slightly	Disagree strongly	
... well structured	☐1	☐2	☐3	☐4	(14)
... well indexed	☐1	☐2	☐3	☐4	(15)
... well illustrated with photos, drawings & diagrams	☐1	☐2	☐3	☐4	(16)
... easy to put into practice	☐1	☐2	☐3	☐4	(17)
... generally too expensive to implement	☐1	☐2	☐3	☐4	(18)
... too focused on birds; it doesn't take other land management objectives into account sufficiently	☐1	☐2	☐3	☐4	(19)

5 Have you yourself taken any action as a result of reading something in the handbook?

Yes ☐1 (20)
Not yet, but I definitely intend to ☐2
Not yet, but I probably will ☐3
No, and I never will ☐4
Not applicable – I'm not a land manager myself ☐5

6 Have you passed on any advice from the handbook to someone else?

Yes ☐1 (21)
Not yet, but I definitely intend to ☐2
Not yet, but I probably will ☐3
No, and I never will ☐4
Not applicable – I'm not an adviser myself ☐5

7 Which of these best describes your current role?

Minerals company employee ☐1 (22)
Conservation site manager ☐2
Conservation adviser ☐3
Consultant ☐4
Local authority planning officer/ecologist ☐5
Something else ** ☐6 ______________________

**Please describe your involvement in mineral restoration

8 How could we improve this handbook for you personally?

for birds • for people • for ever

FIRST FOLD

FLAP A

A stamp will
mean more
money can go
towards
conservation
Thank you.

The RSPB
Conservation Management Advice
FREEPOST ANG6335
The Lodge
Sandy
Bedfordshire
SG19 2BR

Registered charity no 207076

FLAP B

SECOND FOLD

THIRD FOLD

FOURTH FOLD

Fold in sequence along the lines shown (first fold, then second fold etc).

Then tuck flap A into flap B.

You should not need to use tape or staples